Dance as Text

RES MONOGRAPHS ON ANTHROPOLOGY AND AESTHETICS

Series Editor
Francesco Pellizzi

Advisory Board
Joseph Rykwert, University of Pennsylvania
Gianni Vattino, University of Turin

Other books in the series
*The Anatomy of Architecture: Ontology and Metaphor in Batammaliba
Architectural Expression,* by Suzanne Preston Blier
    Winner of the Arnold Rubin Outstanding Publication Award
*Learning from Mount Hua: A Chinese Physician's Illustrated Travel
Record and Painting Theory,* by Kathlyn Liscomb
"The Four Elements of Architecture" and Other Writings, by Gottfried
Semper, edited by Harry Francis Mallgrave
*The Wild Bull in the Sacred Forest: Form, Meaning, and Change in
Senegambian Initiation Masks,* by Peter Mark

Dance as Text
Ideologies of the Baroque Body

Mark Franko

CAMBRIDGE
UNIVERSITY PRESS

Published by the Press Syndicate of the University of Cambridge
The Pitt Building, Trumpington Street, Cambridge CB2 1RP
40 West 20th Street, New York, NY 10011-4211, USA
10 Stamford Road, Oakleigh, Melbourne 3166, Australia

First published 1993
Reprinted 1993

Printed in the United States of America

Library of Congress Cataloging-in-Publication Data available.

A catalogue record for this book is available from the British Library.

ISBN 0-521-43392-4 hardback

For Juliet with Alessio
and Louis Marin, in memoriam

The irreducible political power that everybody has, his bodily behavior in the space that he occupies.

Paul Goodman, *Speaking and Language: Defense of Poetry*

The people . . . enjoy a spectacle which, basically, is always aimed at pleasing them, and all our subjects, in general, are delighted to see that we share their tastes for what they do best.

Louis XIV, *Mémoires for the Instruction of the Dauphin*

The study of dance and theater is the study of how a particular group of people overcome stage fright.

Randy Martin, *Performance as Political Act*

This is precisely what the tyrant does. He causes this lack of self-presence in the body politic which is simultaneously a loss of language.

Vincent Farenga, "Periphrasis on the Origin of Rhetoric"

Dance as Text: Ideologies of the Baroque Body is a historical and theoretical examination of French court ballet over a hundred-year period, beginning in 1573, that spans the late Renaissance and the early baroque. Utilizing aesthetic and ideological criteria, Mark Franko analyzes court ballet librettos, contemporary performance theory, and related commentary on dance and movement in the literature of this period. Examining the formal choreographic apparatus that characterizes late Valois and early Bourbon ballet spectacle, Franko postulates that the evolving aesthetic ultimately reflected the political situation of the noble class, which devised and performed court ballets. He shows how the body emerged from verbal theater as a self-sufficient text whose autonomy had varied ideological connotations, most important among which was the expression of noble resistance to the increasingly absolutist monarchy. Franko's analysis blends archival research with critical and cultural theory in order to resituate the burlesque tradition in its politically volatile context. *Dance as Text* thus provides a picture of the complex theoretical underpinnings of composite spectacle, the ideological tensions underlying experiments with autonomous dance, and finally, the subversiveness of Molière's use of court ballet traditions.

CONTENTS

ILLUSTRATIONS

SERIES EDITOR'S PREFACE

Imaginative studies on the history of dance and choreography are not common, and this is particularly true of Renaissance ballet. Surviving documents, scarce and often of a circumstantial nature, tend to leave out precisely those *performative* aspects of Renaissance dance events that would be most revealing, and in the interpretation of the librettos that have survived it is rare for scholars to have the dance and choreographic experience necessary for a full evaluation. Mark Franko, a distinguished scholar in the history of ballet (and of French culture), but also a theoretician, choreographer, and performer of contemporary avant-garde dance, is not dazzled by the slavish "splendor" evoked in the old official descriptions of court performances, but neither does he fall for the fashionable sociological and semiological jargons of today.

In the emerging field of the "anthropology of the historical body" – of which Rudolf zür Lippe has been a noteworthy champion – *Dance as Text: Ideologies of the Baroque Body* distinguishes itself by emphasizing "text and ideology." Rather than attempting a literal reconstruction of court ballets – as if they were lost texts to be retrieved – or simply weaving a historical narrative of their development, the author establishes a theoretical profile of their development by evoking their ephemeral effect and reconstructing their audience: he thus reveals what he calls the "textual identity" of the dancing body as a key element in the transmutations of aesthetics throughout the entire span of baroque France (1570–1670). His definition of choreographic mannerism, in fact, proposes a new model for aesthetic theory that not only redefines the canon of dance history in its inclusion of the burlesque, but also challenges the position that the Platonic paradigm was the dominant one throughout the late sixteenth and seventeenth centuries.

By viewing the emerging burlesque trend as a form of choreographic mannerism, a "conceptual art" whose theory was inherent in baroque court ballet itself, the author develops a method of theoretical analysis that transcends particular historical periods and demonstrates the historical elasticity of stylistic terms such as "Renaissance," "baroque," and "mannerism" itself. *Dance as Text* exemplifies a kind of "reconstructive" thinking that will affect the methodology of choreographic studies by recasting the dimension of "dance literacy" as an essential historical component in the interpretation of dance events: what are reconstructed are not just the formal and philological features of court ballet but the whole discourse that linked performers and audiences as they created and experienced them.

The book also offers an original examination of the subtle interconnections between politics and aesthetics in a previously neglected period of Western choreography – roughly corresponding to the reign of Louis XIII – in which a burlesque character prevailed in aristocratic ballet, in contrast to the "stately" formal affairs that preceded and followed it. A striking paradox emerges: how is it that a new sense of individuality (or personal "freedom") – a sort of *défoulement* of the (aristocratic) body, by way of the introduction of popular, carnivalesque elements, into the most sophisticated form of "high" performance – could take hold among the highest nobles and be expressed and furthered by them in the very cradle of the rising centralized form of political authority? It is as if for the waning ruling class of the time dissent caused by the loss of real power had been a condition for a sort of ribald repossession and reaffirmation of the individual self. It is most interesting to learn, in this context, that the king himself, taking active part in these exercises, appears as if torn between his two identities – as "absolute monarch" and as himself a feudal lord, *primus inter pares*: his adoption of the "mask" of popular bawdiness, for a time, appears more as a means to transcend this intrinsic contradiction (and control its potentially eversive effects) within the political and cultural structure of the court than as a "spontaneous" rise of prelibertine fashions. Later, as the author demonstrates, the burlesque element was reabsorbed and disguised within the revival of the "comedy interlude" structure (as in Molière), but never vanished.

In his detailed analysis of the inner workings of a "textual" dialectic in ballet, Mark Franko brings to bear his experience as a practicing dancer and choreographer, highlighting the key role played by the performing arts in the development of a modern expressive awareness. French court ballet, in the author's perspective, is both an artistic "avant-garde" manifestation and a "ritual" in the full anthropological sense of the word: it represents, *in itself*, the reaffirmation of a certain political power, as well as the discovery and exploration of a certain kind of *knowledge*, of a new form of artistic expression.

By opening a "dialogue between forms and periods on the basis of style, vocabulary, and theory, rather than history alone," *Dance as Text* truly belongs in the program of the RES Monographs on Anthropology and Aesthetics. It also pertains to the series in the way it evokes the invisible and ephemeral in performance, taking theory itself as a model in discovering its "effect" and reconstructing its audience. In harmony with Margaret McGowan's belief that theory can engender new choreography, the book's epilogue proves that the study of the past can be an integral part of the most advanced experiments of the present. Its insights and implications go beyond its contribution to historical understanding: issues inherited from baroque aesthetics are still relevant to modern dance.

Francesco Pellizzi

ACKNOWLEDGMENTS

In developing this manuscript since 1985, I have benefited inestimably from the close readings and critical advice of Evan Alderson, Gini Alhadeff, Selma-Jeanne Cohen, Susan Foster, Lionel Gossman, Djelal Kadir, Louis Marin, Margaret M. McGowan, Juliet Neidish, Francesco Pellizzi, David Lee Rubin, Joseph Rykwert, Jochen Schulte-Sasse, and Karl Uitti. Each in his or her own way provided fantasmatic sparks animating positions ultimately assumed.

Dance as Text extends research begun in the late 1970s for an earlier study on Renaissance social dance. My interest in French dance history took form in Louis Marin's seminars on seventeenth-century historiography held at Columbia University in 1976–7 and continued in Paris at the Ecole des hautes études in 1979–80. There was excitement in Paris of the late 1970s over the body as a category of intellectual inquiry, an excitement that has since voyaged to America.

Appreciation and thanks go to the students of my graduate seminars at Princeton and Purdue universities, those who worked with me on the problems and contexts of this book, especially John Stout, Anna Creese, Catherine Bothe, and Magalie Hanquier. Earlier versions of some chapters were published elsewhere: Chapter 2 appeared in *Continuum*, Chapter 3 in *Romance Languages Annual*, and the Epilogue in *Theatre Journal*. I wish to thank these publications for permission to reprint here. John H. Baron kindly provided me with a copy of the little-known synopsis of *Les Fées*. I am recognizant of librarians of the Bibliothèque nationale, the Mazarine, the Arsenal, the Paris Opera, and the Dance Collection of Lincoln Center Library for the Performing Arts in New York City for their resourceful help. Valerie Wise offered a true meeting of the minds in the first stages of editing, and Becky Brimacombe contributed significantly to bringing this book into its final form. I would also like to thank Mary Racine and Robert Racine for their work on the final stages of production.

Grateful thanks are extended to the American Council of Learned Societies, the Princeton University Committee on Research in the Humanities and Social Sciences, and the Committee on Research of the University of

California at Santa Cruz for financial aid at key moments in this project and to the dancers of Novantiqua, without whom I would not have thought. The work of live performance has been a constant stimulation to my research.

Finally, the influence of Michel de Certeau as a colleague and friend has been significant; he is sorely missed. I also extend my thanks to Roz Seelen and Arthur Seelen of the Drama Book Shop, the study group at the Warren Street Performance Loft, Maestro Karoly Zsedenyi for teaching me so much over so many years, and my parents.

ABBREVIATIONS

BC   Beaujoyeulx, *Le Balet comique de la Royne* in the French edition by McGowan and the English edition by MacClintock and MacClintock

E   Montaigne, *Essais*

L   Lacroix, *Ballets et mascarades de cour*

TC   Molière, *Théâtre complet*

PROLOGUE
Constructing the Baroque Body

Court ballet accommodated a potentially chaotic melange of music, decor, costumes, props, declamation, distributed librettos, and the audience's active participation, as well as dancing, acting, improvisation, miming, and mumming. Its illusionary universe was much closer – in material density if not in philosophical outlook – to twentieth-century performance art than to classical ballet. Displaced by or absorbed into this vertiginous complexity of collateral arts, the body seems often to have been no more than a spectacular accessory. In fact, many historians conclude that court ballet did not prefigure theatrical dancing as such but the more diffuse spectacle of opera, the genre of excess and displacement par excellence. Although the body was not the dominant artistic component of court ballet spectacle, it was nevertheless central to court ballet as a theatrical projection of noble and royal subjectivity. Court ballets magnified and, in the process, distorted the acceptable forms of contemporaneous noble sociability in accordance with conflicting, first- and second-estate visions of the dancer as subject, and of royal subjects in their specular totality: the nation. In other terms, court ballet was the mannerist scene of a power struggle. This study traces a vastly eccentric foray of manners into the mutating mirror of spectacle and the ideological bases of that performance.[1]

Late-twentieth-century reconstructions of the baroque grandee's dance frequently bring a chastened body to mind, a masked and quasi-desexualized body enacting rituals of opaque self-transparency. Because reconstructions accent past facts of performance, they tend to leave us with an aesthetic carapace.[2] Can we delve beneath its surface to recover the performance's original lines of force? What were the cultural politics of baroque dance? What repercussions did that politics have on court ballet aesthetics? Can a different history of the dancer's body be written, one that does not glorify dance history for the needs of the present, but unveils instead the life-and-death stakes of its performance in the there-and-then?

Cultural historians not directly concerned with dance history provide some useful parameters. Paul Bénichou used the phrase "pride proffering itself as spectacle" to characterize the early-seventeenth-century French noble.[3] In a less romantic vein, Norbert Elias thought the French aristocrat's penchant for self-display was a direct consequence of social constraints.[4] Whether heroic or conformist, the physical theatricality of dance was evidently integral to the noble's quest for prestige as well as to his strategy for survival.[5] Our vision of the cultural, social, and political elites of late Renaissance and early baroque France is, justifiably, filtered through a theatrical metaphor. At the heart of that metaphor lies the court ballet, the noble's most conspicuous arena of self-display and transformation. Yet as this book attempts to show, dance was more than an emblem of court society in its own theatricalized terms. It was also a real theater of ideological tensions:[6] in the early seventeenth century, some ballets were less consistently responsive to the dominant ideology than is commonly supposed.

Court ballet undergoes several distinct stages of evolution in the course of its brief existence, but it can nevertheless be considered one entity, unified by its characteristically anti-Aristotelian qualities.[7] The early baroque period, marked by burlesque and mannerist elements in art, literature, and performance, challenges what will become French neoclassicism and academism.[8] Throughout this study, however, my interest is drawn to marked shifts in the formal balance between dance and text. I believe that intensive focus on such shifts reveals the process of ideological investment in dance in a better way than connected chronological exposition. Therefore, although I proceed in chronological order, my intent is not to rehearse the chronology for its own sake, but rather to interpret court ballet's evolution through its most radically distinctive forms.[9] For the purposes of this study, those forms are exemplified by the first major court ballet, *Le Balet comique de la Royne* (1581),[10] the first well-documented burlesque ballet, *Les Fées des forests de Saint Germain* (1625), and Molière's comedy-ballets, notably *Les Fâcheux* (1661) and *Le Bourgeois Gentilhomme* (1670).

The vast majority of court ballet librettos were first collected in 1868 by Paul Lacroix.[11] Since then, chiefly British scholars from and in the wake of the Warburg school have investigated the social, political, and general aesthetic significance of court ballet.[12] But none have privileged dance and choreography as disciplines most instrumental to that significance. In staking out and developing the field, scholars have studied choreography as a relatively unproblematic feature of the surrounding spectacle and its sociohistorical setting.[13] Laying essential groundwork has displaced close readings of court ballet's choreographic technologies.

Building on Lacroix's work in bibliography, as well as on subsequent research by Henry Prunières and Frances A. Yates,[14] Margaret M. McGowan established a clear-cut periodization of court ballets. She classifies them as predominantly allegorical and political between 1581 and 1610, as melodramatic from 1610 to 1620, and as burlesque from 1620 until 1636.[15] This book is indebted to McGowan's work with which it frequently enters into fruitful dialogue.[16] My own reading of court ballet in the Valois period (1515–98), however, falls more recognizably within the critical tradition of Yates, who stressed the political uses of court ballet as those of mediation. For Yates, Valois festivities aspired to create harmonious accord between the warring factions of Protestant and Catholic extremists. My work extends to the aesthetics of political aspiration rather than separating aesthetics in a self-enclosed domain of ideal forms such as praise. Although praise certainly was one of court ballet's raisons d'être, two other functions nuanced celebratory intent: a politics of rapprochement under the late Valois kings and an ironic ambivalence under the early Bourbons. In the wake of Yates's contribution, much work has been done on early Valois court ballet (1564–84) by McGowan and Roy C. Strong.[17] Much work has also been accomplished on the period of "flowering" (1643–72) by Françoise Christout, Charles I. Silin, and Robert M. Isherwood.[18] The intervening period of seriocomic ambivalence, or burlesque (c. 1620–36), has not received equal attention. In particular, no one has ventured a strong interpretive position on the burlesque period. The present study endeavors to complement what has been written about the late Renaissance while widening the interpretive scope possible to analysis of the burlesque.[19]

The term *baroque*, a category that includes the burlesque, here refers to a period earlier than contemporary dance reconstructors usually designate.[20] Their major sources of dance notation for the seventeenth century were published after 1700 and do not refer to dance earlier than the 1660s. My use of the term *baroque* coincides more exactly with its use in the context of French literature and cultural history. Rather than speak of the period often associated with baroque dance reconstruction (1660–1750), I am concerned with the preceding period (1580–1660).[21] The period in which reconstructed dance usually originates was essentially academic because it postdates the foundation of the Royal Academy of Dance by Louise XIV in 1662. Because the pre-Academy period bridges the sixteenth and seventeenth centuries, it might, to use an art historical term, also be called mannerist. Yet the complexity of the issues surrounding mannerism and the baroque, although they might well be profitably reconsidered in the light of dance history, would distract at this stage from my focus on dance. Moreover, traditions of French cultural history lean toward the designation of the late Renaissance as a beginning of the baroque sensibility. Thus, Jean Rousset identified court ballet as typical of the French baroque style of literature, often characterized as either burlesque or pastoral until 1665.[22] Victor L. Tapié characterized the reign of Louis XIII (1610–43) as baroque because of its "liberal spirit, still full of fantasy, which is not scandalized by anything in life."[23] Most pertinently, José Antonio Maravall has qualified all baroque art as "the gesticulating submission of the individual to the confines of the social order."[24] The oppressive confines of the social order enmeshed the grandee-dancer in economic depression, class conflict leading to social and political uncertainty, and philosophical perplexity.[25]

A theoretical interest has recently emerged in some Continental scholarship with the relationship of dance to law.[26] Rudolf zur Lippe shows that French court ballet was essential to the legitimation of the monarch in his double status as real and ideal body.[27] Pierre Legendre explores more generally how the notion of legality has shaped dance ideology in Western culture.[28] In the present study, I shall wed ideological analysis more closely to the technologies of choreography than do either of these writers. For example, I do not agree with zur Lippe that the lack of a developed choreographic art in the seventeenth century actually favored a political use of court ballet.[29] Rather, the evidence indicates that choreographic structures and dance technique had a distinctly theoretical basis that needs elucidation before ideological analysis of the period can be complete.

That theoretical basis can be grasped through an analysis of the relationship of dance to text in court ballet. Much of what we know, or surmise, about dance is indicated in librettos distributed to the audience before performances or published afterward to commemorate them. Throughout this book, I question whether the body and the playing text (as found in extant librettos) were not "dramatically" counterposed. Thus, I regard both body and text as theatrical elements whose modes of collaboration or conflict determined court ballet aesthetics. In this study texts are considered in their nonverbal or choreographic configuration, in their verbal presence within dance performance, and as acts of a play that use dance as transitional interludes. In the period of burlesque ballets, the term *text* signifies what choreography sought to discard as extraneous to its own concerns: the spoken text of conventional theater. At this characteristic moment of the baroque period, dance undertook to discard the textual model for theater. In its place, choreographers set a series of live images with no more than incidental recourse to narrative. The history traced in this study shows a clear turn away from the interlude structure with its visually choreographed texts toward a virtually "textless" performance, an event legible in its own terms alone. (By "textless" I mean a performance in which the text's meaning is sensibly reduced or ambiguated.) The final phase of this evolution is marked by a reversion to the old interlude structure: Molière integrates dance more successfully with the concerns of conventional theater.

This study, however, does not endeavor to evaluate these different developments from only an aesthetic viewpoint. By gauging a dance–text differential in court ballet over approximately one hundred years, we come to realize that the radical moment of burlesque ballet is both preceded and followed by a contrary and apparently conservative tendency, one that construes dance as textual in every conceivable way short of having dancers speak. Not coincidentally, during these so-called textual periods monarchical ideology dominates court ballet. For example, in the Valois period, exemplified by composite spectacles such as *Le Balet comique*, choreography emulated texts graphically. Being hieroglyphic in their choreographic conceits, these dances needed to be deciphered. Many of the figures formed by the dancers, all noble subjects, led them to act out a sort of physical spelling: their bodies were subservient to texts designed to aggrandize the monarch. Dancers moved and held their bodies in positions choreographed to figure forth the letters of his name or patterns symbolic of his name's glorious attributes. In this sense, their movements were not their own.

In reaction to geometrical dance, antitextual, or burlesque, dance was an attempt to establish a legibility for dance independent of verbal means.[30] Such aesthetic autonomy had political significance when a body, independent of language, could mean something "more" or other than what language said it did. Dance history reveals a striking correlation between political resistance and the body's freedom from, or ironic rapport with, the text in performance. The choreographic struggle between dance and text in the burlesque reveals the text to be a metaphor for autocratic power. Consequently, a body wresting itself – as in burlesque ballet – from the control of an explicative text is potentially subversive. Such are the historicotheoretical premises I shall demonstrate in the following chapters. After the burlesque experiment with choreographic autonomy from texts, Molière returned dance to its role in verbal theater. The experiment with physical self-referentiality had been provocative and controversial in an art of such cultural centrality as was court ballet in seventeenth-century France. Burlesque performance did not stop at pornography as a means for oppositional statement. By proceeding from the burlesque works of the 1620s to Molière's comedy-ballets of the 1660s and 1670s, I am concerned to trace an aftermath of the burlesque trend, which is the central focus of this study. I am interested in the concatenation of events and amassing of facts inasmuch as they illuminate the issue of body and text, but not inasmuch as they speak for themselves.

By a "textless" body I mean two interrelated things: first of all, an independence from verbal, Aristotelian theater whose model is the rhetorical one of verbal and phonetic communication and whose goal is the imitation of human action in a progressive and linear sense, and the psychological consistency of character that imitation also implies. Second, the text-opposed body signifies a political autonomy aspired to by many of those who planned, created, and actually performed court ballets. Burlesque ballets were often the work of the highest aristocrats and princes of the blood: the duke of Vendôme, Gaston d'Orléans, the dukes of Guise, Nevers, and Nemours. These grandees used court ballets to theatricalize a privileged subculture.[31] Late humanist emphasis on skepticism and stoicism, the political attitudes of Gallicanism in France, and a more intangible yet widespread impiety and cynicism – probably the result of France's long history of religious civil wars – must all have contributed to the satiric impulse of the baroque era.[32] Yet it was the nobility's political precariousness that most directly fueled that critical and satiric impulse in court ballets. The period of the most virulently critical burlesque ballets, from 1624 until 1627, coincided with the first years of Richelieu's administration. At this time, Richelieu's ministry was engaged in suppressing the political power of Protestants and princes in order to consolidate centralization.[33] The princely magnates attempted a failed palace coup against Richelieu in 1626. Concurrently, they exercised political resistance by satirizing heroic ballets promoted by Richelieu: part of their satire's meaning, as well as its built-in safety mechanism, was the reduction of the use of words as a context for ideological control. Distance from the text, however, was achieved at the price of eroticism and obscenity. The popular tradition of carnivalesque reversals and low style was endemic to the kind of satire that burlesque performance produced. Still, the motif of royal glorification continued to assert itself in these works alongside contradictory and opposing elements. Burlesque ballets were not conceived and performed in isolation by separate factions but enacted with the participation of Louis XIII. Court ballet of the early 1600s reveals a society struggling to define its political culture in performance before similar attempts were made through the seditious actions of the Frondes.

The period of burlesque ballet allowed for an intentionally ambivalent performance practice in which the body may have come closer to being an autonomous sign than at any other time before the modern period.[34] Yet paradoxically, one can claim relative self-referentiality for the dancing body at this time precisely because its meaning is so dynamically divided as to suggest that it meant nothing or simply itself.[35] The burlesque can be at odds with a number of possible meanings and with the idea of meaning itself. Thus, the dancing body hovers between the semblance of pure play and political statement. Burlesque ballet puts ideology into play, threatening to alter it at every turn. According to Yates's interpretation of late Renaissance culture, court ballets were originally part of a strategy to obtain political compromise among warring religious factions.[36] The notion of a more complex political intent than praise can be extended – though in quite different terms – to the early seventeenth century. That is, the topos of court ballet as propagandistic celebration of the royal house – illusion of power – can be nuanced by more critical and liberal goals vis-à-vis centralization. I will argue that burlesque ballet extends the notion of performance designed to engender compromise toward that of a compromising performance *tout court*. Nevertheless, burlesque ballet manifested a plurality of voices and views; Louis XIII himself danced in many burlesque works, turning some to "good" effect.

Mikhail Bakhtin remarked that the carnivalesque grotesque survived the Renaissance: according to Bakhtin, a carnivalized or grotesque element was still operative in the seventeenth-century novel, burlesque court ballets (also called "travesty"), as well as in Molière's comedy-ballets.[37] Most important for my argument, Bakhtin recognized that burlesque court ballet expressed opposition to official culture.[38] Bakhtin's understanding of that opposition as degenerate could result only from the limitations of his ideological position, not from a conviction that court ballet expressed official culture exclusively (clearly it did not) or was the "private" moral dilemma of a dissipated nobility. Even an imperfectly realized grotesque, Bakhtin wrote, "frees human consciousness, thought and imagination for new potentialities."[39] For Bakhtin, the notion of renewal or regeneration was the desired consequence of carnivalesque distortion, of the latter's plunge into physical and material baseness. Yet he felt the pointed lewdness of burlesque style was devoid of regenerative energy: it was cynical. Reduced laughter doesn't resonate; it fails to stimulate glimpses of an alternative yet still distant new order. Nonetheless, the question remains unanswered how carnivalesque motifs indigenous to medieval and Renaissance popular culture found their way into the upper echelons of baroque culture.[40] What was the rationale for a carnivalized court ballet feigning to represent court society to itself?[41]

If Bakhtin's definition of Renaissance carnival acknowledges seventeenth-century court ballet's burlesque qualities while declining their interpretation, his description of Menippean satire applies to the burlesque with fewer ideological strings attached. After *Rabelais and His World*, Bakhtin became interested in a seriocomic tradition that blended praise and blame. Revived by Varro in the first century A.D., Menippean satire threads uninterruptedly through the history of Western culture.[42] Burlesque ballet shares all of the qualities that Bakhtin attributes to Menippean satire: a profound connection to the present that gives the performance an unfinished quality; "free invention" – imaginative and fantastic, as well as scandalously eccentric – along with a cynical relationship to tradition; an intentional plurality of styles in the quotation of earlier traditional motifs; brusque transformations, violent contrast, and oxymoronic structures that reject dogmatic truths; and, finally, an evident involvement in contemporary sociopolitical problems and an ideologically polemical stance taken toward them. Highly innovative in its forms, burlesque ballet was opposed to epic and classical expressions of dance and theater alike.

When the independently minded though veiled burlesque counterculture had run its course, Louis XIV maximized the potential for propaganda formerly inherent in royal spectacle under the Valois. Between 1651 and 1670 he danced in court ballets. "The age of Louis XIV," writes dance historian Curt Sachs, "marks a peak in the artistic development of dance."[43] In this study, however, I focus more on the aborted autonomy of burlesque ballet than on the glorious apotheosis of the Sun King proclaiming his autocratic centrality. I do not trace the development of the "noble style" in the art of spectacular dancing but rather the precedents for later choreographic theory in the so-called low style.[44] In my view, what transpired in the generally reviled earlier experimentation with burlesque ballet was more significant to the modern development of choreographic art.

Certain modern artists of the twentieth-century centered their creative work on the issue of autonomy. Thus, for example, Edward Gordon Craig and Oskar Schlemmer were fascinated with the idea of the dancer and/or actor as machines, with the automization of the body. Some American, German, and French modern dance (e.g., that of Graham, Wigman, and Saint-Point)[45] and related incursions of the body into twentieth-century theater — Artaud, in particular, comes to mind — take conceptual root in earlier French dance history. I want to suggest that the groundwork for choreographic and theatrical autonomy as a variegated modernist motif was laid in the cultural milieu of the French baroque. This book, then, argues that French baroque court ballet was, for a time, much more experimental and politically volatile than has previously been acknowledged. I suggest a radical rereading of dance history in the baroque era and, by implication, of dance modernism in the twentieth century as a one-way street that led from America to France.

Ballet was initially conceived of as a composite entity that included the other major art forms and was intended to illustrate the political unity of the late Valois dynasty. My study begins with an account of geometrical dance, a choreographic genre germane to court ballet prior to the burlesque phenomenon.[46] Geometrical dance constitutes the earliest European experiment with the body in theatrical space and also betrays a concern with the idea of a text rendered choreographically. It was part of a complex theoretical structure dictated by the idea that the arts of poetry, music, and dance should be fused in the theatrical form called ballet. Within this theoretical structure, geometrical dance existed as an aesthetic midpoint between text and music. It was connected to the drama of the text without really reenacting it, and it obeyed music while not partaking of music's abstraction. It was an indeterminate art form relative to the more established genres to which it could intermittently allude but with which it could never decisively merge. Although geometrical dance employed steps drawn from the prestigious vocabulary of social dance forms such as the *branle* and the *basse danse,* theatrical dancing itself was the "other" of Western aesthetics. At its inception in French court spectacle, geometrical dance drew on a spatial visualization of the text and a physical rendering of the metrical structures of music. Those metrical structures were, in their turn, subservient to poetic meter. Thus, the aesthetic circuitry of composite spectacle enabled textuality to generate theatrical dancing. Yet when one examines the structure of an entire work such as *Le Balet comique* (1581), dance appears to be the fulcrum on which the other arts are balanced. Through an analysis of the kinetic principle of *fantasmata,* inherited from the Italian Renaissance, it will be shown how geometrical dance was able to coordinate a variety of aesthetic and theoretical concerns in *Le Balet comique.*

Although *Le Balet comique* was not strictly speaking the very first court ballet,[47] it is the most significant early example of this form from a structural point of view. Its structure involves a dichotomy between geometrical dance and dramatic narrative as well as an attempt to transcend that dichotomy. Examining the theory and practice of *Le Balet comique* leads one to reevaluate the meaning of harmony and the role of dance in rendering the concept of harmony – with all of its concomitant social, political, and aesthetic aspects – in theatrical terms. In *Le Balet comique,* the dancing body is seen to act on the model of the voice and, as such, is dependent on a text. The voice had the mobility to move between the various artistic modalities of word, song, and physicality. Indeed, the dancing body can be seen to usurp the central and mobile position of the voice with regard to the ballet's structure and theory, if not with regard to its embodied form. Thus, ultimately, the body can be seen in this work as a textural surrogate whose potential as an autonomous entity is theoretical but not fully realized. Although the dance seemed to be emerging as an autonomous form on a theoretical level, it still remained far from this independence in its artistic embodiment.

If *Le Balet comique*'s libretto is the first comprehensive text of a composite spectacle, *Les Fées des forests de Saint Germain* (1625) is the first well-documented example of the burlesque style in court ballet. This work also reveals different traditions of social dance: its choreography lies between earlier social uses and a new theatrical context. In fact, *Les Fées* is about dance itself – its theme is the various sociocultural connotations of dance. In this sense, it is mannerist: it attempts to establish its own internal dance history. Along with other burlesque works to follow, it seeks to establish theater dance as a form independent of verbal theater or composite spectacle. On an aesthetic level, burlesque ballet renders theater dance self-reflexive. Text and decor are intentionally neglected as components of court ballet. In their place, an elaborately costumed dancing figure, whose physical body is often concealed within deforming constructed shapes, occupies the stage. The visual impact of this figure – by turns noble, grotesquely distorted, or highly intellectualized by visible allegory – is the focal point of this type of ballet. Both the aesthetic autonomy of these works from the canon of "good taste" and the autonomy of the dancing body from an encompassing textual structure have political analogies. The noble participant in burlesque performance displays himself prodigally, as in other more codified instances of his social existence, in order to affirm his own identity and place in courtly society. Yet in this particular genre, the exhibition of the self is accomplished is a subversive or libertine spirit betokening criticism and political resistance. Burlesque ballet presents a contestatory body placing unity, harmony, and textual obedience in question. In the Valois period, court ballets commemorated occasions; under Louis XIII they became potential occasions of their own: if the earlier ballets were like incantations, those of the burlesque period were similar to failed prophecies. Moreover, the burlesque phenomenon situates us at an odd interpretive crossroad between two critically dominant historical visions of Renaissance and baroque society and artistic creation, those of Elias and Bakhtin.

According to Norbert Elias, the noble is a developing *homo clausus,* or closed personality, in the process of internalizing external constraints.[48] *Homo clausus* becomes "civilized" by relinquishing the empire of his drives over his actions. As we know from interpretations of the "feudal" aspect of noble self-consciousness in the baroque, this also entails relinquishing his political aspirations in favor of a concept of civilization in keeping with contemporary state formation.[49] On the other hand, Bakhtin's notion of carnival, much closer in its aesthetic manifestation to burlesque art, is enacted by the lower classes. Bakhtin's *homo ludens* never realizes his political force consciously: he is part of a vaster process of dialectical materialism.[50] Neither the *homo clausus* nor the *homo ludens* holds out hope for an interpretive account of burlesque ballet. Its particularly libertine spirit leads me to posit an intermediate figure who shares the class attributes of Elias's construct and the transgressive attitude of Bakhtin's. *Homo strategicus* is somewhere between the conscious resignation or burgeoning self-control of Elias's *homo clausus* and the relatively unconscious play of Bakhtin's *homo ludens*. *Homo strategicus* is one who can suggest change playfully, resisting the status quo by feigning to play.[51] The noble engaged in burlesque ballet was just such a being. Thus, in addition to reading dance history against the grain by placing positive emphasis at new and unusual junctures, I intentionally revise the traditional views of Lacroix, Fournel, and Kirstein, who believe that burlesque ballet was nothing other than a regrettable instance of moral dissolution.[52] The shift I propose inevitably engages questions of canonicity in dance history. Writing burlesque ballet into the canon implies rewriting the canon. This book is partially an attempt to question the foundations of canonical history by rehistoricizing burlesque ballet as politicized game playing.

Following the dominance of geometrical dance at the close of the sixteenth century and burlesque style ballets in the early seventeenth century, Molière's invention of comedy-ballet represents the third most significant innovation in baroque theater dance.[53] The first work of this genre, *Les Fâcheux* (1661), raises familiar issues of dance and text. And precisely because of the relevance of the dance–text dialectic to Molière, his comedy-ballets constitute an important chapter of court ballet history. But since, until now, they have not been apprehended in the context of dance history with any theoretical scope, the critical landscape changes at this stage of the argument. If in the first part of this study my references are predominantly to Yates, McGowan, and zur Lippe, I refer to an entirely different set of commentators toward the end. Although the texts of Benserade, the most famous of seventeenth-century librettists, are usually associated with the high point of French court ballet tradition, Molière's contribution proves to have had a greater effect on the subsequent development of choreography. Whereas Benserade made ballet an adjunct of lyric opera, Molière attempted to integrate dance and theater by returning to the origins of their combination.[54] The dance material he employed in *Les Fâcheux* (1661) derived from the burlesque tradition that had preceded him, but the way in which he used burlesque style recalled the earlier structural aesthetic of *Le Balet comique*. Grafting burlesque *entrées* onto the acts of his play, Molière rehabilitated the use of interlude. Dance was again bounded on both sides by dramatic texts. Yet in another sense, Molière also discovered a new form of generic harmony.

It is significant that *Les Fâcheux* was commissioned by the superintendent of finances, Nicolas Fouquet, for his fête in honor of the young Louis XIV at the former's château Vaux-le-Vicomte.[55] The result of this magnificence produced by Fouquet moved Louis XIV to imprison him two weeks later. The fall of Fouquet signals the symbolic demise of the Fronde movements – a series of challenges to the programs of centralism under Mazarin – just as Molière's comedy-ballet brings burlesque dance again within the pale of textual control and monarchical surveillance.[56] These two events occur at the beginning of the personal reign of Louis XIV. If burlesque ballet had represented a form of veiled protest in its curious autonomy, and an obvious critique through its satire, the events surrounding *Les Fâcheux* mark the death of any such activism. Moreover, they mark the beginning of a studied transformation of the potentially autonomous noble into an impotent court-ier. The very formal experiments *Les Fâcheux* indulges in can be read as a reflection of a return to political control over the body. Interlude – "playing between" – was to be included rather than excluded. But the underlying strategy of court festivity was to undermine the dissident potential of in-terlude by this very inclusion, to infiltrate autonomy and redirect its diver-sions. Louis XIV's politics with regard to spectacle would be announced in his *Lettres patentes pour l'etablissement de l'Académie royale de danse* of 1662. They would become only too evident in the most carefully engineered of his entertainments at Versailles: *Les Plaisirs de l'île enchantée* (1664) and *Le Grand Divertissement royal de Versailles* (1668).[57]

Studying late Renaissance and early baroque dance in its political and aes-thetic contexts, one virtually reconstructs that dance in one's mind, and then on paper. This act of reconstruction presupposes the theatrical one of live performance. In fact, my interest in this subject was aroused by a reverse process. This book, and much of the research that precedes it, grew from a dissatisfaction with the reconstruction of historical dance as practiced in the late twentieth century. Reconstructions appeared to me for the most part as mechanical reproductions that, while rendering a modicum of literal accur-acy, were nevertheless devoid of true theatrical, and therefore historical, di-mension. The allusion to Walter Benjamin's "The Work of Art in the Age of Mechanical Reproduction" is not accidental. What has been missing in most reconstruction is precisely the uniqueness of the original as a quality of the performance. Benjamin thought of uniqueness as "inseparable from [the work's] being in the fabric of tradition."[58] Without the presence of tradition – the reconstruction of the conditions of reception – reconstruction simulates the past in the manner of a copy. Nothing could be more adverse to the very medium of live performance. And yet the reconstruction of the audience is also an impossible project. In the case of burlesque ballet, it would imply reproducing the political predicament of the dancer as shared by the audience rather than as dramatized for it. The very historical impossibility of this theatrical goal renders the reconstructive project an uncomfortable paradox.

Why were reconstructions lifeless? It seemed to me that dance *re*-construc-tion typically posited performance as a retrievable text. The original "histor-ical" performance, however, was never inscribed in anything more durable than contemporaneous time and space: its textual remnants – librettos, notes, drawings – could only be marginally helpful. Moreover, unlike the sixteenth and eighteenth centuries, the early seventeenth lacks explicit sources elucidating its dance vocabulary and style. Therefore, the common theory of reconstruction that viewed dance as a lost text was doomed to failure because of its very literalism. The "text," because of its partial nature, could never be retrieved as a literal entity. Or rather, its very literalism in performance compromised its historical force. The more scientific and exacting reconstruction becomes, the more it results in a choreographic fashion show, one in which dances are paraded by bodies like garments on mannequins. I was thus led to reflect on the relationship between dance and text on a theoretical as well as a historical level. My hypothesis is that the baroque period itself, while presently being the object of so much reconstructive activity, has something to tell us about the textual status of dance, and consequently about its own stylistic translation into the present.[59] I came to accept that one should reflect on the concept of reconstruction itself. Rethinking the idea of reconstruction seemed a necessary preamble to the reenactment of anything "historical." This book's method is to present that rethinking using seventeenth-century court ballet as its historical touchstone. In so doing, it implicitly sets forth an approach to the performance of historical material that I call "constructive" rather than reconstructive. Construction is a form of mannerism that replaces simulation with theoretical analysis. Construction aims above all at retrieving a theory of effects that can be theatrically experienced as unique in the contemporary moment while still purveying historicalness. Thus, my research methodology and my performance practice are intertwined: I understand and "construct" the historical event through the theory of its effects.

In the Epilogue, I return to the question of reconstruction that inspired these chapters. I examine the assumptions that reconstruction and a particular strand of theatrical theory have clandestinely shared. Since Molière, the body has exerted a powerful impact on theatrical theory. Denis Diderot in France, Heinrich von Kleist in Germany, and Edward Gordon Craig in England each pursued an ideal of inexpressive stage practice recalling aspects of court ballet. Although they did not, like Molière, necessarily return to its characteristic forms, they prolonged some implications of court ballet theory through the elaboration of a partially theoretical and partially practical theatrical entity: the marionette. In the work of these theorists, the marionette or automaton comes to represent perfected theatrical gesture as repeatable. It implies that the best performance practice is always already reconstructed. The marionette signifies both a highly articulated movement technology and a theatrical ideal of the definitive become, in many respects, uncanny. It prefigures the dance work in the age of mechanical reconstruction. In the marionette figure, the issues of autonomy and textuality are conjoined: the new issue that emerges entails repeating (textualizing) dance without draining the energy associated with its original appearance. In Benjamin's dialectic, mechanical reproduction can foster revolutionary critique: textuality (the hypothetical possibility that dance could remain stable, present, and self-identical) can resist prevailing ideology. In the light of this dialectic, the mar-

tation and choreographic flux and diversity in its three-dimensional and voluminous presentation counteracted other mimetic considerations of the dance. The actions performed before the eyes of an audience were those of constructing and dissolving hieroglyphs. They had little or nothing to do with the expression of emotion. The movement leading up to and away from these symbolic figures left dancers in a conceptual limbo. By performing a geometrical dance, they neither imitated lifelike actions nor abstracted their own human presence as formal bodies in space. Rather, in the interim between pattern and the matrix from which it emerged, they theorized, by dancing, on their alternately textual and nontextual status.

The verb *to read* (*lego, legere*) applied to Henry III's spectatorship of *Le Balet des Polonais* might well have been the Greek verb *theorein*: to look at, to contemplate, to survey. Geometrical dance suggests an approach to a problem in dance aesthetics, the problem of how theatrical dancing constructs its meaning. The evidence studied suggests that dance constructs meaning neither through pure *aesthesis* – sensual apprehension – nor through unswerving intellection.[52] Rather, meaning in dance is constructed through a contemplation and inference significantly connected to the root meaning of *theory*. For Aristotle, the term *theory* signifies the spectator's active contemplation of the performance. *Praxis,* on the other hand, is not opposed to theory as active to passive. Praxis is the act of performing itself. "In *theoria,*" writes Frances Fergusson "the matter is 'to grasp and understand' some truth. It may be translated as 'contemplation,' if one remembers that, for Aristotle, contemplation is intensely active."[53] Aristotle discusses *theoria* in the context of his idea that poetry is an imitation. The interpretation of poetry, its *theoria,* begins with the game of analogy suggested by likeness. And that sort of analogical, rather than representational, imitation found through likeness is precisely the work of the figure. Such theorizing, if it has hermeneutic value, is not limited to the spectator. The development of a belated dance theory seems to depend, at least in part, on grasping how theory is implicit in the act of dancing itself. Not only is theory a way to create meaningful order in ideas about dancing, but dancing itself is an inherently theoretical act. Dance theory is not thought through "after" choreography; it is constitutive of choreography itself.

Clearly, geometrical dance assimilated the individual performer to the group, just as it assimilated the patterns of the group to a simulacrum of language. In geometrical dance, the body of the courtier or of the maid of honor to the queen was reduced to a signifying element or semantic particle of the sovereign's proper name or of a visual figure containing some message about the sovereign.[54] Thus, the text exerted a power over the body's action, absorbing each individual will within the "idea of a social body constituted by the universality of wills."[55] The aristocrat's body was thus poised between the "feudal" pride of its cast and "lexico-organic" manipulation by the monarch. His or her body is displayed gloriously while being in the service of a pattern whose meaning transcended and semantically absorbed individual presence. Geometrical dance projected a physical lexicon whose signatory was the king. Its figures were produced under constraint and, indeed, as an effect of metaphorical paralysis. Yet one should always bear in mind that flight from the figure – liberation from Medusa's disempowering stare – was a necessary condition for the theatrical translation of paralyzing power.

UT VOX CORPUS, 1581

"Viens donc, Nymphe royalle, et oppose au sçavoir
Des demons ennemis le celeste pouvoir."
"Come forth, royal Nymph, and oppose demons' knowledge
Of the enemy with celestial power."

*Ballet représentéz devant le roy à la venue
de Madame à Tours* (1593)

Ballet spectacle in the late Renaissance began as a hybrid of preexisting art forms: dance, drama, and music. Indeed, the term *ballet* then referred both to an entire spectacle and to its danced segments. The latter were often segregated from dramatic action just as interludes were separate from the acts of a play. Combining the arts in spectacle called "ballet" had both ideological and aesthetic significance for the Renaissance mind. Clearly, one should look to Renaissance thought on politics and music when seeking to understand the nature and necessity of collective unity in early modern *Gesamtkunstwerk*.

The ideological aim of such performance was for ballet's harmonic being to act persuasively on France's political reality. In the Renaissance, the body politic was often symbolized by the members of a harmoniously articulated body. Each physical member, aware of "degree," knew its place and function. Fittingly, *Le Balet comique de la Royne*'s choreographer, Balthazar de Beaujoyeulx, called the entire work "un corps bien proportionné" ("a well-proportioned body") (BC, "Au lecteur"). It could demonstrate measured proportion not only by presenting bodies exemplarily, but also through the ballet's very organization and its choreography. The structured joining of both the different arts and the choreography within and between them produced metaphors of harmony in the aural and sociopolitical senses.

As the philosophical basis of musical harmony from which they would extrapolate politically and artistically, Italian and French musical humanists

– from Zarlino, Artusi, and Mei through Pontus de Tyard and Mersenne – stressed the interval. This chapter will demonstrate how influential the harmonic notion of the interval was for *Le Balet comique*. At the same time, it will show that early theatrical choreography of Western dance promoted the body as a metaphor for theoretical ideas about harmony as much or more than as an emotional response to it. In other words, theatrical dancing originally appeared as a visual manifestation and physical embodiment of social, political, and cosmic theories of order to the virtual exclusion of individual expressivity. Whereas early modern performance is often assumed to have belabored rudimentary physical expression, the dancing body in *Le Balet comique* appears as a mediator of concepts with only minimal recourse to the representation of human emotion.

I will argue on historical grounds against Francis Sparshott's view of dance. Following Hegel, Sparshott claims: "Any dance that models the cosmos is boring. Or, at least, the cosmic symbolism and the aesthetic interest are at odds."[1] Most commentators of *Le Balet comique* argue for its unity and cohesiveness on some level. Obviously, they are defending it against the disparaging view that court ballet was at best hybrid (i.e., generically uncertain), accidental (because collaborative), and artificial (since performance was stressed over text). The negative view of this period of dance history (which Sparshott seems to share) asserts that cosmic allegory impeded the aesthetic potential inherent in dance, that cosmic symbolism reduced court ballet to a purely ceremonious function devoid of theatrical and, consequently, poetic vitality.

In my view, the key to the perhaps unconventional unity of *Le Balet comique* lies in the relationship of the danced segments (interludes or "divertissements") to the entire work. In fact, the notion of interval affords an interpretive strategy for choreographic, dramatic, and musical coherence. But this is neither to redeem the work as emotionally engaging, as advocates of unity might, nor to fault it as aesthetically unmotivated, as a modern-day detractor would. It is simply to claim for court ballet an intellectualized spectatorship. *Le Balet comique* should not be dismissed as a spectacle too primitive for serious consideration in dance history, or worthy of that consideration only because it is a "first" – unless we deny that dancing has any historical dimension.[2] Although the values at stake in *Le Balet comique* may at first appear exclusively choreographic, they nevertheless derive from an aesthetic of bodily movement. Moreover, the leap from that dancing body to the body politic is also something more than a cliché. In her book *The Valois Tapestries,* Frances A. Yates has shown that court ballets in the broader contexts of other festivities were designed to equilibrate a precarious political and religious conflict of enormous European consequence. The evangelical movement of the early sixteenth century survived in the later efforts of the en rond, et de plusieurs et diverses façons, et aussi tost en triangle, accompagné de quelque autre petit quarré, et autres petites figures" ("and these all exact and well-planned in their shapes, sometimes square, sometimes round, in several diverse fashions; then in triangles accompanied by a small square, and other small figures") (BC, 55v–56r:90).

Once again, the precise configuration of patterns in the *entrée* and in the grand ballet remains vague. Yet there is one important nuance. In the grand ballet two subgroups move in tandem so that pattern and flux are played against one another not only sequentially but also spatially. They form a visual contrast to each other in their very simultaneity: "Lesquelles figures n'estoyent si tost marquees par les douze Naiades, vestues de blanc . . . que les quatre Dryades habillees de verd ne les veinssent rompre: de sorte que l'une finissant, l'autre soudain prenoit son commencement" ("These figures were no sooner formed by the Naiads, dressed in white, than the four Dryads, dressed in green, arrived to change the shape, so that as one ended, the other began) (BC, 56r:90–1). In different terms, one group breaks a pattern at the precise moment when another group begins to hold a pattern. No longer do pose and movement merely succeed one another; rather, there is a visual and kinetic tension created between them, as they oppose and generate each other contrapuntally. This effect is doubtless supported by four identifiable groups of dancers – Naiads, Dryads, Nereids, and Oreads – each group distinguished by a predominant color.[22]

Apart from the grand bal – which followed the grand ballet and in which audience and performers alike could engage in *branles* and other social dances – all the formal choreography in *Le Balet comique* is contained in the two *entrées* and the grand ballet. Having isolated *strictu sensu* dance from the surrounding context, let us see how dance embodies a theory of harmony in the ballet.

Beaujoyeulx's preface announces the novelty of a new mixed theatrical genre that harmoniously incorporates dance, music, and poetry. A close inspection of the preface shows that one kind of harmony is that of poetry with music:

Je me suis advisé qu'il ne seroit point indecent de mesler l'un et l'autre ensemblément, et diversifier la musique de poesie, et entrelacer la poesie de musique, et le plus souvent les confondre toutes deux ensemble. (BC, "Au lecteur": 33)

I decided it would not be a bad idea to mix one and the other together, and to diversify the music with poetry and weave poetry with music, and most often to merge the two together.

At first it appears that harmony is taken in its apparent sense such as Pontus de Tyard formulated it in 1555: "Une douce confusion de l'un en l'autre . . . ils ne deviennent quasi qu'un son" ("A sweet blending of one into the other . . . they become as if one sound").[23] The harmony of dance and theater is modeled on that of poetry and music:

Ainsi j'ay animé et fait parler le Balet, et chanter et resonner la Comedie: et y adjoustant plusieurs rares et riches representations et ornements, je puis dire avoir contenté en un corps bien proportionné, l'oeil, l'oreille, et l'entendement. (BC, "Au lecteur": 33)

Thus I have animated and made Ballet speak, and Comedy sing and resound, and have added many rare and rich scenes and ornaments. I may say that within a single well-proportioned body I have pleased eye, ear and mind.

Under the auspices of a new genre, harmonic identity, the exchange between dance and theater actually concerns song and word: the dance would "speak" and theater "sing." The enumeration of the harmonic triad of poetry, dance, and music is expressed at best as two sets of couples rather than as a triple blending.[24] The three different genres are not present in equal proportion; nor do they interact or exchange artistic functions to an equal degree, in theory or in practice. In fact, each couple merely serves to restate the pairing of voice and poetic text that renders dance extraneous to the triad. If we are to take the preface at its face value, dance exists only as luxurious addition, a separable ornament, albeit "rare" and "rich."

Having deprived dancing proper of any effective role in the realization of harmony, Beaujoyeulx retreats from the idea of an exchange of artistic functions and restates harmony as a form of juxtaposition: "Je ne pouvais tout attribuer au Balet sans faire tort à la Comédie, distinctement representee par ses scenes et actes: ny à la Comédie sans prejudicier au Balet, qui honore, esgaye et remplit d'harmonieux récits le beau sens de la Comédie" ("I could not attribute all to the Ballet without wronging Comedy, distinctly represented by its scenes and acts, nor to Comedy without prejudice to the Ballet, which honors, enlivens and fills out the sense of Comedy with harmonious récits") (BC, a.iij.:28). *Récit* seems to be a term for the danced part of the ballet, yet there are examples of the *récit* as a sung text before the dance.[25] Like *intermezzo*, the term *récit* is not used with great consistency. Harmony was not, in all likelihood, conceived as the simultaneous occurrence of, and exchanging forms between, several artistic genres – dance, music, and poetry. Rather, harmony consists in a serial occurrence of different forms that create intervals between themselves: music, dance, and poetry interrupt, overlap on, and are juxtaposed against each other, concordantly. Menestrier puts these questions into some perspective when he writes:

Comme les Representations en Musique s'interrompent quelquefois par des entrées de Ballets; on peut aussi interrompre les entrées de Ballets par des recits en Musique. Au Ballet du Triomphe de l'Amour . . . Diane chantoit au milieu des Danses de ses Nymphes.[26]

Just as musical Representations can sometimes be interrupted by balletic *entrées,* one can also interrupt *entrées* by sung *récits*. In the Ballet du Triomphe de l'Amour . . . Diane sung in the midst of the dances of her nymphs.

One senses in Menestrier's description that harmony for the baroque sensibility was conceived of as an interruptive space between forms, even in their very simultaneity.[27] The different arts set each other off in a contrastive manner rather than blend indistinguishably within one another. In fact, the integral presence of each art almost seems for a time to obliterate the memory of the others.

In Beaujoyeulx's preface, it would appear that dance, although granted "le premier tiltre et honneur" ("first place and honor"), is evicted from the primarily vocal figure of harmony. Beaujoyeulx's comments on harmony in the work's preface give theoretical importance to the voice as a principle of movement and exchange. He illustrates the idea that fusion of the arts occurs with respect to the voice alone as a medium of transference between song and text. In this performance, dance subsists as an eccentric ornament, in fact, as an intermezzo whose function is to mark the divisions of acts.[28] In the prefatory "Au lecteur," Beaujoyeulx describes the whole ballet as a well-proportioned body that pleases the eye, the ear, and the mind, which correspond, of course, to the three components of the work's harmony. Dance was meant to please the eye, song the ear, and poetry the mind. Yet in the preface, Beaujoyeulx also restates the idea of a three-part harmony. Although the preface apparently points to the celebrated Horatian dictum "ut pictura poesis" ("poetry should be like painting"), when applied to dance and theater, closer scrutiny reveals that "ut comedia choreia" ("dancing should be like theater") is not its true message. Where, then, can we locate harmony in this succession of acts and intermezzos? I think that the answer lies in the theoretical import of the work's very structure, as illuminated by the conceits of the preface. I want to argue that the work itself contains the vision of a body whose dance movement has the attributes of a voice. The truly applicable formula is "ut vox corpus" ("bodies should be like voices"). Dancing is a visual intermediary between the spectator and harmony: in seeing dancing we see voice, not only as a conciliatory image, but also as a third term, a genuine hybrid, a sort of conceptual androgyne.

Charles Delmas has proposed the theory that the act and the intermezzo correspond to "a double necessity, triumphal and dramatic."[29] The intermezzo, whether in the form of a procession, song, or *entrée,* would celebrate the triumphal return of the golden age, while the dramatic or spoken sequences would maintain the tension of "fear before the obstacle" to the golden age, which is Circe's threat of chaos and diversity. An interlacing of acts and intermezzos would create, for Delmas, what he calls "the essential unity of the ballet," because the processions, which are somewhat premature celebrations, have a tendency to defuse the action while, by the same token, they become progressively more integrated "into the dramatic movement."[30] That is to say, theater relinquishes action to become more strictly verbal. Hence, it can become less dramatic as it takes on a more strictly celebrating function that is essentially musical. Dance, on the other hand, becomes progressively more dramatic as the ballet proceeds, as the dramatic representation of a festivity in the final grand ballet rather than a divertissement. But to do so, dance is also accompanied by music. At this culminating point, when text is pure song and dance is dramatic action, harmony of the genres is achieved by an exchange of functions, justified dramatically by the presence of music. For Delmas, "Music is the mediator that unites the two genres." Furthermore, in this process, he says that choreography aspires to be "an articulated language" thanks to its increasing mimetic capacity.[31] What theater progressively loses in action is recouped by the dance. This chiasmus is, for Delmas, at the root of what can be called the harmony of the piece.

Consider, however, that dance is much more circumscribed in *Le Balet comique* than is commonly assumed. The evidence reveals that, far from being interchangeable with the act, dance only coalesces with the act at the end of each intermezzo. The true fusion of act and intermezzo occurs only when geometrical dance is interrupted. When dramatic action intersects the act of dancing, dance is also perceived as a dramatic act. What had at first appeared pure pageantry takes on the qualities of dramatic progress. Therefore, dance enjoys drama's "active" rather than mere processional or celebratory status at the very moment of its interruption. In *Le Balet comique*, metamorphosis itself exemplifies interruption as a structural principle. Human beings and goddesses, who lose their capacity for speech or movement, are *interrupted* and become part of a dramatic action. This encompasses their suspended (verbal and motor) functions, ironically, as dramatic acts.

Circe sees the dance of the nymphs and decides to bewitch them by her immobilizing wand:

[Circé] sortit en grande colere, tenant en sa main droicte sa verge d'or hault eslevee et s'en vint tout le long de la salle au lieu ou estoyent les nymphes (placees en forme d'un croissant, ayans leur faces tournees vers leurs maiestez) les touchant l'une après l'autre avec sa verge d'or, duquel attouchement elles demeurerent soudain immobiles comme statues.[32]

She emerged, very angry, holding her golden wand high in her hand. She came forward the whole length of the hall, to where the nymphs stood (arranged in a crescent facing their Majesties); she touched them one after another with her golden wand, and at her touch each became motionless as a statue.

By halting the dance, Circe renders it part of the dramatic action. Dance is absorbed into the narrative only when it loses its characteristic aspect, movement. It is literally reduced to a statuary and statuesque figure. Moreover, the incorporation of the *entrée* into the act occurs by transforming the former into a tableau vivant. Circe immobilizes the musicians as well, and thus as movement modulates into inaction, so also music modulates into silence. Since all playing and singing have been halted, music does not mediate the fusion of dance and theater.[33] Circe's gesture with her wand draws dance into the narrative circumference of the act: the narrative import of her gesture is to interrupt the dance, whereas its theoretical import is to endow the interrupted action with narrative significance. Once she is defeated, the resumption of dancing in the grand ballet is a direct narrative consequence of the undoing of the spell. For the second time in this piece, dance functions as a full-fledged and substantive act rather than as an agent diverting attention from the meaning of dramatized acts.

Far from connoting aspirations to an articulated language, as Delmas would have it, loss of speech accompanies the immobilization of the dancers. Indeed, the libretto places silence on the same level as physical immobility:

Les Deesses des eaux, de sa verge enchantees,
Sont devant son chasteau sur les pieds arrestees
Sans aucun mouvement, sans haleine, ny voix,
Immobiles ainsi qu'une souche de bois.[34]

The Water goddesses, bewitched by her wand,
are standing before her castle, without movement,
without breath or voice, motionless as logs.

The libretto explains that the goddesses have lost their reason: "sans la raison bien peu sert l'eloquence" ("without reason eloquence has no value").[35] The metamorphosis of divinities into figures resembling statues is the divine equivalent of the transformation of men into beasts. Thus, the goddesses lack the harmony implicit in a well-proportioned body, as well as the intellectual capacity to perform geometrical dances.

If the Nymphs do not appeal to their audience as verbally articulate beings (even as they obtain a clearly dramatic dimension), where lies the choreographic contribution to the work's harmony? To understand what harmony meant to the creators of *Le Balet comique*, we should bear in mind the alternative views that contemporaneous musical theory held of harmony. In Pontus de Tyard's reflection on geometrical harmony in music, *Le Solitaire second*, he explains that harmony results *not* from the union of voices but from their proportion:

Il faut donq à fin que de la proportion des deux, la Harmonie procede, que l'un soit different à l'autre: Aussi sourd icy la difficulté, car tous dissonans, ne sont accordans ou rapportables l'un à l'autre en Harmonieuse proportion.[36]

For Harmony to proceed from the proportion of the two, one must be different from the other: Here a difficulty arises, for all things dissonant are not able to be brought together in a Harmonious proportion.

For there to be harmony, a sound (a voice) must "sonne[r] inegalement à celuy auquel il est rapporté" ("sound unequally with one to which it is joined"). That is to say that, within the mix of the two, one must still be able to "discerner *l'espace du mouvement*" ("discern *the space of movement*").[37] The perception of space between chords must be understood as a dissonance that permits the harmony to be heard. Artusi writes that "non puo essere Consonanza, senza che fra le sue Cordi non habbi la Dissonanza" ("there can be no consonance without there being dissonance between the chords").[38] The term *movement* implies an oscillating motion between clear-cut consonance and proportional, and therefore harmonious, dissonance. In geometrical harmony, "les parties s'entre-rapportent en egale proportion et non pas en egale difference" ("the parts relate to one another in equal proportion but not in equal difference").[39] Harmony is thus conceptualized as an effect of proportion applied to sounds in relation to one another. Again, harmony does not imply the identity of several sounds in a fused whole – a Platonic concept – but rather the perception of unequal sounds in a pleasing and intuited dissonance – a Heraclitean idea. It demands that the listener account for the comparability of the unequal intervals of those sounds. They are inaudible to the casual listener: "Ancora nella Musica non si puo udire lo spatio, che si trova dalla voce acuta a quelle che è grave, quando si canta: conciosia che solamente si possa intendere e non udire" ("In music one cannot hear the space that is to be found between high and low sounds during song: they can only be understood, not heard").[40] Harmony, then, must involve at least three voices creating distinctly unequal intervals. The interval is understood as the distance between voices, and the proportion as the comparable distances between two intervals. With regard to the production of harmony – which, after all, has no likeness, no possible representation – each sound is conceptualized as a point in space: "Viene [un Cadimento di voce] considerato nella Musica, come il ponto nella Geometria" ("Each voiced sound in Music is considered as a point would be in Geometry").[41] In a like manner, the dancers representing voiced sounds are considered as points on a flat plane. The intervals can be visualized as the space between them as they hold their geometrical patterns. Thus, choreographic space offers an illustration of the principles of vocal harmony. But like vocal harmony, this illustration is more intelligible than visual. More specifically, the body is a signature or mark of what the voice accomplishes as it weds text to melody. The body is a sign of harmony, not its true manifestation. The conjuncture is assured not by the resemblance that rhythm, the great aligner of genres, affords, but through the similarities that can be noted in intervening spaces. Thus, a particular use of space suggests an analogy cementing the physical sign to its meaning. This meaning as illustration is both visual and intelligible because its sense depends on a theoretical grasp of musical proportion applied to choreographic space. Withal, the relationship of bodies to each other in space is not conceived expressively – through their human significance – but indexically, in that their positioning relative to one another indicates the space between as proportionate distance. By the same token, the body does not *express* harmony. The body is likened to the voice not as a vehicle of language but in the musical sense of a voice part constituted by musical intervals in relation to other voices. Dancing bodies fulfill the same transitional function, formally speaking, as do voice parts in intervalic relationships. And similarly, the harmony of *Le Balet comique* is produced by the perceptible intervals between genres, intervals that are unequal in quantity but nevertheless proportionate. Thus, within likeness, two concepts of the intermediary emerge: the intermediary can be a channel guiding the spectator to meaning, but it can also be a space *between* that holds the spectator fascinated and suspends meaning. That is, the likeness founding analogical interpretation can, in fact, be like or unlike: a transparent membrane such as the voice, or an interruptive and opaque mass such as the body. Dissonance may be the mark of conjunction, but it is also the proof that harmony is suspended in its own conceptuality. Therefore, I stress that this proportion is a form of analogy in which the tension of unlikeness is never wholly resolved. It is similar to the most radical sort of literary metaphor.[42]

The dancing body of *Le Balet comique* should be understood as a unifying presence, doing what the voice does in the ballet's preface: uniting word and song, text and music. It does not, however, do this in narrative terms. Despite the ballet's narrative, much of the choreography can only be justified in theoretical terms, not in dramatic or processional ones. In geometrical dance, the body renders the harmonic theory of the interval usually illustrated by the voice in spatial terms. Dance, music, and text do not coalesce in an exchange of identities or attributes; instead, they stand off from one another so that we may appreciate their mathematical relationship. It is fitting that the Nymphs of *Le Balet comique* represent the voice as a theoretical entity (one not part of the ballet's plot) instrumental to the materialization of harmony. In so doing, dancers did not portray harmony visually, as they did in Guillaume Colletet's *Ballet de l'harmonie* (Paris, 1632). In that work, five dancers portrayed the winds, "car cet element est la matiere et le sujet principal des sons dont se forme l'Harmonie" ("for that element is the matter and principal subject of sounds from which Harmony is formed").[43] In this *entrée*, dance is called on, in unspecified ways, to represent music and its harmonies:

Ils danseront ensemble un Balet, comme s'ils vouloient faire voir par là que l'air, susceptible de toutes sortes de mouvement, est capable aussi de tous les sons differents qui entrent dans la composition d'une parfaite musique.[44]

They will dance a ballet together, as if they wanted to show that the air, which is susceptible to all kinds of movement, is capable also of all kinds of different sounds which enter into the composition of perfect music.

For Colletet, it is natural that one can see and hear harmony in ballets. In fact, in his explanation musical harmony and dance seem to be in a reversible rapport vis-à-vis one another: each one's theory can be translated into the other's practice – ut vox corpus. Although they are apparently quite different, "l'un semble estre le principe de l'autre" ("one seems to be the principle of the other") (L, 4:208). This is what Foucault meant by saying: "The sixteenth century superimposed hermeneutics and semiology in the form of similitude. To search for a meaning is to bring to light a resemblance."[45] In Le Balet comique, however, Nymphs don't "behave" like sound, assuming this were possible. Rather, their patterns indicate harmony's theoretical explanation of unequal but proportionate intervals. Early humanist choreography was neither dramatic nor ornamental, but profoundly intellectual and theoretical. Just as Elie Garel, in his allegorical explanation of Le Ballet de Madame (Paris, 1615) divided vocal harmony into apparent and latent components, so, in Le Balet comique, one can see a surface dance – that of the nymphs – and a "dance in depth," or a theoretical dance beneath the surface.[46] The dancer can embody musical concepts because dance movements index the voice, wind, or sound: themselves understood as moving bodies. Like Ovid's nymph Echo in Metamorphoses, the dancers relay voices in harmonious consort without simulating their flattering presence. What they communicate is not brought forth from themselves as immanent. Rather, its significance is repeated as though from afar: from some external source to them, and from them to the spectator. The dancer points, or indexes, the way.

Dancing to music in order to express one's accord with its harmony would be a less theoretical, more popular manner of visualizing a rapport between these two arts. But the theatrical representation of harmony is indexical when dancing is construed as a visual counterpart of musical theory in terms set up by that very theory. Colletet's preface makes clear that the dancing body performs both as an indexical image of harmony and as an expressive one:

A quoy [l'harmonie] elle [l'Ame] se plaist de telle sorte qu'elle sortiroit volontiers hors de soy-mesme pour aller à sa rencontre, et en jouyr plus parfaitement. Mais si elle a des obstacles qui l'empeschent de retourner entierement à cette felicité naturelle, en l'estat ou elle se trouve à present, cela n'empesche qu'elle n'ait aussi la puissance d'obliger le corps qui la retient à s'y rendre conforme par le mouvement de la danse; elle se peut donc nommer une conformité du corps à l'âme, et de l'âme à la Musique. (L, 4:208–9)

At which [harmony] it [the soul] draws such pleasure that it would voluntarily move out of itself to join music and delight in it more perfectly. But if, in its present state, the soul has obstacles preventing it from returning to that natural felicity, the soul can still oblige the body that constrains it to conform to music by dancing. Harmony can therefore be called a conformity of the body to the soul, and of the soul to Music.

Inasmuch as the dancing body furnishes an expressive image of harmony, its theoretical import is lessened. The union of the soul with the body producing movement is a second-order union in default of the soul's ability to move in unison with music itself. In fact, the body would seem to express the harmony of the soul with music by preventing the soul from entering into that union. The soul would move the body, as it were, in lieu of moving itself. Thus, even within the expressive concept of movement, physical movement indexes spiritual movement, which itself constitutes the true and authentic dance.

Many aesthetic determinations in *Le Balet comique* were attained through an application of harmonic theory to bodies in time and space. It is as though sound were considered a viable, visually available choreographic model. The narrative level of the ballet tells us that the nymphs have come to announce the advent of a golden age, but choreographically they represent vocal loci or postures from which harmony issues. Their relationship to the golden age is realized indexically rather than dramatically as patterns mapping harmony's production.

My point is that the earliest theatrical choreography of the Western tradition is *both* theoretical and dramaturgical. The theoretical matrix of *Le Balet comique* obviously offered the choreographer Beaujoyeulx a series of formal constraints within and against which to work: those of an esoteric cosmology backed by contemporaneous musical theory. To the extent he respected those constraints, his dance appeared to index an implicit theory or nonexpressive meaning. To the degree that he resisted those constraints, he most likely fell back on an expressive mode of self-connoting humanity. Although no one can say how the work actually looked in performance – because both it and the conditions of its reception are forever gone – critical theory has enabled an understanding of this double articulation of indexical and expressive modes in the choreographic fabric, and in the structure of the work as a whole. These criteria could be exploited in future restaging of the work.[47]

This chapter began with the remark that the term *ballet* originally transcended the sole or exclusive reference to dance in and of itself. I wish to distinguish, however, the evidence as presented here from certain conclusions reached by Francis Sparshott regarding court ballet. He writes:

The court ballet, in fact, is not a dance, though it contains dances. It is more of a parade, a spectacle, a masque, as contemporary descriptions make perfectly clear.

The dances as units have little significance, the steps have none. The figures danced on the floor have some geometric and symbolic significance, but not much. No fine art of dance could ever be generated from such practices.[48]

I submit that *Le Balet comique* did not lack what Sparshott calls "a strictly dance organization and significance."[49] It is merely necessary to historicize one's definition of dance in order to get at that organization and significance.[50] The kinesthetic principle of *fantasmata*, originally derived from courtly social dancing and subsequently extended to theatrical choreography, translates all the aspects of *Le Balet comique*'s significance. In other words, *fantasmata* is the physical embodiment of the notion of dyssymmetrical yet proportionate interval and "discordante concordia"[51] that allowed geometrical dance to take its assigned place in the larger ballet. Through its aesthetic of interrupted textures, *fantasmata* supplies a physical microcosm of the ballet's theory of *generic* interruption. *Fantasmata* entered the French dance aesthetic partially through Italian influence, but also through the particular adaptability of that aesthetic to the ideological import of Valois court ballet, its *politique* desire to reconcile Catholics and Protestants.[52]

I see no discrepancy, as does Sparshott, between "crass display" with a political and economic message, and cosmological generalities.[53] *Le Balet comique*, viewed in its structural complexity, evidences its politics and aesthetics in dancing terms. The fact that dance in the work occupies the status of "divertissement" does not point to a conflict between crass politics and spiritualized aesthetic concerns. Rather, as we have seen, the interruptive quality of the divertissement is fundamental to the notion of harmonic interval underlying those spiritual concerns. And spiritual concerns lie, in true Renaissance fashion, along a continuum adjoining worldly and political ones.

INTERLUDE
Montaigne's Dance, 1580s

Dissonance (and its counterparts in the visual arts) – the trademark, as it were, of modernism – lets in the beguiling moment of sensuousness by transfiguring it into its antithesis . . . pain. . . . Dissonance is the truth about harmony. Harmony is unattainable. . . . Dissonance is the same as expression; whereas consonance and harmony seek to do away with expression. . . . Expression cannot be conceived except as expression of suffering.

Theodor Adorno, *Aesthetic Theory*

This chapter is interludic because it diverts attention from the story of court ballet's historical progression. Yet Montaigne's reflections on the body are of undeniable theoretical import for dance history. Montaigne, in his thinking, grappled with the theoretical implications of improvisation for the cohesiveness of reactionary social order and radical individual identity. Montaigne announced the developments, already surfacing in the 1590s, that were to culminate in burlesque ballet of the 1620s. Although not a performer, Montaigne prefigured early baroque performance through his reflections on fixity and fluidity and his call for a stability that would not negate the inevitability of change. Furthermore, his project of self-portraiture, an attempt to reconstruct his prior selves, has repercussions for a period concept of dance reconstruction. Should not dance reconstruction reconstruct lost selves rather than merely lost manners of moving? Is not the very idea of moving *again*, as if for the first time, without the rediscovery of a prior self, in fact, the continuous theme flowing beneath the *Essais*? Indeed, Montaigne progressively puts into question whether a prior self can ever exist *again* as it originally once did. Montaigne's growing conviction about a ceaselessly renewed improvisation at the base of any form of cultural integrity was the kernel of his moral philosophy. In the light of Montaigne's thought, twentieth-century concepts of Renaissance dance reconstruction are clearly seen to derive from concepts of self-identity foreign to the Renaissance.[1]

The body is a metaphor for being in the *Essais* because Montaigne refers to his self-analysis quite often in physical terms. "Je m'estalle entier," he writes in "De l'exercitation," "c'est un *skeletos* ou, d'une veüe, les veines, les muscles, les tendons paraissent, chaque piece en son siege" ("I expose myself entire: my portrait is a cadaver on which the veins, the muscles, and the tendons appear at a glance, each part in its place").[2] The thorough description of his *esprit* ("mind"), "les profondeurs opaques de ses replis internes" ("the opaque depths of its innermost folds") (E, 2:6:414/273) is, however, also a literary portrait. Montaigne's presence to himself and to the world – the portrait of his *jugement* ("judgment") – far outweighs limitations suggested by purely physical description. Yet the metaphor of self-portrait as painting –for all its inherent literality as bodily rather than intellectual image – is adroitly maintained: "Je m'estudie plus qu'autre subject. C'est ma metaphisique, c'est ma phisique" ("I study myself more than any other subject. That is my metaphysics, that is my physics") (E, 3:13:525/821). For Montaigne's writing to gain the fluidity required for miming, indeed mirroring, the self, that writing is often portrayed metaphorically as an extension of his own voice: "Le ton et mouvement de la voix a quelque expression et signification de mon sens" ("The tone and movement of my voice express and signify my meaning") (E, 3:13:543/834). Only his own voice can carry those indigenously self-reflexive qualities that would make the writing indubitably *self*-portraiture and ensure that words convey ancillary images of self. Just as in contemporaneous theatrical dancing, Montaigne conceptualizes the body's significant movement as vocal movement.[3] The aesthetic goal of essay writing – "tel sur le papier qu'à la bouche" ("the same on paper as in the mouth") (E, 1:26:185/127) – is to capture a "subjet informe" ("shapeless subject") in another body: "ce corps aërée de la voix" ("this airy medium of words") (E, 2:7:416/274). Because the voice is also corporal, the reflexivity of "verbal" portraiture, voice over body, nicely encapsulates the reflexivity of Montaigne's project: a portrait *of* consciousness *by* consciousness. By the same token, listening to oneself talk is an apt emblem of self-indulgence in the autoportraitist. The aesthetic concerns of orality tend to maintain Montaigne's writing practices in a natural relationship to his physical processes. That is, at any given time, his body can organize his discourse. It is thus interesting to observe Montaigne's self emerging from his writing by alternately affirming and denying the illustrative value of the body and the ethics of bodily movement, his own and others'.

In this sense, Montaigne announces a bodily poetics new to his time and a philosophical basis for what would be worked through in the coming decades theatrically as burlesque ballet.[4] The 1570s and 1580s knew intense experimentation with theatrical spectacle often understood as ritual. Although, unlike Baïf, Montaigne staged no mascarades, unlike Ronsard or Dorat, he wrote no ballet librettos, and unlike Brantôme, he did not chronicle court spectacle, Montaigne did implicitly elaborate a theory of movement that can be understood as a way of rehearsing self-knowledge. In fact, Montaigne employs gestural metaphor frequently in order to lend conceptual coherence to a wide variety of issues that today would be considered the separate domains of sociology, anthropology, politics, linguistics, history, literature, cultural critique, aesthetics, philosophy, theology, and/or autobiography.

A fundamental position of Montaigne's moral philosophy is that human beings are expressive: there is a truth to be gleaned from observing oneself, and by extension, from observing Montaigne: "Si mon visage ne respondoit pour moy, si on ne lisoit en mes yeux et en ma voix la simplicité de mon intention, je n'eusse pas duré sans querelle et sans offence si long temps" ("If my face did not answer for me, if people did not read in my eyes and my voice the innocence of my intentions, I would not have lasted so long without quarrel and without harm") (E, 3:12:515/814). Montaigne conceives of expressive gesture as largely unconscious, or un-self-conscious, calling it "le naturel pli" ("natural posture"):

Il n'est pas inconvenient d'avoir des conditions et des propensions si propres et si incorporées en nous, que nous n'ayons pas moyen de les sentir et reconnoistre. Et de telles inclinations naturelles, le corps en retient volontiers quelque pli sans nostre sceu et consentement. (E, 2:7:32/479)

It is not unbecoming to have characteristics and propensities so much our own and so incorporated into us that we have no way of sensing and recognizing them. And of such natural inclinations the body is likely to retain a certain bent, without our knowledge or consent.

Rendering "le naturel pli" is the objective of the self-portrait wherein physical and moral being coincide: "Je me presente debout et couché, le devant et le derriere, à droite et à gauche, et en tous mes naturels plis" ("I present myself standing and lying down, front and rear, on the right and the left, and in all my natural postures") (E, 3:8:381/721). Yet the truth inherent in human morphology and expressive behavior, and the politically conciliatory qualities Montaigne's personal expression exudes, is not equally present in all human action.[5] Since the development of *civilité* in Western Europe of the Renaissance, the regulation of gesture constituted both a bond of human society and a source of duplicity. Particularly sensitive to this development, Montaigne analyzes the authentic and the inauthentic, the essential and the accidental aspects of gesture with scrupulous precision. Indeed, he develops a scathing and sustained critique of the coded physical behavior emanating from the upper class.

Fundamentally opposed to rhetorical forms of culture, Montaigne rejects *la ceremonie* ("ceremony") as necessarily artificial: "Nous ne sommes que ceremonie; la ceremonie nous emporte, et laissons la substance de choses; nous nous tenons aux branches et abandonnons le tronc et corps" ("We are nothing but ceremony; ceremony carries us away, and we leave the substance of things; we hang on the branches and abandon the trunk and body") (E, 2:17:31/478–9). Ceremony designates codified formal behavior "aux lieux de respect et de prudence ceremonieuse" ("in places full of respect and ceremonious prudence") (E, 3:3:243/625). The realm of ceremony is the public act: "Les vies publiques se doivent à la ceremonie" ("public lives are owed to ceremony") (E, 3:8:540/831). The adjectival epithets of ceremony are *superficiel* ("superficial"), *artificiel* ("artificial"), and *emprunté* ("borrowed"). To ceremony, Montaigne opposes "nature": authentic movement, spontaneous utterance. The adjectival epithets of nature are most often *vrai* ("true"), *essentiel* ("essential"), *naïf* ("naive").

Montaigne does not argue against ceremonial behavior indiscriminately. Rather, he acknowledges gestural spontaneity only when fully and visibly motivated. His most striking example of a desired gestural spontaneity is motivated by pain:

Au demourant, j'ay toujours trouvé ce precepte ceremonieux, qui ordonne si rigoureusement et exactement de tenir bonne contenance et un maintien desdaigneux et posé à la tollerance des maux. Pourquoy la philosophie, qui ne regarde que le vif et les effects, se va elle amusant à ces apparences externes? Qu'elle laisse ce soing aux farceurs et maistres de Rhetorique qui font tant d'estat de nos gestes.[6]

Moreover, I have always considered that precept formalistic which so rigorously and precisely orders us to maintain a good countenance and a disdainful and composed bearing in the endurance of pain. Why does philosophy, which has regard only for real substance and actions, go playing around with these external appearances? Let her leave this care to the actors and the teachers of rhetoric who set so much store by our gestures.

To the Stoic principles of constancy that characterizes the early Montaigne, finding their paradoxical complement in the physical containment of *civilité*,[7] Montaigne ultimately opposes a notion of diversion that suggests a radical reinterpretation of interlude and is fundamentally a theory of decentered and unpatterned movement:

Si le corps se soulage en se plaignant, qu'il le face; si l'agitation luy plaist, qu'il se tourneboule et tracasse à sa fantasie; s'il luy semble que le mal s'évapore aucunement . . . pour pousser hors la voix avec plus grande violence, ou, s'il en amuse son tourment, qu'il crie tout à faict. (E, 2:37:172/577)

If the body finds relief in complaining, let it do so. If it likes agitation, let it tumble and toss at its pleasure. If it thinks that the pain evaporates somewhat . . . for crying out more violently, or if that distracts its torment, let it shout right out.

Yet he is careful not to endow action with a natural status if, unlike the example that pain provides, the individual is not imbued to overflowing with the feelings and sensations that dictate action as a conscious experience:

Chacun sçait par experience qu'il y a des parties qui se branslent, dressent et cou-chent souvent sans son congé. Or ces passions [impressions] qui ne nous touchent que par l'escorse, ne se peuvent dire nostres. Pour les faire nostres, il faut que l'homme y soit engagé tout entier; et les douleurs que le pied ou la main sentent pendant que nous dormons, ne sont pas à nous. (E, 2:6:412/271)

Every man knows by experience that there are parts that often move, stand up, and lie down, without his leave. Now these passions which touch only the rind of us cannot be called ours. To make them ours, the whole man must be involved; and the pains which the foot or the hand feel while we are asleep are not ours.

It is particularly interesting to compare movement consciousness and un-consciousness with Montaigne's views on courtly social dance. For when it comes to dance, he also divides action into two categories – the controlled and circumspect as opposed to the vertiginous:

Tout ainsi qu'en nos bals, ces hommes de vile condition, qui en tiennent escole, pour ne pouvoir representer le port et la decence de nostre noblesse, cherchent à se recommander par des sauts perilleux et autres mouvemens estranges et bateleresques. Et les Dames ont meilleur marché de leur contenance aux danses où il y a diverses descoupeures [figures] et agitation de corps, qu'en certains autres danses de parade, où elles n'ont simplement qu'a marcher un pas naturel et representer un port naïf et leur grace ordinaire. (E, 2:10:453/300)

Just as at our balls these men of low condition who keep dancing schools, not being able to imitate the bearing and fitness of our nobility, seek to recommend themselves by perilous leaps and other strange mountebank's antics. And the ladies can more cheaply show off their carriage in the dances where there are various contortions and twistings of the body, than in certain other formal dances where they need only walk with a natural step and display a natural bearing and their ordinary grace.

The dance steps that Montaigne favors in this passage appear to be those of the *basse danse* and the *branle*. These were the very dances that formed the basic vocabulary of geometrical dance in its early stages. The movements Montaigne opposes are characterized by aerial elevation and twisting, the hallmarks of burlesque dance vocabulary. In courtly social dance, contain-ment was an attribute of simplicity and nature whereas abandon was a sign of vainglory.[8] Yet Montaigne's way of theorizing movements of pain and move-ments of dance are not incompatible. There is nothing inherently wrong, for Montaigne, with excessive and apparently uncontrolled movement. It is sim-ply that this movement should be honestly produced. That is, the feeling or sensation that animates it must be fully adequate to the scale of the movement. If there is a discrepancy between outward movement and its inner source, then that movement is artificial, "borrowed," based on an unauthentic model that could be termed "ceremonious." Montaigne's movement aesthetic seems poised between the politically conciliatory practices of composite spectacle as practiced by the Valois and the intensely personal motivations that led to burlesque works in the 1600s.

The value placed on the natural as opposed to the artificial dovetails nicely with the project of self-portraiture, the study of the author's own nature in writing. In his "Au lecteur," Montaigne distinguishes as sharply between the public and the private as between ceremony and nature: "Si c'eust [le livre] esté pour rechercher la faveur du monde, je me fusse mieux paré et me presenterois en une marche estudiée" ("If I had written to seek the world's favor, I should have bedecked myself better, and should present myself in a studied posture") (E, "Au lecteur":1/2). The self portrait is not to be that of a public but of a private self: "Je veus qu'on m'y voie en ma façon simple, naturelle et ordinaire, sans contantion et artifice: car c'est moy que je peins" ("I want to be seen here in my simple, natural, ordinary fashion, without straining or artifice; for it is myself that I portray") (ibid.). Concomitant to the notion of Montaigne's private being is the constant pain of the kidney stone on which so much description is lavished. At the outset, therefore, Montaigne opposes artifice to nature, limiting nature only by custom: "Que si j'eusse esté entre ces nations qu'on dict vivre encore sous la douce liberté des premieres loix de nature, je t'asseure que je m'y fusse très-volontiers peint tout entier, et tout nud" ("Had I been placed among those nations which are said to live still in the sweet freedom of nature's first laws, I assure you I should very gladly have portrayed myself here entire and wholly naked") (ibid.).

Coustume ("custom") is a term that, in many instances, mediates between "ceremony" and "nature."[9] Although not a synonym of "ceremony," it does designate the layer of ceremoniousness that, like customary law, precedes "ceremony" as belief does opinion. We are blinded to the relativity of *coustume* by *accoustumance* ("habit").[10] For Montaigne there is, and there will always be, in each act and feeling an element of conditioning, an *emprunt* or borrowing from convention that stands between nature and its own undivided singularity, which is a good argument for cultural pluralism but also, in the European context of the Renaissance, for cultural skepticism. A full awareness of the power of custom is disillusioning. Cutting across the dichotomy of the natural and the artificial, custom predetermines what is natural as partially acquired. The truth of custom demystifies the myth of spontaneity: "C'est à la coustume de donner forme à nostre vie, telle qu'il luy plaist; elle peut tout en cela: c'est le breuvage de Circé, qui diversifie notre nature comme bon luy semble" ("It is for habit to give form to our life, just as it pleases; it is all-powerful in that; it is Circe's drink, which varies our nature as it sees fit").[11] In this citation from "De l'experience" ("Of Experience"), the unsettling figure of Circe, representative of threatening diversity in *Le Balet comique de la Royne,* overrides the sanctity of the individual subject, rendering us similar to others but different from our true selves. Conformity is social monstrosity. To sum up, *coustume* is, at its best, naive ceremony, ceremony at its least arbitrary, its most "natural." At its worst, *coustume* is exposed as the artifice of nature. "Nous appelons contre nature ce qui advient contre la coustume" ("We call contrary to nature what happens contrary to custom"), he writes in "D'un enfant monstrueux" ("Of a Monstrous Child") (E, 2:30:118/539). In that essay, Montaigne claims that custom blinds us to a desired cultural relativism. Custom is responsible for our perception of the unusual as monstrous.[12] Moreover, the monstrous has a secondary definition as "ennemie de communication et de société" ("inimical to social intercourse") (E, 1:26:179/123).[13]

It is mostly because of the power of *coustume* that nature is not easily available to consciousness: "Je n'ay rien mien que moy; et si, en est la possession en partie manque et empruntée" ("I have nothing of my own but myself, and even there my possession is partly defective and borrowed") (E, 3:9:408/470). We are all, Montaigne seems to say, culturally contaminated. Only God enjoys the full presence of his self to himself: "Dieu, qui est en soy toute plenitude et le comble de toute perfection, il ne peut s'augmenter et accrosire au dedans" ("God, who is himself all fullness and the acme of all perfection, cannot grow and increase within") (E, 2:16:15/468). Only He merits praise because only He is so abundantly substantial that an unchanging sign – his name – can stand for him in his absence. The substance of human beings, by contrast, is too unstable and inconsistent to be represented with anything other than a constantly altered or recalibrated name. This human onomastics is frequently referred to in the *Essais* as *voix* (voice"): "Nous sommes tous creux et vuides; ce n'est pas de vent et de voix que nous avons à nous remplir; il nous faut de la substance plus solide à nous reparer" ("We are all hollow and empty. It is not with wind and sound that we have to fill ourselves; we need more solid substance to repair us") (E, 2:16:16/468). As with the term *custom,* the voice can be valorized in contradictory senses: it can be a model for transparency of expressional intention emerging from within, or singled out as an emblem of metaphysical emptiness syphoned from an outside. Ideally, for Montaigne, proper names should be reinvented at each instant to ensure authentic connection to human beings. In the aristocratic system of honor and reputation, proper names were the emblems of glorious actions, long outliving their real performance.[14] Thus, the glorious proper name for Montaigne is the very emblem of the discrepancy between action and intention. Only severe pain or absolute virtue can establish a consistency between action and its motivating feeling. Paradoxically, in the instance of pain, the gestural language is authentic because it is chaotic and unique to the moment. One might say that it is improvised with utter, though unrepeatable, conviction. This is, in essence, Montaigne's nominalist position. No word, and a fortiori no proper name, has an essential connection to the identity it marks. Nor, one might add, does any repeatable movement coincide inevitably with cosmic order or individual subjectivity. With his famous dichotomy between *le nom* and *la chose* (names and things) in "De la gloire," he inaugurates that nominalist position through a linguistic theory of proper names that are, as Mill would say, disembodied.[15] In that essay, proper names are considered as the equivalents of arbitrary though ceremonious gestures to which public consensus attributes meaning.[16] Thus, the danger of ceremony is to presuppose universals – unchanging contents – falsely guaranteed by all varieties of cultural performance: mourning, eloquence, *civilité,* bad literature, law, dance, medicine, theater, to name only those most frequently cited by Montaigne. He frequently overdetermines the critique of a particular cultural practice by conflating several endeavors. For example, in the following quote, mourning, oratory, and theater are used as descriptive systems for one another:

Est-ce raison que les arts mesmes se servent et facent leur proufit de nostre imbecilité et bestise naturelle? L'Orateur, dict la rethorique, en cette farce de son plaidoier s'esmouvera par le son de sa voix et par ses agitations feintes, et se lairra piper a la passion qu'il représente. Il s'imprimera un vray deuil et essentiel, par le moyen de ce battelage qu'il joüe. (E, 3:4, 259/636)

Is it reasonable for the arts themselves to make their use and profit of our natural feeble-mindedness and stupidity? The orator, rhetoric says, in that farce that is his plea, will be moved by the sound of his own voice and his own feigned emotions, and will let himself be tricked into the passion he is portraying. He will imprint on himself a real and essential sorrow by means of this mummery that he enacts.

Thus, the problem of the self-portrait in the *Essais* becomes increasingly bound up with the changing definition of gesture. For example, in "De l'exercitation," Montaigne writes, "ce ne sont pas mes gestes que j'ecris, c'est moy, c'est mon essence" ("It is not my deeds that I write down; it is myself, it is my essence") (E, 2:6, 416/274). This essentialist view of the self is subsequently overturned in favor of a processive one when Montaigne writes: "Je ne peints pas l'estre. Je peints le passage" ("I do not portray being: I portray passing") (E, 3:2:222/611). In the first instance, "essence" is distinguished from transient and superficial gesture; in the second instance, being is attributed, paradoxically, only to the trajectory between states: interstitial movement: "Nostre vie n'est que movement" ("Our life is nothing but movement") (E, 3:13:553/840). A semantic instability inhabits Montaigne's terminology, indicating a split between ontological and epistemological conceptions of the self-portrait. "Essence" obtains a positive reading with regard to gesture, while its synonym *etre* ("being") can only be understood negatively when compared with *le passage* ("passing"). In a similar manner, *coustume* should be read positively in the context of *ceremonie* but negatively against "nature." *Coustume* signifies by turns a superior ceremony but an inferior nature. The same relative redemption does not befall the proper name or any equivalent linguistic phenomenon in the *Essais*.[17] Gesture, however, *does* accede to an unexpected theoretical flexibility in the course of the work.

These and similarly shifting thresholds of meaning are frequently referred to by Montaigne as movement: *branle*. "Le monde n'est qu'une branloire perenne" ("The world is but a perennial movement"), he writes in "Du repentir" (E, 3:2:222/610), thus evoking that social dance most directly connected to Renaissance belief systems. In its circular pattern of joined hands and its constant though uneven shifts from side to side, the *branle* evokes cosmic harmony even as it affirms change. James Miller's *Measures of Wisdom* sets forth the complex and extraordinarily rich traditions of this performance concept in Western culture. It is worth noting that the *branle* was unique in late Renaissance France for being the only social and theatrical dance that transcended class barriers. Given to much popular elaboration, it also maintained a privileged place in court ballet well into the seventeenth century, particularly through geometrical dance. In 1635, the librettist of *Le Balet du Roy* writes of that work:

Le sujet de ce Balet triomphant estoit une representation de la vissicitude des choses humaines, dont le branle continuel n'a point d'hieroglyphe plus significatif que celuy de la danse. (L, 5:58)

The subject of this triumphal ballet was a picture of human vissicitude, whose continual movement (*branle*) has no more significant hieroglyph than that of dancing.

The *branle* clearly served as an emblem of the general sociocultural import of dance for late Renaissance and early baroque France. And that import was not far from Montaigne's message about change and instability. In other terms, the *branle* was at the nerve of dancing as a practice, one that had great cultural centrality. Montaigne's "branloire perenne" ("perennial movement") suggests both a shifting and unstable universe and a dance floor on which a shifting dance is performed to acknowledge and compensate for cosmic instability. Dancing the *branle* in Renaissance France was a manner of rehearsal – in the performative sense – of social, political, and personal opposites in a "condition mixte": "Nostre vie est composée, comme l'armonie du monde, de choses contraires" ("Our life is composed, like the harmony of the world, of contrary things) (E, 3:13:545/835). The "branloire perenne" suggests both a metaphysical problem and a cultural "performance" designed to address that problem.[18] Montaigne thus redefines harmony as Heraclitean by placing its static and hierarchical aspects in question.

The "branloire perenne" is probably the most well-known of Montaigne's references to dance. Yet in "De l'institution des enfants" ("Of the Education of Children"), Montaigne calls on dance as a paradigmatic example of intellectual training. As he opposes rote learning to the true formation of judgement, Montaigne draws the seminal distinction between words and their "substance." Bad learning allows the student to confuse specific texts with the true end of education: "Il les transformera et confondera, pour en faire un ouvrage tout sien, à sçavoir son jugement. Son institution, son travail et estude ne vise qu'à le former" ("He will transform and blend them to make a work that is all his own, to wit, his judgment. His education, work, and study aim only at forming this") (E, 1:26:162/110). Surprisingly, at this juncture, the model of true instruction or education is given as the learning of a dance step:

Je voudrais que le Paluël ou Pompée [two famous Milanese dancing masters], ces beaux danseurs de mon temps, apprinsent des caprioles à les voir seulement faire, sans nous bouger de nos places, comme ceux-cy [bad teachers] veulent instruire notre entendement, sans l'esbranler. (E, 1:26:163/112)

I wish Paluel or Pompey, those fine dancers of my time, could teach us capers just by performing them before us and without moving us from our seats, as those people want to train our understanding without setting it in motion.

Montaigne probably had recourse to a dancing example because he considered it most persuasive at this point in his argument. No one can reasonably well imagine that learning an aerial dance step without moving – exercising one's faculties – is possible. But the example is interesting for another reason. Despite his own theatrical prejudices, this quote reveals that dancing is not uniquely an emblem of rhetorical patterning resisted throughout the *Essais*. In fact, here, *patron* is associated with bookish study: "Ce qu'on sçait droittement, on en dispose, sans regarder au patron, sans tourner les yeux vers son livre. Facheuse suffisance qu'une suffisance pure livresque" ("What we know rightly we dispose of, without looking at the model, without turning our eyes toward our book. Sad competence, a purely bookish competence").[19] Reading is opposed to doing, study to practice. Or, more exactly, reading is advocated as a form of exercise. Dance is not only a potent metaphor for universal uncertainty and the wisdom of cosmic sympathy, it is also a model for that polar opposite in Montaigne's mental universe: the formation of individual judgement.

In his recent *Les Métamorphoses de Montaigne*, François Rigolot claims that Montaigne the moralist rejects dance as a practice (even while retaining it as model for the essays themselves as play) in the name of judgement, the latter defined as an "inner pattern": "Man's duty," writes Rigolot glossing Montaigne's thought, "is to withdraw from the dance of life to establish a personal, inner pattern."[20] Rigolot misinterprets the sense of *branle* as popular dance only, and therefore as, vertiginous movement.[21] Montaigne does favor a simple and noble dance over a popular and inflated one, but the *branle* fits into neither category. In fact, the *branle* provides a model for that most anticultural of concepts in Montaigne's essays: movement and flux. The very process of writing the essays entails judgement confronting personal and universal instability and seeking resolution in movement. Although by nature unpredictable and unregulated, that movement is already aesthetically patterned by the cultural practice of Renaissance dance.[22]

By exploring differences between the dancer and the dance, Montaigne implicitly points to gestural rehearsal as a metaphor for the epistemological process of self-knowledge. For Montaigne, gesture is not reified in any pattern, but its improvisatory space does have culturally determined limits. The different possibilities of movement rehearsed reflect the ontological project of the *moy* in a specular way, as epistemological spectacle. Montaigne's faith in the adaptability of human performance to a metaphysics of uncertainty makes him a key theorist of court ballet prior to Louis XIV's institutionalization of dance in the Royal Academy. Montaigne can be read, although this claim may displace the glorious position he already enjoys in the literary canon, as the de Pure and Menestrier of early baroque festival. Montaigne points prophetically to developments in later court ballet and French court society that were to transform emblems of cosmic harmony into idiosyncratic practices of improvisation and eccentric self-portraiture.

POLITICAL EROTICS OF
BURLESQUE BALLET, 1624–1627

> We will believe, then, that the Precious and the Burlesque are like crises
> through which language must pass.
>
>   Ferdinand Brunetière, "La Maladie du burlesque"

The moral universe of *Le Balet comique de la Royne* is not as sharply divided
between good and evil as its propagandistic mission in the service of the
Valois might lead one to expect. Actually, Circe's monologues betray a sym-
pathetic treatment of human mutability. Although she says "Seule cause je
suis de tout ce changement" ("I am the sole cause of all this change") (BC,
26v:62), Circe does not generate change as much as allegorize its natural
presence in the world. She represents the human subject, a quintessential
victim of change. While far from the stoicism required of virtue by some
Renaissance moral philosophy – in particular that of the early Montaigne –
Circe's monologues do not portray mutability as intentional evil. Rather, the
most negative vision of metamorphosis in *Le Balet comique* renders an allegorical vision of inconsistency or moral ambivalence. Circe invokes the spec-
ter of Montaigne's customary improvisation. She opposes the textuality of
geometrical dance but can replace its suspended moments only with the
tabula rasa of frozen immobility. Although she interrupts the evolution of
figures, she does not generate a new figureless dance. Thus, while Circe
points to the dissolution of textual fixity, her presence can only presage
movement alternatives that are left undanced in *Le Balet comique*.

Le Balet comique theatricalizes a characteristic dilemma of late Renaissance moral philosophy. Montaigne was also fascinated with, though sus-
picious of, the amoral force of diversity. In strikingly similar terms, two
visions of the dancing body were repeatedly debated in France from 1550
until 1603: for the Protestant tradition, dance exemplified morally reprehen-
sible action symbolized by the quest for variety in movement. Proponents of

dance, on the other hand, discerned the order and consistency of dance movement. The terms of this polemic are echoed in *Le Balet comique* where geometrical dance represents social and political cohesiveness in the terms of ordered shape, rhythmical measure, and relative legibility. Opposed to this order, Circe represents a natural temptation toward mutability, indicated in *Le Balet comique* by the interruption of ordered dancing but expressed only through Circe's reputation as sorceress with the power to bewitch and transform.

In the decades following *Le Balet comique*, choreographers would experiment more boldly with the moral and political ambivalence of dancing itself as an emblem of mutability. In 1614, ten gentlemen dressed uniformly in green, the "dix verds," became symbolically variegated (*divers*) by shedding their outer green to reveal an array of colors underneath:

Mais laissons-là ces habits verds,
Je vois vostre oeil [Grand Roy] qui nous demande
Pourquoy nous sommes tous divers. (L, 2:14)

But let us quit our green garments,
I notice your eye [Great King] enquiring
Why we are all different [all "ten green"].

Through a verbal pun whose sense relies on a visual effect, mutability was presented as a hidden attribute of unity and celebrated, at least in this work, as a principle of stability rather than as a threat to order:[1]

Chasque saison, chasque element
Chasque astre est fait diversement;
Et tout iroit à la renverse,
Si par des changements divers,
La Nature tousjours diverse
N'entretenoit cest Univers. (L, 2:14)

Each season, each element
Each star is made differently;
And everything would become topsy-turvy,
If by diverse changes,
Always diverse Nature
Did not maintain the Universe.

The *récit* of the ten green, yet diverse, gentlemen announces that change and variety underlie stability. A dance of movement begins to supplant a dance of position in early seventeenth-century court ballet; a dance emerges that could more properly have been that of Circe herself – lubricious, everchanging, diverse – than of her nymphs staidly marking the perimeters of geometrical figures. Burlesque ballets stage no geometrical figures, but they do enlarge upon the transitions between the figures. Burlesque dance deconstructs geometrical dance by magnifying the latter's barely perceptible transitions. Burlesque dance also prefers the individual, or a miscellaneous collection of individuals, to the homogeneous group. Burlesque dancers twist about the axes of their own bodies rather than join in mapping a collective social space.

Bakhtin has described the collectivity experienced by the populace at festival time as nongeometrical, "more complex and differentiated."[2] Similarly, one can think of the baroque in purely stylistic terms as "rebellion against earlier fear of dissonance."[3] Dissonance in court ballet was signaled by eroticism, thinly veiled obscenity, and transvestism, all recurrent features of burlesque works. In *Le Ballet des secretaires de Saint Innocent* (c. 1605–10), perhaps the cleverest of the early genre, clerks address the ladies of the audience as follows:

> Aux Dames
>
> Vous portez un aymant si doux,
> Qu'il dresse nos plumes vers vous
> Par une puissance incognue
>
> . . . .
>
> Nos plumes fermes par le bout,
> Que nous faisons marquer par tout,
> Laissent de si bons caracteres,
> Que quand elles sont en leur point,
> Les femmes ne se lassent point
> D'employer de tels secretaires (L, 1:198).

> To the Ladies
>
> You carry such a sweet magnet
> That it raises our quills towards you
> By an unknown power
>
> . . . .
>
> Our quills, hard at the ends,
> Which leave their traces everywhere,
> Leave such skillful characters,
> That when they are in good shape,
> Ladies never tire
> Of using such clerks.

In this ballet, the conceit of writing is extended to a frankly sexual domain. The allegory of the clerk's pen as phallus was doubtless overlain with the visual oxymoron of softness (feathers) as rigidity. One can deduce that the *plumes* were worn by performers as enormous quilled pens. The play on the term and the visual object *plume* (writing instrument, phallus, and feather) adds a visual irony to the verbal punning. The pun, in other words, is incomplete without the "spectacular" visual addition of feathers.

> I was a very handsome boy,
> And I had the allure
> That one sees in royal ones
> Who are in close proximity to crowns,
> When, through my strong attachment
> To the fair sex which I love so
> By dressing as it dresses
> I finally became a girl.

The cross-dressed courtier is "out of control" and therefore in a subservient position.

The noble dancer also suggested ambivalence toward his own economic plight by portraying the bourgeois as more financially privileged than himself. In the *Balet du naufrage heureux*, a bourgeois has the following *récit*:

> Les Bourgeois en rien ne ressemblent
> A tant de Courtisans . . .
> . . . .
>
> Ils [les Courtisans] sont couverts d'or et d'argent
> Et n'en ont point dedans la bourse.[20]
>
> Bourgeois don't resemble
> Courtiers in any way . . .
> . . . .
>
> The latter are covered with gold and silver
> But have none in their purses.

The *Ballet des infatigables* introduced the theme of appearance versus essence in the guise of reversals: the reversibility of youth and age, ugliness and beauty.[21] Nevertheless, the statement of reversibility is above all a prologue to the critique of courtiers:

> Courtisans dont les coeurs s'en vont toujours de biais,
> Et de qui les discours sont pures moqueries:
> Nous voyons si constans vous nous appelez niais,
> Car la constance en Cour n'est qu'une niaiserie.[22]
>
> Courtiers whose hearts are twisted
> And whose discourses are pure mockeries:
> We [bourgeois] see so clearly that you call us stupid,
> For constancy in the Court is a stupidity.

Monsieur le Comte de More's *récit* as a bourgeois allows him to reflect on the performance's strategy, thus engaging a theoretical dimension also typical of burlesque ballet. His *récit* suggests the possibility of carnivalesque role reversals. That is, by lowering his social rank he suggests switching roles with the king:

Tantost c'est mon plaisir de paroistre Bourgeois,
Tantost valet de pied, tant j'ayme la vitesse,
Pour obeir soudain aux adorables loys
De celle qu'un grand Dieu voudroit bien pour Maistresse.

A quoy ne suys-je propre? aux alarmes de Mars
J'ay reçeu des lauriers par les mains de la gloire:
Et quand je fays sortir le feu de mes regards,
Chacun me va nommant Maistre de la Victoire.

Toutes mes actions me font croire un Soleil:
Comme celuy des Cieux jamais je ne repose,
Et si Mars m'a tousjours estimé sans pareil,
La bouche de l'Amour en dit la mesme chose.

M'a-t-on pas vu reluire à nostre grand Ballet?
Et là j'ay bien monstré tant de grace et d'adresse,
Qu'on diroit, me voyant soubs l'habit d'un valet,
Que je meriterois le coeur d'une Déesse.

A la guerre, à la chasse avec sa Majesté,
Et de coeur et de corps je suis infatigable:
La mort pour son service est l'immortalité,
Et je n'ay pour ma fin que ce but honorable. (L, 3:28)

At times it is my pleasure to appear a Bourgeois,
At times a valet, I favor quick change,
To obey with alacrity the adorable laws
Of she whom a great God would like as Mistress.

What can I not do? I have received laurels
In the alarms of Mars from the hands of glory:
And when I emit the flames of my glance,
I am called the Master of Victory by all.

All my actions indicate I am a Sun:
Like the actual sun I never rest,
And if Mars has always thought me without equal,
The same opinion issues from the mouth of Love.

Did you see me resplendent in our grand Ballet?
I demonstrated such grace and skill therein,
That it was said, though I was disguised as a valet,
That I merited the heart of a Goddess.

In war, in the hunt with his Majesty,
I am tireless both in body and heart:
To die in his service is my immortality,
and all I have as an end is this honorable goal.

De More suggests that his role playing provides an illusory social mobility
spanning identities as diverse as bourgeois, servant, and master. He also
suggests that he plays to please the king's mistress in the first stanza; yet by

Rounded projections from the shoulders and hips, conelike volume to the skirts often, but not always, reaching the ground, and voluminous sleeves widening away from the torso in unexpected directions were some typical traits of burlesque costuming (Figure 7). The organic body was segmented from within or overwhelmed from without by triangular, spherical, and conical distortions. The body became a locus of allegorical meaning not only by carrying symbolic properties, but by projecting them physically into space as extensions of itself. This displacement of the organic body is also symptomatic of the concern for choreographic autonomy: the dancing figure becomes autonomous from the "natural" body in a project whose artistic outcome is not bound up with assumptions about psychology and human action resumed in narrative. Some costumes reduced the body to one anatomical feature, such as an enormous head or legs walking without a trunk[48] (Figure 8). Others were densely cluttered pieces of walking architecture determined by the allegorical attributes of a particular *métier*.[49]

By deforming the body's natural outlines within constructed shapes, allegorical costumes dictated, in large measure, the way the body moved. The notion of compositeness once applied to the structure of ballets was now applied to the body itself. Moreover, if dancers still appeared in groups in burlesque works – as most illustrations do attest – they are nevertheless often depicted as moving individually. And a greater number of *récits* are for individuals rather than for uniform groups. The dancing body was thus differentiated from the mass and encouraged to move in energetic and original ways. Françoise Christout notes that despite the frequent presence of enveloping constructed shapes, the dancer's legs were as often unencumbered.[50] It is important to note that baroque experimentation with autonomy was carried out on two potentially contradictory levels: that of costume, which, when carried to extremes, could inhibit or radically define movement, and that of unencumbered physical movement. Part and parcel of both excessive formal constraints on the body and unwonted liberation of its movement potential are the "postures merveilleuses" ("marvelous postures"),[51] an aesthetic of ageometrical twisting markedly opposed to the earlier aesthetic formalization of geometrical pattern.

Although the verse of burlesque ballet appears to border on the nonsensical, its sense resides in its particularly reductive use of motifs. Each theme interlocks with another, yet all appear to resolve themselves into triviality. Thus, burlesque ballets erode the intention to praise while still appearing to be about nothing: "pur caprice." The object of a dancer's impersonation was frequently commented on by *cartels:* small scrolls handed or thrown, and sometimes shot with an arrow, by the performers to members of the audience for them to read aloud. Similar hints were provided by *récits* sung by non-dancing figures whose allegorical appearance was often more elaborately contrived than that of the dancers themselves. Walter Benjamin characterized the spoken word in seventeenth-century German tragedy as "a commentary on the images, spoken by the images themselves." He also alluded to speech used as "captions" that declare "the stage setting to be allegorical."[52] Both of these comments are relevant to French court ballet as well. Text and action were frequently detached from one another: since the dancer never spoke, the functions of act and voice were splintered between a dancing and a nondancing performer. Further, the *récits* themselves frequently ironized on the player and his role, creating an awareness of the subject as both in and apart from his impersonated role object. The motif of voicelessness isolated the body per se from other interpretive cues, maintaining an ironic rapport with an already ironic and incomplete text. Unlike composite spectacle in which the body stood for the voice promoting artistic consanguinity in a harmonistic world view, physical and textual aspects of burlesque ballet remained aloof from one another. To the degree that the dancing body approximated an autonomous status during these performances, it resisted reading and controlled interpretation of the spectacle.

Burlesque ballets particularly desirous of ambivalence explored ways of suggesting theatrical reversal in ironic contrasts between words and actions. In *Le Ballet du monde renversé* (1625), one *récit* proclaims:

> Voici le monde renversé
> Où chacun faict son personnage,
> Tel pense y estre bien versé
> Qui n'est que dans l'apprentissage. (L, 3:49)

> Here is the world upside down
> Where everyone is playing a role,
> Someone thinks he does it well
> Who is just learning how it's done.

This particular kind of self-conscious theatricality lends burlesque ballet an unfinished, open-ended feeling consonant with Bakhtin's sense of Menippean satire. The text was frequently part of the ballet on condition that it be contradicted by dancing or, at least, be the object of ironic commentary through movement.

Although burlesque ballets consisted of visual spectacle, diversions solely "for the eyes,"[53] theorists of the period would have them be as intelligible as verbal theater. The most frequent apologists of court ballet were Jesuit professors of rhetoric who thought of ballet as an exercise in the production of figures. Whereas the figure in geometrical dance was taken literally as an embodied theatrical sign, the concept of figure in burlesque ballet extended to the thematic relevance of an *entrée* to the entire ballet. Each *entrée* was a synecdoche of the whole, a thematic variation on a larger thought. The queens. Mercury, god of thieves, enters to abjure all thievery short of "larcins d'amour" ("love larceny"). Revering the beauteous nymphs leads to erotic verse in praise of them. This reversal is reinforced by the costumes of the king and his courtiers: they are called both *voleurs* and *volés,* both "thieves" and "stolen." Ambivalent warrior figures (courtiers dressed as thieves) are vanquished by love: they are both strong and weak. In these reversals one notes again the deliberate confusion of sexual subject and object.

The theme of games and gaming in the first *entrée* of *Les Fées* reflects the aesthetic of choreographic improvisation and novelty central to the form. Lack of existing dance notation supports the hypothesis that improvisation was typical of the genre. The claim to have improvised an entire ballet in very little time is frequent in the literature.[74] Court ballets cultivated the aura of *impromptus,* which Molière subsequently turned into a genre that could stage criticism and theory. Later, Molière employed the "lack of control" trope frequently to characterize the production of his own court performances.[75] The importance of improvisation points in turn to the idea that burlesque ballets had more than one choreographer. If burlesque ballets were the product of a group effort under one or several organizers, their destabilizing intentions can be understood as a historical reality. The license to improvise without ultimate responsibility for the work left ample space for any dancer to work against the text of his *récit,* producing unexpected ironies. The intention to have court ballet appear an impromptu form also corresponds to its bathos: the appearance of the ordinary, and even the grotesquely realistic or utterly fantastic, in a sublime context. Yet the dichotomy of serious matters versus diverting ones is eroded because power and eroticism are viewed as two sides of one coin, both in language and in movement. Thus, the enormous cynicism and ambivalent ideology of this satire. In the interstices of conventionally condoned experimentation, with its requisite negativity, a space of critique becomes possible.

On the one hand, we have seen that games frequently have erotic connotations in burlesque ballet. We have also seen that, just as frequently, they have political referents by suggesting a different course of events or the reversibility of political fortunes. Similarly, we have observed that direct references to erotic play in burlesque ballets inevitably implicate the monarch as a source. Thus, games, erotic play, and political force become intertwined in burlesque works. Structured loosely on improvisation, burlesque ballets are Peirceian icons of a self beyond the text. The presence of the actual bodies whose political destiny is at stake endows the dancer with "firstness": his resemblance to his role object. Erotic subjugation endows the dancer with "secondness": an index of political subjugation. Games of chance manifest the ballet's "thirdness" by producing symbols of political change.[76]

In the *récit* for M. de la Valette playing a debauched courtier, the themes of dance, games, and political allegiances are linked as passions without including the obviously erotic component so frequent elsewhere:

Dans la pompe sont mes plaisirs,
La danse anime mes desirs,
Le demon du jeu me conserve,
Il a pouvoir de m'enflammer;
Mais un Soleil tient en reserve
Le feu qui doit me consumer. (L, 2:321)

In pomp are my pleasures,
Dance animates my desires,
The demon of gambling saves me,
He has the power to enflame me;
But a Sun holds in reserve
The fire that must consume me.

As icons of thematic links constituting court culture, ballets became self-conscious and self-reflecting. Asserting unusual cultural continuities lent burlesque ballets an open-ended quality that itself promoted a critical self-awareness.

The next *entrée* of *Les Fées* takes lunacy as its theme. *Entrées* are performed by four groups: the Dupes (les Embaboüinés), the Half-Mad (les Demy-Foux), the Extravagants (les Fantasques), and the Deft Gentlemen (les Esperlucates). The first two groups suggest carnivalesque reversals of the courtier with which we are already familiar. They recall a plethora of earlier "mad" ballets with titles such as *Ballet de la folie des fols* (1605), *Mascarade de six fous* (1600–1601), or *Ballet des chercheurs de midy à quatorze heures* (1620).

The sources of madness in movement can be traced back to the tradition of Renaissance social dance. In dance treatises of the French sixteenth century, two kinds of dancing were presupposed: the official, permissible dance, for which these treatises constituted an apology, and the unofficial, impermissible dance. Impermissible dance was shunned as a transgression of rule, art, and legality in the direction of vanity, madness, and melancholy. Burlesque ballets rehabilitated the transgressive aspects of earlier social dance by integrating them into theatrical representations of madness. They cultivated an "official" grotesque style, which was above moral reproach.

The depiction of madness in ballet runs the gamut from the primitive and uninstructed to the intoxicated, vicious, and monstrous. In *Les Resveries d'un extravagant* (Dijon, c. 1633) the fifteenth *entrée* presents six nobles, named in the libretto, personifying dancing peasants (Figures 14 and 15).

Figure 14. Entrée of the drunken peasants, danced by nobles, in *Le Ballet du chateau de Bissestre* (1632). Bibliothèque nationale, Paris.

Figure 15. Nobles dancing as peasants, probably in *Le Ballet du chateau de Bissestre* (1632). Louvre, Collection Edmond de Rothschild, Paris.

Their *récit* is as follows:

> Mes Dames, si en nostre danse,
> On ne remarque la cadance,
> N'en faites mauvais jugement,
> Car une simple creature
> N'a jamais aultre mouvement
> Que Celuy qu'apprend la nature. (L, 5:15)

> My Ladies, if in our dance
> We cannot keep to the rhythm,
> Do not judge us ill,
> For a simple creature
> Does not dispose of other movement
> Than the kind nature has taught him.

What is meant in dancing terms by "de geste fol et de posture" is rarely detailed. A similar *récit* from the *Ballet de l'heure du temps* (c. 1622) gives a picture of dancers extending the definition of dancing to unskilled and unstudied "natural" movement:

> Pas un de nous ne sçait danser;
> Nos pas se font sans y penser,
> Nous marchons tous à l'advanture,
> Comme gens qui n'ont point appris;
> Partout nous nous trouvons surpris,
> Hormis au Ballet de nature.
> Sans pas, ny dessein,
> Les pieds croisés, les bras au sein,
> Sans ordre, discours, ny cadence
> Par un bizarre passetemps,
> Nous vous dansons l'heure de temps
> Elle qui tous les jours nous danse. (L, 2:227–8)

> Not one of us knows how to dance;
> Our steps are performed without reflection,
> We walk in any which way,
> As people would who have never learned;
> Everything comes to us as a surprise,
> Except in the Ballet of nature.
> Without steps, without design,
> Our feet crossed, our arms to our breasts
> Without order, discourse or rhythm
> In a strange pass-time,
> We are dancing the time of day for you
> The very one that dances us daily.

It is fair to imagine that these aristocrats accompanied the above *récit* with a dance not unlike the performance of the *gaillarde* which Thoinot Arbeau

Figure 16. Entrée of the beggars, danced by nobles, in *Le Ballet du chateau de Bissestre* (1632). Louvre, Collection Edmond de Rothschild, Paris.

described as unschooled: "Ceulx qui dancent la gaillarde aujourd'huy par les villes, ilz dancent tumultuairement, et se contentent de faire les cinq pas et quelques passages sans aulcune disposition et ne se soucient pourveu qu'ils tumbent en cadance" ("In the towns nowadays the *gaillarde* is danced regardless of rules, and without any orderly arrangement so long as they keep the rhythm").[77] Examples of nobles dressing as peasants are numerous in the literature (Figure 16). The peasant garb is often interpreted as a justification for an erotic stance. In *Ballet de Monseigneur le Prince* (1622), Monsieur de Blinville gives the following reasons for his diguise:

Soubs ce vestement paysan,
Brusle l'âme d'un courtisan
Pour une beauté qu'il adore;
Puisque je cherche à me brusler,
Croyez-vous qu'il me reste encore
Quelque soucy de m'habiller? (L, 2:303)

Beneath this peasant clothing,
Burns the soul of a courtier
For the beauty he adores;
Since I am willing to burn,
Do you think I need
To worry about dressing?

Like the Moor, the peasant is burned out: he wears his heart on his sleeve.

According to the dance theorist Saint Hubert, grotesque dance, at least in its inception, was an extension of the Renaissance notion of "bad dance." Drawing on his own experience as a dancer, he writes:

Quelquefois il y a des entrées où il n'est pas necessaire de sçavoir parfaictement bien dancer. Il me souvient qu'au premier Ballet où j'ay eu l'honneur de dancer devant sa Majesté je representois un Escollier, ou je dancay tout a contretemps et hors de cadence, chacun crut que je le faisois a dessein, et mon entree fut trouvée fort bonne.[78]

Sometimes there are *entrées* which do not require that one know how to dance perfectly. I remember that in the first Ballet in which I had the honor of dancing before his Majesty I played a schoolboy, where I danced everything in syncopation and against the rhythm, everyone thought I was doing it on purpose, and my *entrée* was judged to have been quite good.

The dichotomy between legality and transgression that the Renaissance formalized and ritualized in the *basse danse–gaillarde* pair returns in burlesque ballet in the dichotomy between the noble or serious and the grotesque style: "On fait une danse meslee du Serieux et du Ridicule, du Naturel, et du Chimerique, du Fabuleux et de l'Historique pour faire un juste Ballet" ("To compose a proper ballet, one should combine the Serious and the Ridiculous, the Natural and the Chimerical, the Fabulous and the Historical.")[79] On the most generic level, the serious dances connote what prudence would in social dance. In the ballet entitled *Le Sérieux et le Grotesque* (Paris, 1627), the character of "the serious one" depicts himself in these terms:

Le fils aisné de la Prudence
N'est point serieux comme moy
. . . .
Et ne vay point sans le compas
Dont je mesure tous mes pas. (L, 3:302)

The eldest son of Prudence
Is not as serious as I
. . . .
And I am never without the compass
With which I measure all my steps.

Burlesque ballet represents lunacy variously. It can be entirely fantastic, as with the eight monsters of the *Ballet de Tancrede* (Paris, 1619) who stand on two feet but whose upper bodies are an amalgam of grotesque creatures executing "des pas endiablez et des grimaces du tout extravagantes" ("devilish steps and completely extravagant grimaces") (L, 2:174). But, in general, madness is an effect of erotic seduction. The carnivalesque extremes permit an undifferentiated madness that connotes the courtier's impotence: his status as object vis-à-vis the king.

Frenetic or uncontrolled movement also conveyed unrequited love, through physical gestures. For example, in the *Vers pour "Le Ballet du roy"* (Paris, 1618), the unsympathetic women in the audience are said to be the cause of the performer's gracelessness.

> Pour Monsieur de Blinville, representant un fol
> Beautez de qui l'esprit, plein de perfections,
> Jette un oeil de mespris dessus mes actions,
> Pour n'y voir aujourd'huy ny mesure ny regle
> De grace, pardonnez à cet aveuglement
> Qui trouble tout à faict l'oeil de mon jugement.[80]

> For Monsieur de Blinville, playing a madman
> Beauties whose minds, full of perfections,
> Are looking upon my acts with disdain,
> Since you see neither measure nor rule
> I beg you to pardon this blindness
> Which has completely troubled the eye of my judgement.

Madness is frequently a variant of the courtier's feminization: he is the feminized victim of love in peace even as he is the powerless object of the king's will in war.

After the three groups of madmen perform their *entrées* in *Les Fées*, the Half-Mad (les Demy-Foux) also appear. The first, played by the king's brother, Monsieur, says that "amour et le dieu Mars partagent mes desirs" ("love and the god of war divide my desires"). This prepares several satiric battle scenes: a fully armored and mounted joust, a ground war with fantastic weapons and no casualties, a ballet for "head and arm choppers," and a tilt at the quintain for doctors riding mules. All the combatants in these scenes appear daft and incompetent although the detached arms and rolling heads of the third scene are said, in the synopsis, to have occasioned some fright.

The "head and arm choppers" satirically represent the boastful swashbuckling captain in the tradition of Matamore: "Leurs coups font aux combats, bras et teste voller, / Il est vray qu'elles sont postiches" ("Their blows in combat send arms and heads flying, / It is true that they are not real ones") (L, 3:45). One of the surest signs of this satire is the conceit of the ballet as a "machine de guerre" ("a war machine").[81] See, for example, the *récit* of the "capitaines estropiez" in *Le Ballet des infatigables* (1624):

> Qui ne sçait que les boulets
> Nous plaisent plus que les balets?
> Et celuy qui par nous se dance
> N'est pas de nostre mouvement,
> Amour fit le commandment
> Et nous rendons l'obeissance. (L, 3:27)

> Who doesn't know that canon balls
> Are more to our liking than ballets?
> And he whom we are dancing
> Is not animated by us,
> Love gave the command
> And we the obedience.

The soldiers are preceded by a herald who holds a *cartel* in a presentational manner, perhaps reminding the audience of the discrepancy between the *cartel*'s historical function as challenge to battle and its balletic function as conveyor of a *récit*. The *cartel* inevitably suggested a *scheda provocatoria* or *provocatoria charta*, a written challenge to duel. In popular culture, the herald participated in the "cris de Paris," as Bakhtin explains, "announcing mobilization, siege, war," in the public marketplace.[82] The herald's presence in *Les Fées* seems to underline that the courtiers' warrior status is hollow because purely balletic (Figure 17). Thus the ballet stands for social reality itself, in which bravery is a priori illusory. Burlesque ballets criticize society simply by pointing to their own basis in artifice.

Turning to the two framing scenes of *Les Fées*, one notes an overall progression from disharmony to harmony. The Fay of Music, Capricious Guillemine, states her preference for "la Musique qui ressemble aux Charivaris" ("cacophonous music"). This fay's spell will not enchant, but rather cause its audience to wince at the sound of its cacophonous effects. She places a guitar in the hands of Monsieur le Duc d'Aluyn (a "jeune Mars" – "a young Mars"), who is to serenade his lady with disharmonious sound while he is garbed in feminine attire. Mars, epithet both of Louis XIII (who himself strums a guitar in this scene) and of Spanish music making as an image of cowardice, underlines the work's ambivalence vis-à-vis its own format: spectacle as gallant seduction. The ballet's organizer, le Duc de Nemours, addresses Louis as they play in these terms:

> Le Mars des fleurs de Lis, Roy de mes volontez,
> Anime mon courage ainsi que ma guiterre,
> Scachez donc que je suis, ô Divines Beautez,
> Espagnol au Ballet et François à la guerre. (L, 3:38)

Figure 17. Herald and drummers from *Les Fées des forests de Saint Germain* (1625). Victoria and Albert Museum, London.

> The Mars of the Lily, King of my wills,
> Fires my courage as well as my guitar,
> Know, O divine Beauties, that I am,
> Spanish in Ballet and French in war.

In this dual address to Louis and to the "Dames," this double reference to power and subjugation, the motifs of disorder and sexual ambiguity, as well as those of combat and madness, and their respective reversals, are all resumed. In the final scene, the Fay of Dance enters prepared to withdraw all the ballet's characters as if they were puppets ("des bilboquets que j'esca-motte").[83] Suddenly, however, she realizes that they are all dancing like "demy-Dieux" ("minor Deities"). She states that their transformation has been effected by the beautiful ladies in the audience: "Je dois aux charmes de vos yeux / Ce dernier effect de Magie" ("I owe this final magic effect / to the charms of your eyes"). Thus, in this last of the ballet's transformations, grotesque style takes on a noble shape, thanks only to the sexual rapport between audience and players.

As with other libertine texts in the burlesque tradition, *Les Fées* inaugurates, in the words of Joan DeJean, "polemical dialogue with cliche."[84] It would therefore be unwise to extend Lincoln Kirstein's judgement on the 1653 *Ballet de la nuit* to the burlesque phenomenon that preceded it. Kirstein evaluated the presence of low style in this work as follows: "Popular imagery with precise pantomime served as contrast to exalt the grandiose manner and atmosphere of formal ballet."[85] As we have just shown, *Les Fées* ends with an abrupt reversal of low to high style. Unlike *Le Balet comique*, the restoration of order does not reaffirm a threatened harmony. Rather, it is a magic effect on a par with all the other effects in the work: harmony and order come about by transforming the materials of chaos. In a similar manner, at the close of another famous burlesque work, *Le Ballet du chateau de Bissestre* (1632), harmony is constructed out of chaos:

Puis la Musique du Roy se fit entendre, laquelle fut fermée par le grand Balet dancé aux pieds de Sa Majesté, qui rejoignant en un corps tant de pieces destachées et faisant à son aspect reconnoistre pour gens d'honneur ceux qui paroissoient nagueres plongez dans un cloaque de vices, signifioit combien la vertu de ce Monarque est efficacieuse, puisque le vice ne peut subsister devant luy, et qu'à son abord les Diables mesmes cessent de l'estre. (L, 4:225)

Then the King's Music was heard, which was followed by a grand Ballet at his Majesty's feet, which brought together so many disparate pieces and made us recognize as honorable people those who had just appeared to be plunged in a sewer of vices. It signified how this Monarch is effective, since vice cannot subsist before him, and that in his presence Devils cease to be devils.

This final vision of the monarch occasions a transformation of his vicious subjects into virtuous ones. Yet this scene betrays a critical awareness of the king's perspective in court festival because he does not merely interpret historical reality, he puts a construction on it through his very presence. In burlesque ballet, the nation is no longer the flat state: it is a mosaic of "disparate pieces" open to varying and variable interpretations. The king has the final word, but this final word appears no more conclusive than any one else's. At most, it provides a sense of formal closure for the ballet.

Some dance historians claim that the dancing in burlesque ballet is satirical because purely imitative. It should be emphasized that there is also a great deal of gratuitous fantasy in the genre and that the dancing contains much visible allegory. The component of meaningless fantasy has been stressed since Menestrier. Yet the more meaningless these works are, the more parodic their vision of themselves and society is likely to be. They masquerade as *mascarades*. The dancing figure as such, and its frequently deforming costume, gained precedence over the other arts traditionally participating in court ballets. Visible allegory in burlesque ballet does not entirely depend on the presence of a "dramatic development lending itself to various moral interpretations," in the words of Margaret McGowan.[86] Whereas humanist ballet cultivated dramatic allegory with political and moral significance, burlesque ballet is more architectural in its constructed visual forms, daring in its inventive physicality, and purposefully ironic in its dramatic significance. In fact, burlesque ballets crystallized moments of ideological ambivalence by safeguarding their irresponsible lack of dramatic coherence.

McGowan attributes the period's excessive indulgence in allegory to its taste for pedantic erudition. I see the use of allegory as expressly inimical to the goals of imitative theater in its conventional, Aristotelian sense. Burlesque ballet engendered appearances, not actions. Beyond its pedantic appeal, allegory still has the potential to transcend conventional forms of communicating meaning.[87] Although it traditionally points toward a higher meaning whose synthesis challenges direct apprehension, it also points to the fragmentation of all meaning. In allegory, as Walter Benjamin put it, "any person, any object, any relationship can mean absolutely anything else."[88] Allegorical meaning in burlesque ballet can derive in part from its costume because its allegory is visible rather than dramatic. Thus, it seems logical that costume should have developed to the detriment of decor and text. With the more elaborate forms of burlesque costuming, the body became a composite spectacle in its own right. Burlesque ballets clearly eschew a linear in favor of a spatial deciphering of the visual image. Each body is juxtaposed with the forward movement of performance as a conundrum to be contemplated in depth. Irony encouraged the spectator to linger on the dancing figure's presence, to extract some ultimate meaning from it and it alone. Burlesque ballet was developing a procedure physically equivalent to Peirce's iconic sign, a model for its own reading that would differentiate it from other forms of narrative theater and centering on the body's appearance as much or more than on the body's movement. It is true that in *Les Fées* some dancers portray recognizable types such as soldiers, whereas others are purely allegorical, such as Music as a Female Colossus (Figure 18). But the preponderance of satire in burlesque ballet does not transform the individual exclusively into a type.[89] The many allegorical figures in burlesque ballets are not confined to purely farcical types, limited by historical convention.

It is difficult to attribute the same ideological thrust ordinarily associated with earlier and later performance to burlesque ballets. The eruption of eroticism, in particular, does not square with our received ideas about court ballet in the service of the divine right of kings. Burlesque ballets inaugurate an ambivalent commentary on the wielding of power itself. The king's body is interposed between the desiring male dancer and the eroticized female audience. The noble would feign to occupy the royal body or display his ignoble physical subservience to it. Just as the king is liable to represent untouchable excellence, he is also read across all the negative codes of burlesque ballet. He appears as himself and as a sham. In *Les Fées*, Louis XIII has the following *récit:* "France, qui dans les mains me vois des armes peintes, / Dont les exploits ne sont que des jeux et des feintes . . ." ("France, you see me here with painted arms / My exploits are only games and play . . .") (L, 3:46).

Figure 18. Music as a Female Colossus in *Les Fées des forests de Saint Germain* (1625). Victoria and Albert Museum, London.

Self-conscious theatricality paired with the reduction of text and decor and the experimental distortion of the body's outlines all point beyond symptoms of moral dissoluteness toward a strategy of subversion of norms. This subversion is explored both in pointed satire and in pure aestheticism as well as in erotic posturing. The noble's sense of his growing obsolescence in court society induced him to employ burlesque fashions in the interest of an ironic critique of that society. I do not mean critique in any particularly reasoned or systematic sense, but rather as an expression of nihilistic resistance arising in spiteful and vitally negative statements about himself and his sociopolitical status. Burlesque ballets embodied harsh ironies playfully enacted in the face of insurmountable odds. Therefore, I claim that burlesque ballet was politically volatile. Although recognizing the critical potential of burlesque works, McGowan separates burlesque ballet from what she calls political ballet. Thus, she restricts the politics of performance to official channels. In contrast, I give to the term "political" a nonliteral sense on the margins of statecraft. Burlesque ballet is not political by reflecting royal policy, that is, by framing or camouflaging diplomatic intentions. Clearly, it does neither of these things. Burlesque ballet is ideologically subversive and, therefore, politically destabilizing. Certainly, the links established in this chapter between combativeness, subservience, derangement, and chance outcomes in no way promote, or even suggest, foils for royal power. Burlesque ballet practices resistance, but also ultimately compliance, with the dominant ideology. Its avoidance of narrative makes it an early variety of modernist absolute dance, one whose reflexivity is dictated by considerations of political egoism. The original impetus, historically speaking, for dance autonomy was based in an unsavory political self-interest.

The most potent, and yet unfocused, resistance to the centralized power of the monarch resides in the *disponibilité* of burlesque dance rather than in its satiric barbs. Given that court ballet had previously become an ideological instrument of the sovereign – although created and performed by his noble subjects – its new-found variability and openness to interpretation were provocative. It is on the margin of representation, in the incompleteness or indetermination of meaning, that the body's autonomy is realized. This autonomy is burlesque ballet's innovative and modernist contribution to choreography.

When we interpret theatrical history as a function of literature, early seventeenth-century Cornelian heroism is emblematic of the last gasp of noble individualism. In this perspective, burlesque works are considered indiscriminate satire that belittles and humbles powerful ambition. I maintain, to the contrary, that the satiric thrust of burlesque court ballet should be understood as the corrosive underside of heroic self-absorption: lewd self-debasement. But along with this ignoble self goes the whole sociopolitical structure that it was court ballet's privilege to epitomize. Burlesque ballet appropriates certain aspects of carnivalized culture to its own ends. It cannot be carnivalesque in the full Bakhtinian sense because it demolishes the past without a spirit of regeneration. In place of a regenerative spirit, burlesque ballet's carnivalesque reversals engender a critical self-consciousness. Burlesque ballet is a nondramatized *gloire,* a single-minded pursuit of passions whose stakes have become irrelevant. In this sense, affirmation does emerge from burlesque negation: the affirmation of pure dissent.

Chapter

5

MOLIÈRE AND TEXTUAL CLOSURE
Comedy-Ballet, 1661–1670

C'est dans le jeu qu'on voit les plus grands coups du sort.
In games one sees the greatest intervention of fate.

Molière, *Les Fâcheux*

Toutes les personnes raisonnables la [la Danse] considereront à l'avenir comme . . . un corps qui peut facilement subsister sans estre animé par leur harmonie [des instruments de Musique].

All reasonable people will henceforth consider it [Dance] as . . . a body that can easily subsist without harmonious animation.

Lettres patentes

Even if its ideological disparities did not crystallize until approximately 1624, the burlesque style existed as early as 1595. Although the motifs of reversal inherent in grotesque realism persisted well into the 1650s, by the 1640s the corrosive force of those motifs seems to have faded. It is not that the burlesque disappears entirely: it becomes pastoralized – framed and distanced – consciously costumed as itself and, consequently, ersatz when compared with its originally raw apparition in the 1620s. Pastoral images pervade court ballet librettos between 1643 and 1660, so that by 1670 Molière's Monsieur Jourdain has good cause to complain: "Pourquoi toujours des bergers? On ne voit que cela partout" ("Why always shepherds? That's all one ever sees").[1]

In 1661, Louis XIV acceded to personal power, and Molière created his first comedy-ballet, *Les Fâcheux*. Although apparently unrelated, these two events intersect on both historical and theoretical grounds. Louis XIV was present on August 17, 1661 at the premiere of *Les Fâcheux* in the gardens of Nicolas Fouquet's château Vaux-le-Vicomte. Fouquet was arrested on September 5, 1661, for competing with Louis in the opulent display of which *Les Fâcheux* was a part. Having danced in ballets since childhood, Louis knew

spectacle in the framework of a dramatic text. This work sought a new solution to the old problem of harmonizing dance and theater. Although Molière may originally have conceived *Les Fâcheux* with a purely aesthetic aim in mind, it must have appealed to Louis XIV for the historical and ideological precedents it invoked. Molière and his collaborators were actively working with all the components that had distinguished court ballet as a political statement: text, music, and dance.[17] Having seen *Les Fâcheux* in 1661, Louis surely recognized in Molière the kind of theoretical practitioner he needed. Here was a contemporary playwright and actor-director able to rejuvenate the court ballet form. And although his performance style was highly physical, he was also a man of words. His combined physical and verbal gifts made it likely that Molière would restore composite spectacle's former ideological *éclat*. In 1660, Louis had already given Molière's troupe the Palais royal theater to work in. By 1665, Molière's Illustre théâtre became the King's Troupe, and royal patronage was to last throughout Molière's career.

Les Fâcheux is an important work, not only because it is Molière's first comedy-ballet, but because it reveals he appropriated dance to comedy with a full awareness of older court ballet theory. Thus, I argue that *Les Fâcheux* contains a theoretical reflection on court ballet: it is an experimental work governed by a theoretical outlook.[18] Molière claimed in the preface to *Les Fâcheux* that comedy-ballet was a unique and experimental genre ("C'est un mélange qui est nouveau pour nos théâtres" – "It's a mixture new to our theaters") (TC, 1:399). Of course, the idea of putting dances between the acts of a play was not original. It was Molière's particular way of coordinating act and choreographed interlude that became entirely his own. He nevertheless reverted to a structure familiar to earlier court ballet in which the acts of comedy are interspersed with dance. This is nothing other than the interlude structure that burlesque ballet had collapsed by eliminating any central act. In reviving the interlude structure, Molière caused the *entrée* to lose the autonomy it was developing in burlesque ballet. He placed dance, once again, between the acts of a play. But in modeling the comedy's narrative on the principle of thematic proliferation, Molière constructed a comedy out of the material of interlude.

In his preface to the printed version of *Les Fâcheux*, Molière took two positions on the relationship of interlude to act. First, he seems to indicate an aesthetic of improvisation common to burlesque ballet. In this case the relationship of interlude to act appears relatively fortuitous. He remarks, "On s'avisa de les [les entrées] coudre au sujet du mieux que l'on put" ("We tried to connect them [the *entrées*] to the subject as best we could"). Then he claims to achieve a fusion of ballet and comedy inevitably recalling Beaujoyeulx's preface to *Le Balet comique:* "[On s'avisa de] ne faire qu'une seule chose du ballet et de la comédie" ("[We tried] to make the ballet and the comedy one thing").[19] It is not unusual for Molière to draw upon a Renaissance model at this early stage in his career. Three years before, in 1658, he had adapted his second full-scale comedy, *Le Dépit amoureux*, from an Italian comedy published in 1581, through originally written in 1550. His preoccupations with the fusion of dance and comedy make the comedy-ballet project appear doubly reactionary. It seems to revert back not only to the interlude structure of composite spectacle, but also to the ideology of harmony that characterized that spectacle. What, in fact, is Molière doing in *Les Fâcheux*, and what is original about it? Its originality is more conceptual than formal. The play is driven by the interlude rather than the other way around, in that the play takes its action from the themes that the interlude seems to suggest.

In *Les Fâcheux* (*The Button-holers* or *The Social Bores*), the main character, Eraste, encounters a vast number of tiresomely obstructive acquaintances on his way to a tryst with his beloved Orphise. The acts are punctuated by interludes, and each act itself consists of numerous small scenes. As the play begins, Eraste recounts the episode of a grotesque marquis who interrupts a stage performance. The marquis, a stock butt of satire in many of Molière's other comedies, makes a public nuisance of himself as does every other character in *Les Fâcheux* besides its hero and heroine. Eraste describes the scene of a performance, and the theme of his story is performance interrupted. Indeed, Eraste's monologue sets a precedent for the bores who will plague him: verbose creatures whose long-windedness is time consuming as well as opaque. Eraste's own introduction is typical of the importunate speech acts to follow: "Il faut que je te fasse un récit de l'affaire" ("I have to describe the scene to you") (TC, 1:404). A boorish noble arriving late to a performance disrupts its progress as he chooses a seat. He interrupts the play's best moment, and Eraste cites his dismay at this theatrical intrusion:

'Hé! mon Dieu! nos Français, si souvent redressés,
Ne prendront-ils jamais un air de gens sensés,
Ai-je dit, et faut-il, sur nos défauts extrêmes,
Qu'en théâtre public nous jouions nous-mêmes?' (TC, 1:404)

'Oh! my God! our French, so often excitable,
Won't they ever settle down and be reasonable,
I said, and must we, to our great demerit,
Always play ourselves in public theaters?'

Eraste is a character in a play quoting himself as an audience member of another play. Thus, his own discourse waylays the matter at hand – *Les Fâcheux* – in a paradigmatic way.

Although *Les Fâcheux* stages a series of frustrations, interrupted action is the play's motor. In Eraste's account of the boorish marquis, the theatrical intruder becomes a visual obstruction to the performance by taking a chair center stage: "Et de son large does morguant les spectateurs / Aux trois quarts du parterre a caché les acteurs" ("And with his broad back facing the audience / He hid the actors from most of the audience") (TC, 1:404). In a similar manner, digressive monologues obstruct the intention of the hero to act ("toujours ma flamme divertie" – "my flame always diverted") (TC, 1:416). Similar to *L'Impromptu de Versailles* in this respect, *Les Fâcheux* is a postponed play: it has difficulty getting started.

The dramatis personae of *Les Fâcheux* follow one another across the stage like so many burlesque *entrées*. In their static relation to the narrative they are essentially interchangeable. (Molière himself played all but one of the bores). Yet with regard to the technical specialization of their discourses, the bores are differentiated. In fact, the dense technical vocabulary some deploy frequently renders the sense of their speech practically incomprehensible. Because what they say fulfills no particular narrative function other than that of idling narrative development, their very prolixity appears burlesque. The breadth of these monologues also suggests that speech becomes the action of the play: each character has a story to tell on the model of Eraste's initial story; but by the same token, the physical obstruction that each character occasions is their speech act. The burlesque sentiment purveyed by *Les Fâcheux* is: by speaking I do nothing. This could be viewed as a parody of d'Aubignac's dictum for neoclassical drama: "*Parler, c'est Agir*" ("*Speaking is Action*").[20]

In addition, most of the nuisance discourses in *Les Fâcheux* suggest thematic preoccupations of burlesque ballet. Lysandre, for example, asks Eraste's opinion on a dance air to which he choreographed. He obliges Eraste to dance the piece with him. He is followed by Alcippe, who seeks consolation for a devastating loss at cards. In this way, the link between self-conscious and improvised dance performance and gaming – a prevalent feature of many burlesque works – also becomes a prevalent motif in *Les Fâcheux*. Another burlesque theme is suggested by Orante and Clymène, who seek mediation of their argument over the values of jealousy in love: as with Eraste himself, who must pine impotently as his advances are obstructed, the characters of burlesque ballet are often sick with a love whose outcome hangs in the balance. When Eraste frees himself from his inopportune petitioners to speak to Orphise, the result is misunderstanding. On the one hand, the theme of interruption can suggest anger. "Ah! ne vous fâchez pas, trop sévère beauté," says Eraste ("Ah! Don't become angry [*fâchée*] overly severe beauty"). On the other hand, the notion of the obstacle is a goad to love: "Dans l'obstacle qu'on force il [l'amour] trouve des douceurs" ("In the obstacle overcome [love] finds sweetness"). The obstacle has a double-edged meaning: it is a source of fulfillment and loss. The ambivalent reversals of sentimental/erotic and hierarchical/power themes from burlesque ballet are subtly activated in the title's active connotations. A bore (*fâcheux*) can make one angry (*fâché*), but obstacles (*fâcheux*) incite to action. Dorante, like Eraste himself at the beginning of the play, wishes to relate an encounter with a quintessential bore, thereby suggesting the kind of self-conscious circularity also typical of many burlesque works.

Eraste continues to be accosted by various characters whose demands prevent him from rejoining Orphise. He is asked to be a second in a duel, to present a petition to the king, and to hear a secret in which he has no interest. Finally, Filinte attempts to protect him from an ostensible threat and will not leave his side, again preventing him from meeting Orphise. *Les Fâcheux* is about the interruption of action. Each scene typifies fastidious, drawn out talk as speech acts. These words are actions standing in action's way. *Les Fâcheux* is also constructed in a manner similar to burlesque ballet. In the place of action we have the unfolding of thematic variations on inaction. Only Eraste's need to unite himself with Orphise maintains the impulse of dramatic action, overarching the acts and the *entrées* as an unrealized intention. The *entrées* themselves are also constructed in much the same way as those of burlesque ballet. They employ *déclassé* characters performing for the most part mundane actions that accelerate into a piece of choreography, for example, the *joueurs de mail* ("the croquet players") and the *curieux* ("the curious") at the end of act 1, and the *joueurs de boules* ("boccie players"), *petits frondeurs* ("stone slingers"), *savatiers et savatières* ("shoemakers"), and the *jardinier* ("gardener") at the end of act 2. Molière's preface indicates that a small number of dancers played each interlude, but apart from the "prologue" in which a naiad emerges from a fountain followed by dryads, fauns, and satyrs emerging from trees and columns, the interludes embroider on the theme of obstructive action with reference to the lower classes. In this way too, they play subtly with burlesque ambivalence since the actions of lower classes could hardly be considered as valid visual metaphors for speech acts of the upper classes.

What actions, if any, are performed in the *entrées*? Both the *joueurs de mail* and the *curieux* force Eraste off the stage momentarily, the first group absorbed in their game, the second motivated by idle curiosity and crowding him out. The *joueurs de boule* enlist his aid in settling a dispute, thus mimicking the "jealousy" episode in act 2. Their choreography also recalls, in a more formal sense than that of the *joueurs de mail*, the conceit of a game: they dance "un pas composé de toutes les postures qui sont ordinaries à ce jeu" ("a dance composed of all the postures normally observed in this game") (TC, 1:427). They are displaced by the *frondeurs*, who in turn give way to the *savatiers*. The latter are interrupted by the *jardinier*. At times, transitions between dancers occur when one group chases the other off the stage. In this way, the *entrées* gain a dramatic motivation from the theme of interruption itself.

Louis Eugene Auld calls the use of interlude in this play rather "mechanical," and Claude Abraham suggests it "was flawed as a dramatic entity by yielding too much to the *ballet de cour*."[21] Yet in fact, the comedy's subject adapts to the action that interlude can provide, namely to divert. It is as if Molière's thought process were the following: if dance occurred in interlude that interrupts action, then the only way to make a comedy blending act and dance is to make a comedy about interruption. Thus, far from being mechanical, his use of interlude is precise and technically accurate: motivated by the form's most basic function. The comedy itself is about disruptive moments. In other terms, *Les Fâcheux* explores the "active" or dramatic potential of interlude. Viewed from this standpoint, it is both highly theoretical and original. It is in this mannerist sense that we should understand Molière's claim to originality in the preface. With *Les Fâcheux*, Molière has not simply placed dance and text side by side once again and simulated their marriage in a pleasurable experience. This comedy is in fact interlude reflecting on its own formal structure as a dramatic entity. That is, interlude determines action, rather than the reverse. It is in this sense that acts and interludes are "une seule chose" ("one thing").

Les Fâcheux is a formal experiment demonstrating Molière's acute awareness of the difference between interlude and act. Molière recognized the theoretical premise that the *entrée* was interruptive rather than linear and expressive. Despite this, he proceeded to make comedy and dance adhere by locating those areas of comedy that are like dance. He structures the comedy in such a way that its acts embody the interruptive aspect of interlude. In so doing, the dance–text paradigm becomes subtly inverted because the textual component takes an illustrative role. W. D. Howarth claims that *Les Fâcheux* establishes a theme that is then reflected in the interludes.[22] Rather, the play's theme seems derived from interlude itself, as Molière attempts to find its dramatic equivalent. Molière purposely chooses court ballet as a model for comedy-ballet in order to work out the problem of dance and text. Moreover, once Eraste and Orphise are finally united in act 3 and the theme of inaction appears resolved, the stage is invaded by boisterous *masques* playing "des crins crins et des tambours de Basques" ("noisemakers and drums") rather than violins, which would traditionally herald the grand ballet. These are the last disruptive bores of the play: their role is to frustrate the expectation and suspend the advent of the grand ballet. A final reciprocity between act and interlude is achieved through displacing the conventional expectation of dance and music. The grand ballet is postponed in the very function that brings it closest to dramatic action traditionally, that of celebration. This final obstacle also stems from the need to explore interruption from every possible dramatic angle. It also suggests, however, the kind of generic reversal cultivated in burlesque ballets.

Molière's apparently modest yet brilliant experiment in *Les Fâcheux* had several far-reaching consequences for the creation of subsequent comedy-ballets, notably for *Le Bourgeois Gentilhomme*. It is therefore curious that Molière's comedy-ballets were virtually never considered by literary scholars within the historically significant context of court ballet. Perhaps the importance he accorded dance and music in approximately one-third of his oeuvre was a disappointment, if not an embarrassment, to Molière scholars to whom comedy-ballet seemed insufficiently literary when compared to Molière's earlier, "regular" comedy. Comedy-ballet has gradually been exhumed from scholarly neglect in the twentieth century by Pellisson, Auld, Defaux, and, most recently, Abraham because literary historians are now more willing than previously to consider nonliterary criteria as essential to the analysis of theater. Most of these critics have dealt with Molière's indebtedness to court ballet in order to evaluate his comedy-ballet in its true light.

Court ballet historiography and theory from Yates and McGowan to zur Lippe has not extended its corpus explicitly to the comedy-ballets. Molière has been the professional concern of literary critics on the one hand, and of theatrical producers on the other. Considering Molière's comedy-ballets as an integral part of court ballet, and consequently of dance history, entails the attempt to reconcile two different critical traditions: there is not much overlap between court ballet historiography and Molière scholarship. Even the most experimental of Molière critics have been reluctant to explore the imprint of court ballet on the comedy-ballets. Although they have begun to focus on performance values, Molière scholars with few exceptions have persisted in deriving interpretations of the comedy-ballets that do not integrate the relevant court ballet traditions.[23]

Maurice Pellisson suggested that the performance values of Molière's comedy-ballets might intersect with, and even contribute to, their literary meaning. He did not, however, acknowledge the importance of court ballet to the origin of comedy-ballet. Moreover, he claimed that no court ballets could be considered works of art because they were not harmonious and lacked action.[24] Like other among his contemporaries, Pellisson remained unaware of the conflict between dance and text that had taken root in the seventeenth century.

Auld addressed the question of the structure of comedy-ballets and their inner coherence as theater. Implicit in this method of inquiry is the idea that dance is always secondary to the real business at hand, which is strictly dramaturgical. Nevertheless, he contested the assumption that Molière's "lyric" work was a testing ground for French opera. According to this view, the comedy-ballets are regarded as inherently preliminary, bearing the same relationship to full-fledged opera as would cartoons to a complete fresco.[25] Jean-Baptiste Lully, Molière's musical collaborator on *Les Fâcheux* and many subsequent works, embarked on opera only after the demise of comedy-ballet. Yet the chronological sequence of events – comedy-ballet as prior to French opera – does not have theoretical import.

Defaux has focused on comedy-ballet as the final word of Molière's mature output and stressed the "reflexive dimension" of this part of his artistic evolution. That is, for Defaux the comedy-ballets are part of an implicit critique of conventional comedy because they abandon norms of social wisdom and the chastisement of vice.[26] Nevertheless, Defaux disregards the influence of prior court ballet on Molière by claiming that Molière turned the material of court ballet to good advantage while asserting that court ballet itself was inherently unworthy of any such transformation.[27]

Abraham is much more willing than Defaux to examine the ways in which dance and text effectively interact in Molière's work. Abraham does this at first by contesting Auld's idea that ballet offered Molière an extension of the gestural continuum that he had practiced from farce to imitation of everyday life. Situated at the opposite pole from farce along this continuum, ballet would enhance theater with a stylized version of imitative actions. Unlike the sources of French farce or Italian *lazzi*, which are often considered a matrix of Molière's creativity,[28] ballet would extend theater toward aesthetic formalization rather than toward caricature.[29] According to this argument, the incorporation of ballet is the logical consequence of Molière's interest in gestural stylization. At one end of the spectrum is the grotesque gesture of farce; at the other, the aesthetic gestures of dance.

In an odd twist to this model, Defaux thinks of dance as a form of "pure farce" or aesthetic caricature. Abraham critiques Auld's notion of a continuum, however, because it does not address structural aspects of comedy-ballet. He argues instead for a symbiosis of the arts in Molière. For example, in *Monsieur de Pourceaugnac* he sees an intentional blurring of the difference between theater and *fête*, whereas in *Le Bourgeois Gentilhomme* he sees formal choreographic procedures suggested by the text as determining its dramatic presentation.[30]

Abraham's interpretation, although it constitutes a step forward, only serves to reaffirm the ideology of harmony in the historical combination of dance and text. Ironically, it reflects the theory found in the preface to *Le Balet comique*: the harmonious fusion of the arts. Molière recognized instead the heterogeneous quality of the arts. In arguing Molière's authorship of *Le Ballet des incompatibles* (Montpellier, 1655), Robert McBride stresses Molière's interest in aspects of incompatibility.[31] But McBride's examples pertain to the psychology of Molière's characters, whereas mine encompass his theory of genres and his interest in juxtaposing different levels of language. In exploiting this heterogeneity, Molière forged a dramatic continuity between theatrical genres that privilege speech and gesture differently. This is precisely the aspect of comedy-ballets that can truly be called original,[32] and it occurs primarily in *Les Fâcheux* (1661) and *Le Bourgeois Gentilhomme* (1670).[33]

Molière harmonizes dance and comedy in *Le Bourgeois Gentilhomme* by making dance the self-conscious subject matter of comedy. The main character, an inept but wealthy member of the bourgeoisie, studies dance and has ballets staged for him, both wittingly and unwittingly, in his home. Two plots are pursued simultaneously: Jourdain takes lessons in the noble arts of *savoir-vivre* and seems to be in the process of changing social classes by remolding his physical identity. Intertwined with this plot are the affairs of his own bourgeois family: his wife's disdain for his ambitions and his daughter's betrothal to a nonnoble. Since Jourdain lives in the glow of his own aspirations, these two plots only intersect when he obstructs the marriage plans for his daughter on the basis of her suitor's insufficient social rank. It then becomes necessary for Jourdain's family to disguise the modest suitor, Cléonte, as the son of a Turkish dignitary and to stage Jourdain's mock ennoblement as a "Mamamouchi" as a ruse for integrating the family's realistic plans with Jourdain's preoccupations. The ceremony of ennoblement, made up of dance and song masterminded by Cléonte's valet Covielle, is the site of a Turkish-style burlesque ballet, the so-called *turquerie*, to which I shall return shortly.

A preliminary structural analysis of the play reveals that dance is integrated into the action in two unique ways. To begin with, it is explicitly presented as the action of dancing.[34] By staging a dancing lesson for Jourdain in act 1, Molière renders that dancing self-referential in much the same way as do the *Letters Patent:* the performance of dance in the comedy serves the purpose of representing the autonomous steps and figures in which social dancing consists. At the other end of the spectrum, in act 4, the autonomous apparition of dance is further developed through the staging of a burlesque ballet that is called a *turquerie*, a *mascarade*, and a *bourle*. This violent and phantasmagoric performance within the play itself is crafted to dupe Jourdain into compliance with the family's plans of marriage. It flatters Jourdain with bogus noble status, accomplishing his class elevation in a carnivalesque spirit of debasement. The carnivalesque nature of the *turquerie* enables it to transcend its narrative context and make a symbolic statement that is usually taken as an extended metaphor for Jourdain's psychological state. To conclude this preliminary analysis, the comedy-ballet progresses from courtly social dancing to theatrical dancing. Both sorts of dancing are staged *within* the play rather than as tangential interludes. Yet both are also placed as though within quotation marks because they open a space of autonomous development in which dance takes it course independent of, though not in total disregard of, narrative. Dance in *Le Bourgeois Gentilhomme* has an enormous manipulative potential both pedagogically and theatrically: it is used to thwart, exploit, and satirize the comedy-ballet's protagonist.

At the end of act 1, the dancing master presents Jourdain with a demonstration of dance vocabulary: "Quatre danseurs exécutent tous les mouvements différents et toutes les sortes de pas que le Maître à danser leur commande" ("Four dancers perform all the different movements and all the kinds of steps that the dancing master orders them to do") (TC, 2:720). Thus, dance is integrated into the play's action on a literal level. Although dancing opens a space of divertissement for the audience, it is no longer a formal interruption of the narrative. It only slows the narrative because of the real time it takes to enact a dancing lesson. This fusion addresses one of the goals of *Le Balet comique;* however, dance and action were fused paradoxically through the interruption of dance per se.[35] In *Le Bourgeois Gentilhomme,* Molière fuses dance with action by permitting dance literally to evince its own active qualities. The real time of the dancing coincides with the diegetic time of the narrative, or more precisely, narrative time becomes the real time of dance. What distinguishes Molière's manner of fusion is the quality of dance and text. Although the surrounding structure is clearly textual, the subordination of dance to that textual order is uncertain. There are instances when action fuses with dance rather than the reverse. For example, at the end of the "Ballet des nations," this comedy-ballet's grand ballet, the staged audience applauds to dance and music while singing the work's praises (OC, 2:787). In this case the order of priorities between dance and text appears reversed as the actors reach spontaneously for a new level of expression.[36] In the cases of the lesson and the *turquerie,* however, dance is presented as a plausibly realistic and historicized activity in the consciousness of the play's characters. But, because of its active autonomy, dance is always poised to exceed textual closure.

The dancing lesson is addressed to Jourdain, for whom it is meant as a demonstration and preliminary lesson, while also constituting the first "interlude." Thus, although the term is retained, the digressive status of the interlude is dissolved. "All the different movements and all the kinds of steps" are employed, much as in the croquet game *entrée* of *Les Fâcheux* in which "all the postures" of the game are shown. The *entrée*'s comprehensiveness gives it a pedagogical quality permitting amplification within the narrative role assigned to it. Jourdain's lesson is no longer an *entrée,* however, but a literal demonstration of pedagogy. In both of these instances, even as a new formal apparatus for combining dance and text is being implemented, a critical distance puts the partnership of dance and noble ethos into question. Each use of dance thus described is a demonstration whose professed function bears a label, as it were, abstracting it from its courtly integration. When Jourdain participates to study a *révérence,* the effect is intentionally grotesque. Enacting the thwarted physical apprenticeship of nobility contains a double message: while the noble code is proven inviolable, it is also exposed in its mechanics as learnable. Although Jourdain has no birth right and is thus exaggeratedly gauche in all he undertakes, he does gain access to the physical technologies of class. Innate ability is thus indirectly demystified as a series of "dos" and "don'ts." Jourdain's own comic theatricality constantly diverts our attention as spectators from this essential point.

The rupture between the arts of performance and the noble ethos is not only apparent through Jourdain's will to learn to dance. *Le Bourgeois Gentilhomme* is roughly contemporaneous with a shift in Louis's personal attitude toward dance via his own body. Louis's last appearance in a court ballet was on July 18, 1668 in the *Ballet de Flore*. Eight months prior to *Le Bourgeois Gentilhomme*, Louis declined to appear as scheduled in Molière's comedy-ballet *Les Amants magnifiques*.[37] Racine's negative characterization of the dancing Nero in *Britannicus* (1670) could have dissuaded Louis from further public self-display. His doctor's journal for February 7, 1653, describes Louis becoming overheated while rehearsing a ballet and having contracted a cold that severely inhibited his talking and breathing.[38] This frailty could presumably have worsened. Yet these explanations are only anecdotal because it is impossible to say with certainty why Louis curtailed his performing career.

On a more theoretical level, Apostolidès has hypothesized a cultural crisis in the mythohistorical representation of the king through prestigious classical iconography. According to Apostolidès, in the early 1670s it was no longer deemed necessary by Louis's inner circle to mythologize the royal body in public performance: his personal power was sufficiently consolidated to permit him a private relation to space, one in which his body could retreat from a public staging of history and become real.[39] Louis's body could become detheatricalized because his history had become real. His body would consequently be replaced by the institutions founded to formalize his power. In the case of dancing, for example, the Royal Academy was to professionalize the dancing body, thereby outmoding the real theatrical presence of both the noble and the royal body. The development of technical proficiency to the detriment of a unique "aura" was to become a major problem-idea in enlightenment theatrical theory.[40]

In 1673, there were signs that the king's body had withdrawn personal participation, and possibly a degree of personal favor, from ballet. The opening conversation of the dancing and music masters in *Le Bourgeois gentilhomme* betrays their anxiety over this putative change of heart. On Jourdain's first day of lessons, the masters hopefully project a secure financial future for their arts from the wealthy bourgeois. "Ce nous est une douce rente," says the music master, "que ce Monsieur Jourdain . . . et votre danse et ma musique auraient à souhaiter que tout le monde lui ressemblât" ("This Monsieur Jourdain is a sweet subvention . . . and your dance and my music should wish that everyone resembled him") (TC, 2:712). Although the chief purpose of dance and music was to please the king, these arts now must please "everyone." The music master stresses that Jourdain's purchase of lessons "est de quoi nos arts ont plus besoin que de toute autre chose" ("is what our arts now need more than anything else"). Jourdain, the ignorant but financially well-to-do bourgeois, is more valuable to ballet than Dorante, the knowledgeable but impecunious courtier. The dancing master, idealistic in this regard, thinks financial gain should still be beneath an "honnête homme" such as himself. This detail is significant because it shows that the dancing master is, like Dorante, a noble living in the pre-Academy world where dance is as much an extension of the aristocratic as of the royal ethos. By wishing that Jourdain would acquire taste in dance, the dancing master sustains the naive belief that dance can effect social transformation, an inverted form of belief in its revolutionary power to transform society, just as Jourdain's comic ineptitude is an indirect expression of ruined social orders. The masters' dialogue reveals, however, that as court ballets become less intertwined with royal ideology, dancing becomes increasingly detached from the noble ethos as well. When institutionally neutralized, severed from their natural connection to estate in prestigious bodies, dance and music join the institution of learning as a universal school of etiquette: they become products on a taste market, techniques that can ideally be studied even by those lacking taste as a birthright. This is Molière's far-sighted response to the *Letters Patent*. The brawl between the masters of dance and music with the masters of fencing and philosophy at the end of act 2, scene 3, makes an unmistakable visual statement of this ideological disenfranchisement. As the four figures jostle each other toward the door in a din of imprecations hurled at each other's arts, there evaporates before our eyes the image of a society founded on the complementarity of dance and warfare and cemented by a cosmology in the name of which the arts collaborate to the point of fusion. Molière's visual commentary on the death of composite spectacle as political aspiration contradicts the famous apology of dance vis-à-vis statecraft earlier in the play:

Tous les malheurs des hommes, tous les revers funestes dont les histoires sont remplies, les bévues des politiques, et les manquements des grands capitaines, tout cela n'est venu que faute de savoir danser. (TC, 2:717)

All of mens' misfortunes, all of the fatal setbacks that fill the history books, all of the blunders of statesmen, and the wrong decisions of great commanders, derive from nothing other than lack of skill in dancing.

accomplished with only the sort of nonsensical utterances typical of burlesque ballets. Jourdain's fractured syntax as he aped noble mores ("Madame, ce m'est une gloire bien grande de me voir assez fortuné pour être si heureux . . . " – "Madame, this is a great glory to be so fortunate as to be honored . . . ") (TC, 2:759) here gives way to its obverse, a burlesque conciseness:

Cleonte: Bel-men.
Covielle: Il dit que vous alliez vite avec lui vous préparer pour la cérémonie afin de voir ensuite vous votre fille, et de conclure le mariage.
Monsieur Jourdain: Tant de choses en deux mots?
Covielle: Oui, la langue turque est comme cela, elle dit beaucoup en peu de paroles.
   (TC, 2:768)

Cleonte: Bel-men.
Coveille: He says that you should go quickly with him to prepare the ceremony so that you can then see your daughter and conclude the marriage.
Monsieur Jourdain: So much in two words?
Coveille: Yes, the Turkish language is like that, it says a lot in a few words.

If *Le Bourgeois Gentilhomme* offers the spectacle of language's compression and decomposition, it also offers the genesis of dance's composition and unfurling from pedagogical building blocks to full-fledged performance: the *turquerie*. In the course of the comedy-ballet, dance and text cross one another in opposite directions. The conceit that language must collapse or accede to a hermetic laconism for dance to emerge is a burlesque one. The more reassuring image of a reforming dance is represented by the lingua franca that appears in the *turquerie* but characterizes more markedly the "Ballet des nations." Molière's contemporary noble audience in the château of Chambord in October 1670 could hardly fail to grasp the allusions to "disfigured and corrupting" performance embodied by the *turquerie* and condemned by the *Letters Patent* nine years earlier.

The political reading one can give Jourdain is ambivalent. The *turquerie* evokes burlesque autonomy from the text and from social controls thirty years after the fact because it encases seditious memories within the comedy-ballet *Le Bourgeois Gentilhomme*. The *turquerie* exists both as a reference to antimonarchical burlesque performance and as a proscribed quotation from a banished form. As a quotation, it is poised to exceed its boundaries, yet is diffused by the text that justifies its presence as a prank. Nevertheless, following Larry W. Riggs's interpretation of other works by Molière, I interpret this comedy-ballet as "a kind of cultural, and even political, insurgency."[48]

The "Ballet des nations" that follows the *turquerie* in *Le Bourgeois Gentilhomme* benefits from no such elaborate justification. After a series of ingenious innovations integrating dance and text, this final divertissement is introduced arbitrarily as "un petit ballet qui avait été préparé" ("a little ballet that had been prepared") (TC, 2:779). Its only structural justification is that of burlesque ballet itself as a genre. In those works, a fairly conventional grand ballet would usually recoup the transgressive quality of the ballet as a whole by paying lip service to order and stable values. The "Ballet des nations" is not organically linked to Le Bourgeois Gentilhomme because its audience is staged within the ballet. This new audience is continuous neither with that of the play nor with the play's characters. Abandoning his earlier strategies of progressive integration of dance and text, Molière stresses the exteriority of the final divertissement to the text. He simulates a sense of textual closure.

The "Ballet des nations" is attended by a staged audience clamoring for the ballet's text. As with the Turkish language for which Madame Jourdain sought verbal equivalents in act 5, scene 1 ("Qu'est-ce à dire cela?" and "qu'-est-ce donc que ce jargon-là?" – "What does that mean?" and "What is that jargon?") (TC, 2:772–3), the noble public of the "Ballet des nations" seems insecure about how to interpret the transparent lingua franca ("me muero de amor," "Ay! que locura," "Felice la pena," etc.) of the "Ballet des nations." In addition to nobles, the audience also contains a bourgeois family. The talkative bourgeois couple in the audience reject the performance because it does not afford them enough social mobility. Their daughter, although courted by a noble, cannot obtain a libretto and they are not well seated. The final word of Le Bourgeois Gentilhomme is that the bourgeois is situated close to but outside of the circuit of power to which s/he aspires. Jourdain's madness, by contrast, stands forth in retrospect as the futility of noble unrest in disguise.

The issue confronted throughout this book has been how the body responds to texts that colonize physical environments of performance. By 1670, the control that Louis XIV wished to exert on ballet through Molière is a textual one. Riggs sees autocratic cultural control as "textualization of consciousness, or colonization of subjective 'space' by authoritative discourses concretized in printed texts."[49] Historically speaking, court ballet evidences just such colonization of a subjective choreographic space by an appropriating theatrical text able to fix and limit interpretation of the body's meaning. In Le Bourgeois Gentilhomme, a radicalized burlesque interlude is reframed by a "Ballet des nations" that both supports it and explains it away. In response to Louis XIV, Molière exercised a false compliance with textual colonization.

My goal has been to trace the aesthetic and ideological profile of French court ballet between 1573 and 1670. By analyzing configurations of body and text in late Renaissance composite spectacle, early-seventeenth-century burlesque ballet, and mid-seventeenth-century comedy-ballet, I have shown how those forms evolved in response to varied political agendas. Burlesque ballet at its most controversial suggests that a nobiliary opposition statement emanating from the confines of an officially sanctioned art addressed a multiclassed audience. This is undoubtably a surprising conclusion to draw regarding even a small portion of court ballets. Though it challenges the received image of court ballet, it is amply supported by historical evidence.

The concept of formal idealization stressed by McGowan,[50] like the Platonic concept of harmony whose blending leaves no place for Heraclitean contraries, does not tell the whole story of court ballet aesthetics. The idealization of form, like Platonic harmony, offers a static model. Ballets designed to comment critically on the absolutist project presupposed by celebration and praise infused the figures of harmony with antinomic forces. The political nature of court ballet is not only in the "pièce d'occasion" that reveals direct, circumstantial references to particular events, but also in the devious will to transform the very ideologies subtending both events and performances. Baroque court ballet was a metapolitics. In the choreographic itinerary traced in these pages from geometry to twisting, from hieroglyphs to desire, we can discern a mannerist continuum along which the body enhances its self-referentiality. Satire is the last eccentric outpost of mannerism; that is, satire is still a form of mannerist invention or *sprezzatura* as long as it maintains a faith in its own political efficacy. Mannerism, within this particular historical and artistic perspective, is a corruption of the Renaissance but a hopeful form of the baroque.

Molière's comedy-ballet staged court ballet's nostalgic but ruined image. Molière rehabilitated the integrative project of composite spectacle while also reviving the burlesque style of dancing suggesting disintegration. That is, Molière combined the fundamental historical givens of court ballet in a sort of collage, the result of his extended reflection on French court ballet theory combined with his covert ideological stance on cultural plurality. *Le Bourgeois gentilhomme* symmetrically reverses the social situation of burlesque ballet to which it alludes. In burlesque ballet, nobles perform before a bourgeois audience; in comedy-ballet, bourgeois performers address a noble audience. Burlesque court ballet seems about to become a forum for action, whereas carnivalesque reversals of the 1620s are replayed in comedy-ballet as travesties of the social mobility of the 1670s. Both contain nihilistic social visions: the first disguised as royal entertainment, the second disguised as bourgeois humanism.

Prior to Molière's deft compromises, burlesque practice revealed an impossible aestheticoideological stance or, as Djelal Kadir has phrased it, an untenable ground of self-reminiscence.[51] The advent of theatrical dance in 1581 marks the advent of the body's intextuation in monarchical space. Yet by 1624, the progress of "intextuation" is interrupted by that of "incarnation" or resistance.[52] Physical autonomy – the self-mediated body in theatrical space – was theatricalized by obscenity, political allusiveness, and open-endedness. Kadir, glossing Octavio Paz, throws interpretive light on the historical transition from geometrical dance to Menippean satire that has been the theme of these chapters: "The statement that 'bodies are visible hieroglyphs' clearly implies its differential supplement, that is, the hieratic quality of bodies as signs of an *invisible reality*."[53]

Remembering the example of geometrical dance enables us to link its most baroque characteristics to the burlesque phenomenon. The breaking away from the choreographed text already implicit in the chaotic transit between the figures of geometrical dance culminates historically in the total abandonment of the figure and its mastering text. One can discern a "progress" in court ballet history from characters as written figures to characters as self-possessed personalities. Yet burlesque rejection of the geometrical figure is achieved through a renunciation of the human figure itself, a distortion of its "schematic" rhetorical outlines in favor of overwhelming geometrical shapes. But geometrical shapes in the burlesque figural sense are neither rhetorical nor expressive. They are forms of protest that suspend both forms of theatrical meaning. The figure of the figureless is best represented by the androgyne: a body in transit between gender identities whose presence shatters patterns of dominance and submission. Thus, in the very midst of a rhetorical culture, the body was repossessed by a subject who lived between the lines, as it were, threatening to reemerge as both pure and impure, playful and political. Perhaps it is this very threat, or promise, that constitutes the baroque turn. There is something "fantasmatic" about baroque dance. The baroque body demonstrates a will to occupy the impossible space between movement and pose, text and flesh, metamorphosis and ostentation, aesthetics and politics: the space of theory in act.

This analysis of burlesque ballets inevitably begs the question of how oppositional baroque culture can really have been. I have tended to favor an account of its power in the context of ultimate powerlessness. Baroque contestation nevers "takes off." Other scholars, Maravall in particular, think of baroque culture as always a "guided culture," one in which the space for contestation has been carefully calculated and scrupulously allowed. The nuance causing my interpretation to diverge from Maravall's, and from Elias's as well, lies in an attentiveness to the reality of performance as such. Those, and I include myself among them, reimagining performances as experienced events of substantial impact, subscribe to their power, however limited the political consequences of that power may prove historically to be. In this sense, my work shares equally in the critical influence of Bakhtin and Yates, who – critical renegades in a textual world – perceived the body–text dialectic.[54]

In the context of court ballet, it is traditional to envision performance as entirely subject to the control of political institutions. Yet this view proves too narrow. Power itself is negotiated by performing bodies just as burlesque ballets are crystallizations of class and genre conflict in an ideological conflict. The relationship between ideology and form described in these pages suggests that the theoretical premise of dance as text has proven a useful tool of analysis. It has enabled us to grasp the hidden stakes of baroque dance performance and to propose certain cultural criteria for the interpretation of Molière that had not previously been applied to comedy-ballet. With regard to canonical dance history, we can see that the baroque is more diverse than first thought, and the option remains open to further explore that diversity.

The dance–text dialectic has other ramifications for the discipline of dance history. It shows us that dance autonomy itself has a history: absolute dance is not the original construct of twentieth-century modernism. Neither is "dance theory" a purely postmodern gesture. The choreographic practices of baroque court ballet themselves suggest that the relationship of dance to theory has historical precedents. Theory was embedded in choreography; it was actually intrinsic to the earliest significant choreographic practices of Western theater dance. Dance writers need no longer harp on the necessity of expressive coherence or on concepts of aesthetic unity outmoded for over four hundred years. Nor need they, at the other extreme, overrate the originality of disjunctive aesthetics in some postmodern performance. Traditionally minded dance scholars need no longer complain that theory distorts dance history and aesthetics. The evidence shows that theory and practice share *one* history. They have always done so in the history of Western theater dance. By cultivating the theory of dance, we engage in a fundamentally baroque pursuit: a form of questioning and a questioning of form developed at the historical site of Western theatrical dancing. To paraphrase Djelal Kadir, dance theory as baroque discourse is tautologically synonymous to itself.[55] Dancing, of course, has shifted in its history both away from and back to its inherently theoretical status. But, we need be neither inordinately proud, nor suspiciously fearful, of the theoretical potential in dance. As postmodernists we are belated; as traditionalists we are historically anachronistic: our spectatorship *is* baroque.

EPILOGUE
Repeatability, Reconstruction, and Beyond

In 1988, Susanne Linke began her reconstruction of Dore Hoyer's *Affectos humanos* (1962) by walking, clad only in black work clothes, to a costume rack placed on the stage.[1] Slowly and methodically, Linke donned Hoyer's costume for the first solo, "Pride," in full view of the audience. At the outset, she established a distance between herself as reconstructor and the artist whose work was to be reconstructed. Indeed, each of the dance's four parts was punctuated by a similar meditative interval in which Linke disrobed and recostumed herself. This reconstruction consciously avoided simulation of the original, as the reconstructor alternately embodied, stood apart from, and commented on it. Such effects of distancing are rare in reconstructions of historical dance. But reciprocally, the idea of reconstructing the work of a predecessor has been rare, until recently, among contemporary choreographers.

In the late Renaissance, choreographers wrote ballets that took for granted not only a receptive audience, but an erudite one. Realistically conceived or not, this audience was expected to be at home with all the literary and philosophical allusions subtending a court ballet's structure and action. Choreography, in other terms, was an academic pursuit. It would seem that scholarship and performance have since come to be artistically incompatible. The most logical place to seek the intellectual and theatrical components of choreography in fruitful union would now seem to be, if anywhere, in scholarly reconstructions of earlier dance. Yet the results of research are rarely known to materialize convincingly on the stage. Reconstructions of historical dance have long been shadowy and insubstantial renditions of a period's choreography. Historical dance reconstruction has too often been characterized by a condescending attitude to audience and performer alike. It resulted from a paranoia that choreographers fell prey to regarding the palatability of their material to a general audience. They were led to adopt a patronizing, tongue-in-cheek attitude to compensate for the ostensibly boring nature of the material itself. Those staid and antiquated presentations have since been challenged by a kind that restores a degree of literal accuracy with the requisite theatrical immediacy. In the 1980s we began to see reconstructions conveying something closer to the theatrical force of the original choreography: a force, moreover, that potentially influences new work rather than merely animating a historical artifact.

Most reconstructions today are either of the first works of the early modern period – the courtly social and theater dances from the Renaissance through the baroque[2] – or of experimental dance of early twentieth-century avant-gardes.[3] The focus on seventeenth- and twentieth-century dance to the exclusion of the intervening periods is significant. Choreographers of a reconstructive bent seem vitally concerned about two things they can learn from dance of those periods: the way early twentieth-century experiments prefigured many later developments in dance and, by extension, the radical historicity of dance's beginnings.

Thus, it is through our newly gained distance from the historical avant-gardes of the twentieth century that the baroque period crystallizes in its historical significance. In periods of transition, it is important to look back to origins: our historical perspective on modernism presupposes a more acute sense of the radicality of the baroque. Because the baroque served as a springboard for modernist experimentation, court ballet aesthetics take on added meaning as modernism itself loses its initial impact and becomes an object of deconstructive study.

Yet lest this be too simple an assessment, there is also the question of the relationship of reconstruction to historical references in postmodern art. Do reconstruction and new tendencies deriving from it signify a return to earlier sources of creativity? Does the recycling of historical material serve implicitly to critique modes of creativity and contexts now in vogue? Or does it, as Hal Foster has suggested in reference to much postmodern art, lead to revisionism for an empty culture effect, which is for the sake of gesture alone?[4] The French aesthetician Guy Scarpetta phrased this last idea in another way when he distinguished between a return *to* in a nostalgic sense and a return *of* in an inventively original sense.[5]

One of Foster's prime concerns is the use that a critical art would make of history and historical styles. He faults much postmodern art and architecture for its perverted historicity:

Though the habit of the historicist – to see the *old* in the new – remains with such art, the imperative of the radical – to see the *new* in the old – is lost. Which is to say that this art retains its historical (or "recuperative") aspect, even as it loses its revolutionary (or "redemptive") aspect.[6]

The historicist tendency to see the old in the new is characteristic of recon-struction. Its master conceit is to evoke what no longer is, with the means of what is present. This is particularly true of baroque dance to the degree that most reconstructions of it, as noted earlier, are of post-Academy material and, therefore, suggest a historical continuity with contemporary ballet. Yet as such, they offer little insight into new bases of creativity. Seeing the new in the old, on the other hand, is a pinpointing of radical historicity in former production. The internalized commentary and self-reflection of burlesque work, for example, are postmodern attributes of historical work. Bringing these and similar qualities to the fore in new choreography is a project that I call construction. I regard construction as a mannerism, characterized by the fixation on precise stylistic and theoretical aspects of lost original work.[7] Construction is surely a facet of the postmodern sensibility. Yet my approach here differs from some recent dance criticism in that I do not entertain any iconic notions of dance as postmodern on the basis of its being "quintessen-tially eighties": that is, characterized by quick, nonstop motion and refer-ences to popular culture. Nor do I rely here on chronological/locational signposts in order to endow the term *postmodern dance* with conceptual coherence. Rather, I agree with Umberto Eco, who wrote:

Postmodernism is a trend not to be chronologically defined, but, rather, an ideal category – or, better still, a *Kunstwollen*, a way of operating. We could say that every period has its own postmodernism, just as every period would have its own man-nerism (and, in fact, I wonder if postmodernism is not the modern name for man-nerism as metahistorical category).[8]

While the archeological impulse motivating the mannerist artist leads him or her to give inordinate attention to certain aspects of the model, in so doing an original work is often generated.[9]

Construction sacrifices the reproduction of a work to the replication of its most powerful intended effects. This would be how I, as a choreographer, interpret Foster's dictum of radicality: seeing the new in the old. Separating the effect from the accepted representation of its historical context de-familiarizes it while maintaining its historical prestige. It opens a dialogue between forms and periods on the basis of style, vocabulary, and theory, rather than history alone. Just as burlesque works critiqued court society by altering the forms of its ballets, so new choreography can practice cultural critique by historicizing dance in ways that problematize canonic lexicons and their current reception. For example, the obsession with the vertical posture in Renaissance dance clearly makes it a progenitor of classical ballet. Yet through its weight, tension, angularity, and athleticism, Renaissance dance can also be seen in a theoretical relationship to modern dance. By disrupting conventional associations to vocabulary and style at different periods, construction favors a radical rather than historicist perspective, in Foster's terms. It rethinks dance history as well as its meanings and uses now. In this way, we can begin to figure social realities beneath the aesthetic surface that reconstructive aesthetics both present and mask. Beyond these purely technical examples proper to dance, the influence of burlesque costume design on the visual arts through Arcimboldo and Braccelli have profoundly affected the visions of modernists such as Georgio de Chirico, Jean Cocteau, and the surrealists. Modernist mannerism presents "an alternative that departs from actual historical conditions, one that *pretends* to be in a meta-historical dimension — but only in order to project into the future the bursting forth of present contradictions."[10] This is the ground on which modernism and postmodernism meet, the ground on which postmodernism is seen to prolong and complexify the modernist project.

Choreographic mannerism differs from its analogue in the fine arts because of the lack of an observable dance model. As a result, only a theory of dance can provide a profile, essentially speculative in nature, of the original impact of the choreography. Whereas reconstruction at its weakest tries to recreate a reality without a predetermined effect, construction aims at creating precisely that effect. It suggests, thereby, the necessity of reconstructing the audience. Audience "response," writes Cynthia J. Novack, "constitutes the definition of a culturally significant utterance."[11] Thus far, the importance of reconstituting response *within the spectator* has not been adequately recognized or discussed in the field of historical reproduction.[12] And, given the nature of the reconstructive project, it probably never will be.[13] It is up to a new field — one could designate it as constructive, mannerist, reinventive, appropriative, or the like — to explore this vital area of performance.

The constructive choreographer replaces the frame that historical representation affords the reconstructor with historical theatrical theory. As Walter Benjamin has shown, in a theoretical treatment of art, historical extremes can be seen to acquire the status of "complementary forces."[14] In fact, this insight was linked to his own consideration of baroque drama and twentieth-century avant-garde collage. There was an intellectual component to these periods suggesting a single theoretical sensibility. Similarly, today's intellectual climate favors a collusion between constructive choreography and theatrical theory that may in part be a result of late-twentieth-century American performance art. It frequently cultivated the desultory and seemingly "insignificant" act or task in a social yet ritualized context and could be construed as a deconstruction (on a formal level) of early theatrical protocol. Unlike baroque theater, performance art detheatricalized actions as it unwittingly theatricalized baroque theory.[15] Seventeenth-century *danse noble* established an ideal corporal stance that could serve as a point of departure and return of "elegant" movement while appearing to be executed effortlessly in a social or theatrical context. Much performance art of the 1960s and 1970s[16] seemed to be setting out to dismantle these basic premises, operative since the Renaissance, of the body's theatricality. And it seemed to do this not in a polemical way (though there were other politics involved in this art) but in a highly theoretical yet theatrically palpable way. Performance art meant to undo what had been done, making a theatrical experience out of the realization of what it had eliminated. The missing part, excluded from performance in a conventional sense, can resurface, however, as theory. This was Benjamin's point. And theory, belatedly crystallized, can also engender new choreography.[17]

One result is that choreographers can evolve an aesthetic grounded in a deconstructive analysis of Renaissance or baroque dance. Performance art provided the catalyst for twentieth-century choreographers to look at earlier dance from a new perspective.[18] To "deconstruct" historical dance is to get at its root sources through an analysis of the choreography's theoretical underpinnings. One cannot deconstruct a piece of choreography only by looking at it in reconstruction. The deconstruction needs to be worked out through an analysis of all available primary sources (librettos, theory, pictorial representations, etc.) before it can be implemented in choreography.[19] The move from reconstruction to construction is also a move toward the creation of choreography that actively rethinks historical sources.

My own construction of geometrical dance will illustrate how new work can be structured by historical theory. In late Renaissance and early baroque court ballet, a group of dancers often portraying nymphs would form geometrical or symbolic patterns.[20] To construct such a geometrical dance in *Harmony of the Spheres*,[21] I worked from a kinetic theory: patterns were held with a measure of rigidity, while the movement between them offered no such symmetries, appearing by comparison visually amorphous. Using six dancers, I worked with the idea of realizing patterns as interrupting and suspending movement. Whereas the patterns themselves created a moment of visual stasis, transitions between patterns were visually and emotionally chaotic (Figure 19). From this idea flowed another: in the pattern, each dancer resembles a statue, a metaphor for an object, a frozen work of art (Figure 20). These images were also suggested to me by the eerie atmosphere of stone museums in the South of France: fragmentary bodies, heads with mutilated features, fortuitously gathered in a large dark room, seem to share our presence and yet to converse secretly with one another in a dimension we can only intuit. The dancers were directed to reach out to each other from within the frozen gestures of the patterns as if from this other dimension that we perceive only as a fragment.

The tone of pathos the work then assumed suggested the second broad

Figure 19. Transitional flux in *Harmony of the Spheres* (1987). Novantiqua. Photograph by Lilian Gee.

formal aspect of the dance construction: these nymphs were undergoing a cathartic process of terror and pity abstracted from any particular narrative. The increasing intensity of their emotions experienced beside each other, yet rarely with one another, motivated each succeeding choreographic sequence.

An aesthetic of interruption became another formal aspect of the work. I chose to theatricalize it choreographically as fragments of movement and pose. Edgard Varèse's 1931 score *Ionization* supported this aesthetic by its unpredictable halts and screeches. The air-raid sirens used in this score acted in interruptive contrast to the dancers' flowing robes, endowing them with a lurid quality but at the same time accentuating their historical potential as Renaissance images. Fragmentation was the dramatic figure of the piece, both in the interplay of movement and pose and in the image of statuary. The concept of interruption was furthered by appending part of the "Winter" section of Vivaldi's *Four Seasons* to Varèse's score. This musical fragment created another interruptive transition. Visually at this moment a male dancer dressed as a Greek god reanimates the emotionally exhausted nymphs.

Working on this piece evoked a chain of associations in my mind. I recalled that Isadora Duncan worked from the same sources that stimulated the

Figure 20. Statuesque stillness in *Harmony of the Spheres* (1987). Dancers: Loretta Abbott and Juliet Neidish. Photograph by Midori Shinye.

creation of the first geometrical dances by Balthazar de Beaujoyeulx in the late Renaissance. Although four centuries apart, both choreographers were both looking back to the chorus of ancient Greek tragedy as a model to imitate or reconstruct. In using some vocabulary derived from Duncan juxtaposed to Renaissance and baroque steps and attitudes, I was shaping a work that did not reconstruct dance of the Renaissance or modernist periods per se. Rather, its composition could be experienced as the space of a dialogue long since opened between them, but never represented in choreographic terms. This work is related to the radical historicity of the burlesque if we consider that internalized self-commentary became possible in dance only through burlesque works.

The work was analogous to the special use Oskar Schlemmer had made of baroque sources in his *Triadic Ballet* (1922) (Figures 21 through 26). Schlemmer was also caught up in the historical web of sources and their reinterpretation. In fact, he can be seen in this epilogue as a connector of all its themes, as a multifaceted example of the link between choreography, construction, and theory. Schlemmer was aware of his own indebtedness to tradition and conducted his own research on dance history. Much of his choreographic work was carried out before a backdrop of theatrical theory whose history begins in the early baroque era. Thus, Schlemmer carries forward the modern*ist* tradition of inquiry into the historical roots of modernity.

The rapport between reinvention and theory in Schlemmer's work can best be understood in relation to three key texts: Denis Diderot's *Paradoxe sur le comédien,* Heinrich von Kleist's *Ueber das Marionettentheater,* and Edward Gordon Craig's "The Actor and the Ueber-Marionette."

Schlemmer's Bauhaus dances (1926), reconstructed by Debra McCall with the assistance of Bauhaus artist Andreas Weininger, were influenced by Heinrich von Kleist and Edward Gordon Craig.[22] Schlemmer himself acknowledged the relevance of their writings about the marionette figure in his own letters and essays on choreography. Less attention, however, has been paid to the impact of early baroque court ballet on Schlemmer, especially in regard to its constructed shapes and their adaptations in the *Triadic Ballet,* first performed in 1922. "Why ballet?" writes Schlemmer in a diary entry dated July 5, 1926, "which, they say, is dead or dying. Because the heyday of ballet may be long since past, and the old courtly ballet is certainly dead, but today's entirely changed circumstances give good cause to believe that this particular art form can be revived."[23] Theatrical dance of the French seventeenth century was an open mine for continued experimentation to Schlemmer because court ballet was "free of constraints and thus predestined to furnish time and again the starting point for a theatrical Renaissance."[24] It was specifically the baroque tradition of "bright games, disguises, dissimula-

Figure 21. The Grotesque One from *Le Balet du Sérieux et du Grotesque* (1627). Tobin Collection, McNay Museum, San Antonio, Texas.

tion [and] artificiality" that inspired Schlemmer to consider that a rebirth of theatrical creativity was possible.[25]

Thus, in 1926, Schlemmer sets forth choreographic ideas antithetical to the prevailing dance trends of his time that stressed the human form: "Eurythmics, the chorus of movement developed out of them, and a new cult of strength and beauty."[26] The classical ballet that Schlemmer knew seemed to him an incompatible hybrid of the new "cultic soul dance" and the old "aesthetic mummery." The former was characterized by virtual nakedness, the latter by costume imposing abstract configurations on the human form. Schlemmer refers to this second type of costuming as "shrouding" the body. "And in between," he writes, "one finds the skimpiness and flutteriness of today's ballerinas, whose halfway position makes them shun nakedness as much as costume."[27]

In returning to early baroque dance as a source of inspiration, Schlemmer aligns himself with the tradition of "the artificial human figure," the *Kunstfigur*, on which he elaborated. Inspired by court ballet costume design, he was cognizant of his debt to the past. "We children of *modern times*, i.e. technical and mechanical," he writes in the essay "Mekanisches Ballett," "are only capable of pouring new wine into old skins."[28] The artificial tradition, whose modernist equivalent is mechanical, came to an end, remarks Schlemmer, in 1772 when face masks were abolished.

Schlemmer was also awakened to the idea of the *Kunstfigur* by Kleist's 1810 essay *On the Marionette Theater*. Kleist imagines a dialogue in which a ballet master explains why dancers should study marionettes to attain a superior dance aesthetic.[29] The essay also includes two parables of the perfected gesture as unrepeatable. In the first, an ephebe loses his gracefulness the moment he becomes the observer of his own gesture and tries consciously to reproduce it. In the second, a bear on its hind legs fends off fencing opponents with an uncanny economy and strategy of movement. Both examples of perfection in movement seem beyond the reach of conscious reflection. The ephebe loses his gracefulness once he becomes aware of it, and the bear never risks losing the efficacy of his movement, since he never reflects on it. Perfected gestures can only be achieved un-self-consciously by the child or the animal, or accidentally by rational man. Montaigne's prerequisites for the truly expressive gesture are operative in Kleist's thinking. But the marionette, being neither human nor animal, is closest to the ahistoric, nonhuman innocence of the god: "Here [in the marionette]," says the ballet master "is the point where the two ends of the circular world meet." In other words, the ignorant and the all-knowing are two extremes that meet in the marionette because its movement is perfect and repeatable. Paradoxically, the guarantee of authentic expression becomes the possibility of its mechanical reproduction. The marionette is a middle figure standing for the combination of the mechanical and the Godly, thereby resolving technique and inspiration. It is a symbol of perfected theatrical performance as both trans- and subhuman, beyond and before man's conscious grasp. Neither mechanical regularity nor Godlike inspiration can be within the reach of conscious control per se.[30]

Court ballet and Kleist are an intriguing combination of sources that invites further investigation. The former is by now an archaic phenomenon of dance overlapping the Renaissance and baroque periods; the latter occurred on the threshold of modernism both in theater and dance. Indeed, Kleist can be regarded as prefiguring the opposition between nonexpressive and emotional dance that we are familiar with today.[31]

The problem of the contrived versus the naturalistic approach to stage action and movement can be retraced to Noverre's treatise *Lettres sur la danse* (1760) and Diderot's fictional dialogue *Paradoxe sur le comédien* (1773).[32] Schlemmer's references to court ballet take on their true significance relative to this issue in eighteenth-century theatrical theory. Moreover, Kleist and Craig can also be seen to rephrase (albeit more radically) the position advocating control over *sensibilité*.

Diderot explores in depth the problem of naturalism by raising the question of the actor's craft in terms of naturalness versus technique. *The Paradox of Acting* pits two interlocutors against one another: the first maintains that the imitative actor, described as "an unmoved and disinterested onlooker [who must have] no sensibility," is ultimately superior to the emotional actor who works from the depths of his own feelings.[33] The sensitive or emotional actor, so the argument goes, cannot "play the same part twice running with the same spirit and success."[34] So the imitative actor's technique, his or her ability to repeat a role's performance with the same degree of perfection each time, is opposed to the actor's emotions, which can on occasion produce sublime results but are at best unpredictable. The imitative actor's "talent depends not, as you think, upon feeling, but upon rendering so exactly the outward signs of feeling, that you fall into the trap."[35] The trap refers to performance as a persuasive mechanism.

In defending his view of the actor or actress as a machine for producing feeling in the spectator rather than as a conduit of sensitivity, Diderot comes to picture him or her as an automaton. In reference to the actress Clairon, Diderot states, "She is the informing soul of a huge mannekin which is her outward casing, and in which her efforts have enclosed her."[36] Although Diderot is not referring to an actual marionette, to the degree that he is designating the actor as an unfeeling being, he does touch the question of a performance machine capable of reproducing perfected theatrical acts ad infinitum. Thus, Diderot suggests the outlines of Kleist's marionette. His work, read from this perspective, also suggests that one of the recurrent themes of Western theatrical theory is the issue of repeatability, and that a strand of theatrical theory of the nineteenth and twentieth centuries made unconscious reference to burlesque dance forms and to Montaigne in order to illustrate a point.

Both Diderot and Noverre were inspired by the English actor David Garrick in their reform of theater and dance. For Noverre, unlike the later Diderot of the *Paradox,* only the use of real feeling could animate stage action. He divided dance into its technique ("danse *mécanique ou d'exécution*" – "*mechanical or technical* dancing") and its artistic component ("danse *pantomime ou en action*" – "*pantomimic or narrative* dancing"). Because dancers already possessed a physical technique (he calls them "machine men" at their most technical), Noverre looks to the dancer's *acting* technique as an instinctual and emotional enhancement of stage presence.[37] The dancer, he explains, is like a stringed instrument whose sounds can express passion. "When the strings are touched by the soul, the heart will determine all of its vibrations."[38] Although concerned with different art forms, both Diderot and Noverre focus obsessively on the importance of gestural expression that constitutes pantomime in their terms. For Diderot, pantomime is clearly more gestural than verbal and stresses the pictorial aspect of each theatrical moment as tableau vivant. For Noverre, pantomime adds dramatic action to dance and therefore moves dance closer to drama. Obviously, pantomime transcends either art form taken alone. Pantomime, whose impact was first theoretical and only secondarily experiential, seems to exist as a theatrical effect in a space of dialogue between the two texts as well as between two genres.[39] Theatrical theory itself tended to cross over genre boundaries before these boundaries were blurred by theatrical practice.

Noverre likens the expressive part of dance, both in the structure of a ballet and in individual performance, to the principle of dramatic action. Action is rendered by gesture and ballets were in need of it. Without expressive gesture, Noverre felt that the art of ballet would lapse into sterility. But, for Noverre, the dancer's gesture is dictated by emotional inspiration. "Can set precepts be given for pantomimic gesture?" he asks: "Aren't gestures the work of the soul and the faithful interpretors of its movements?"[40] These remarks render Noverre's differences with the Diderot of the *Paradox* explicit.[41]

The issue of the use of spontaneous feeling versus the calculation of every effect by technique resurfaces in the opposition suggested much later by Schlemmer between the unclothed and the shrouded body. It would be perverse to suggest that Diderot was inspired like Schlemmer by the baroque, yet the consequences of Diderot's theory have repercussions for Schlemmer's aesthetic stance.[42] But if that is the case, why did Schlemmer claim only Kleist and Craig as his forerunners? Because only beginning with Kleist does the mechanical body appear as a theatrical option. Diderot theorized about the mechanism of acting without wishing to transform the actor into a machine as did Kleist and Craig. Nevertheless, there is a theoretical continuity from Diderot to Kleist in their mutual desire for perfect repeatable action in a theatrical context.

Kleist's marionette can be regarded as an extension of Diderot's moral and theoretical paradox into a theological dimension. Kleist's tale of a ballet master who admires the grace of puppets addresses the problem of the perfect theatrical act. It does not matter whether this act is destined to portray emotion persuasively or to give the aesthetic pleasure of grace. Mastering the theatrical act in Kleist's context means mastering movement per se. The ballet master explains the consonance of the soul and body as a technical control of the marionette's *Schwerpunkt* (center of gravity) by the puppeteer: "Each movement," he said, "had its center of gravity: it would suffice to control this within the puppet; the limbs, which are only pendulums, follow mechanically of their own accord – without further help."[43] The lines described by the movement of these mechanical bodies in perfect balance at all times are called "the path taken by the dancer's soul."[44]

The marionettes are superior dancers because their bodies follow their souls' movement, as it were. Each body moves with its soul, the body's *vis motrix,* shadowing its impulses from without. Yet these souls are not real ones: they are fabricated by the puppeteer's technique. Nevertheless, this description of movement, like the earlier ones in Diderot, is inconceivable without a concept of passion as itself a physiological event. It presupposes an internal movement within the body that dictates a response in the form of external movement. Kleist's is merely an aestheticized extrapolation of the idea of expressivity.[45] Diderot's paradox is displaced, but it is still very much present. Furthermore, one can begin to see how the marionette figure shall allow choreography a means to reflect on the theory that underlies expressivity.[46] This is ultimately part of Schlemmer's contribution in staging the marionette figure.

Kleist's paradox is that the live dancer cannot attain perfect movement any more than postlapsarian man can go back to paradise. The dancer cannot find his or her own center of gravity any more readily than the actor can impose on him- or herself at will the experiential reality of an emotion. The dancer's body divorced from its *Schwerpunkt* reveals its own fall from grace simply by its own physicality. To abandon one's mind to (and place one's center in) the *Schwerpunkt* is to be entirely innocent, as is the ephebe for a brief time, and as is the bear. The puppet has the kind of innocence of pure mechanism that can be rivaled only by that of a deity: "Only a god could equal inanimate matter in this respect."[47] A state of grace, with all of the implied theatrical and religious overtones, is available only to the utterly ignorant ("innocent" or mechanical) or to the infinitely knowledgeable: the god. In Diderot's moral terms, a state of grace is only available to the flatterer

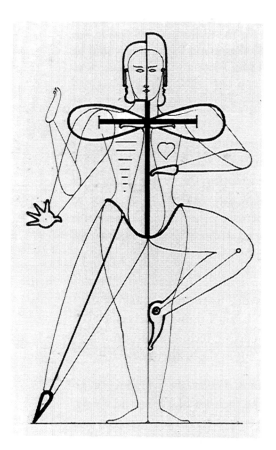

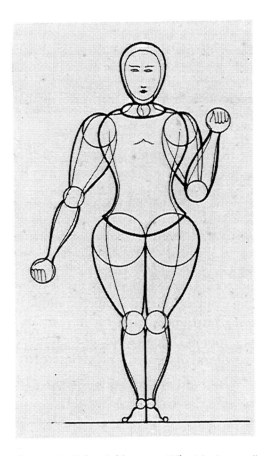

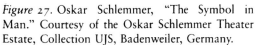

Figure 27. Oskar Schlemmer, "The Symbol in Man." Courtesy of the Oskar Schlemmer Theater Estate, Collection UJS, Badenweiler, Germany.

Figure 28. Oskar Schlemmer, "The Marionette." Courtesy of the Oskar Schlemmer Theater Estate, Collection UJS, Badenweiler, Germany.

figures of the Bauhaus dances once again rehumanize the dematerialized body as if from within or behind the shell of mechanism (Figure 29). Schlemmer's piece opened a dialogue between his early fascination for the baroque distortion of the body's outlines and his apparent interest in human expressivity. Within the encasing figure is human consciousness. "The two ends of the circular world meet," here again thanks to a marionette figure. But with Schlemmer, that meeting is deconstructive and theoretical. His choreography, in this respect, stages an analysis of theatrical theory. This would be another of the radical objectives of construction.[54]

A curious exchange occurs between theatrical theory and the project of reconstruction. The former is forward looking in its utopian vision of an unattainable form of theater. It generates manifestos. The latter is reactionary, seeking the truth in its own "still life" reproduction. It generates performance

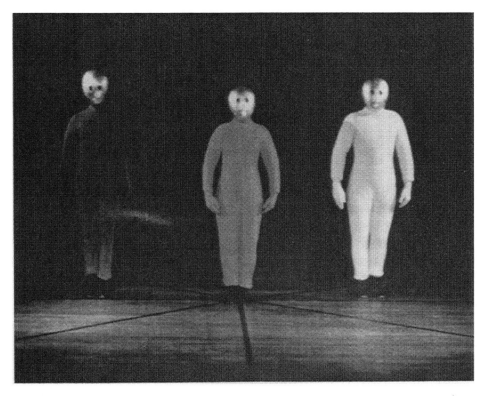

Figure 29. Marionette-like figures, but no longer ambulant architecture. "Space Dance" from Schlemmer's Bauhaus dances (1926). Dancers: Marsha Blank, Juliet Neidish, Jan Hanvik. Reconstruction by Debra McCall (1982). Photograph by Craig Massey.

museums. Yet it has been shown that theatrical theory since the eighteenth century contains an obsession with repeatability at its core. Repeatability is indeed the goal of much theatrical theory and can be understood as the desire to endow performance with a textual status. Reconstruction also derives its underlying rationale from a similar need to render performance unchanging, or in some way stable and permanently present. Paradoxically, both theatrical theory and reconstruction see performance as inherently perfect or desirable because it is absent: either yet to be or lost in the past.

With some critical distance, reconstruction can begin to be viewed as a consequence of Western theatrical theory's obsession with repeatability. The concept of reconstruction can rely on the fascination with the theatrical act itself as repeatable, except that the act in question is now a choreographic one. Choreography suggests a broader realm of cultural pattern than does the individual act of performance, and by the same token, choreographic construction could become the nexus for awareness of cultural relativity. In this spirit, zur Lippe envisages psychoanalysis as a social practice parallel to cultural history.[55] Access to the unconscious has analogies with access to the constitution of ideology for "social man": it illuminates interiorized constraints and repressions. For zur Lippe, quattrocento social dance contained an unexploited historical potential for *different* social relations. He proposes that psychoanalysis and politics share this common ground of the future potential since they both study "distant objects of our understanding."[56] To bring quattrocento social dance into the present – not as a repetition of early dance but as a realization of the anomalous potential for altered social interraction contained in it but subsequently repressed – is the political challenge of construction. Each reconstruction of historical dance inevitably *constructs* the cultural act it means to replicate. Reconstruction is an act that actually implies, although it may internally reject, multiple distancing.[57] Construction theorizes more openly, indeed theatrically, on the significance of origins and ways to represent them by encoding that reflection in the choreography itself. Performance theorizing implies subjective reminiscence and defamiliarization. In order to translate one culture, or state of culture, into another, one is absorbed in, and yet critically distant from, both. The textual status performance aspires to in the West should no longer be one of repeated presence. Rather, the textual status of performance to be desired is inherently in between. Poised between the apprehension of the object and the creation of the object, it can both serve cultural critique and foster new creativity.

Dance theorizing should replace the old myth of repeatability. There are many analogies to it in what Susan Foster has called "writing dancing"[58] that "permits parlance among mediums," affirms "the possibility of conceptual resonances," and immerses viewer, dancer, and choreographer "in a playful yet critical interpretive practice."[59] In a similar manner, I am suggesting that construction can practice cultural critique as a form of active theorizing on dance history. It consists of inscribing the plurality of visions restoring, conceptualizing, and/or inventing the act.

NOTES ON *CHARACTERS OF DANCE*

Characters of Dance is an evening-length work choreographed in 1990. The following are preparatory notes interspersed with descriptions of the finished work and presented in the form of a project.

Project. To choreograph a "new" baroque work. Guidelines: fanciful atmosphere, corrosive statement, doing impossible things in dance (i.e., using dance to represent abstract concepts).

Title. This piece was inspired by a title of a baroque dance suite, Jean-Ferry Rebel's *Les Caractères de la danse* (1715). None of Rebel's music, however, was used in the new work. Rebel mapped dance moods as generated by musical forms. The character of each musical segment indicated the character of the dance performed to it. Rebel thus characterized dance moods through musical stimuli. *Characters of Dance,* on the other hand, recycled dance vocabularies (historical, classical, modern) and their eccentric uses by characters. Here, the emphasis is no longer on dance forms as rhythmic behavior. Instead, dancers articulate erratically different styles in new constructs.

Methods. Convey the historical past as a personal past: another way of dealing with the unconscious. Choreographic lesson: thinking backward – to analyze the conventions of choreographic structure; to dance that theme.

Costumes. Designer Susan Hogan has been doing relief paintings using the brass mesh material that she molds here into shapes that appear at once baroque and physically organic. A fine brass mesh molded over black unitards to suggest components of the baroque panoply – collars, panniers, etc. – as well as gender: biocultural protuberances or "cages" (Figure 30). The costumes suggest an armature and an interspace. We experiment with the way this mesh moves with/on bodies in space. The costumes are "bent out of

IX

Les deliberations qui seront prises concernant le fait de la Danse, par lesdits Anciens assemblez comme dessus, seront executées selon leur forme & teneur, tant par lesdits Anciens que par les autres faisans profession de la Danse & aspirans à ladite Academie, aux peines cy-dessus, & de cent cinquante livres d'amende contre chacun des contrevenans.

X

Pourront lesdits Anciens Academistes, & leurs enfans, monstrer & enseigner en cette ville & faubourgs de Paris, & ailleurs en l'étenduë du Royaume, toute sorte de Danses, sans qu'ils puissent estre, pour quelque cause ou prétexte que ce soit, obligez, necessitez ou contraints, de prendre à cause de ce aucunes Lettres de Maistrise, ny autre pouvoir que celuy qui leur sera pour ce donné par ladite Academie, en la maniere & dans les formes cy-dessus.

XI

Le Roy ayant besoin de personnes capables d'entrer & Danser dans les Ballets & autre divertissemens de cette qualité, sa Majesté faisant l'honneur à ladite Academie de l'en faire avertir, lesdits Anciens sont tenus de luy en fournir incessamment d'entre eux ou autres tel nombre qu'il plaira à sa Majesté d'ordonner.

XII

Les affaires communes de ladite Academie seront poursuivies, soustenües & défendües par lesdits Academistes, à frais communs dont le fond sera regalé & fait entre eux, ainsi qu'il sera à cet effet par eux avisé à la pluralité des voix, eux à cet effet assemblez en la maniere cy-dessus.

Enregistrement

Registrez, ouï, & ce consentant le Procureur General du Roy, pour estre executez selon leur forme & teneur, suivant l'Arrest de Verification de ce jour, à Paris en Parlement le 30 mars 1662. DU TILLET.

DELIBERATION DE L'ACADEMIE ROYALE DE DANSE, CONTENANT LA RECEPTION DU SIEUR BERNARD DE MANTHE, EN LA PLACE DU FEU SIEUR LE VACHER, & LE REGLEMENT DES RANGS ET SEANCES DES ACADEMISTES, DU 16 AVRIL 1662

Assemblez en Academie les Sieurs François Galand sieur du Desert, Maître à Danser de la Reine, Jean Renauld Maistre à Danser du Roy, en survivance de

Monsieur Prevost, & Maistre à Danser de Monsieur, Frere du Roy, Guillaume Queru, Hilaire d'Olivet, Bernard de Manthe, Jean Reynal, Nicolas de l'Orge, Guillaume Renauld, Jean Piquet, Florent Galand du Desert, Jean de Grigny & Guillaume Reynal, Maistre à Danser de Monseigneur le Dauphin.

Par le Sieur du Desert a esté represente que le Sieur le Vacher cy-devant nommé par le Roy, pour remplir l'une des places de l'Academie, estant mort, & estant necessaire de faire choix d'une personne capable pour mettre en son lieu, sous le bon plaisir de sa Majesté; il croit que la compagnie ne pourroit faire un meilleur choix que celuy du Sieur Bernard de Manthe, qui a le service & les qualitez requises pour cela, & a prié la compagnie d'y déliberer.

SURQUOY, ledit Sieur de Manthe estant sorty, il a esté resolu d'une commune voix qu'il seroit receu, & à l'instant estant rentré, il a presté le serment en tel cas requis, d'observer les Statuts & ordres de l'Academie, & a pris sa place.

Et ayant aussi esté proposé de regler les rangs des Academistes, afin qu'il n'arrive jamais aucune contestation entre eux, & qu'ils puissent conserver l'union & l'intelligence qui y est si necessaire, pour faire subsister & fleurir leur Academie; Il a esté resolu qu'en tous Actes & Assemblées generales & particulieres, Contrats & Déliberations, lesdits Academistes seront rangez suivant que leur noms, sont écrits en la presente Déliberation, sans que cet ordre puisse à l'avenir estre interrompu pour quelque cause & occasion que ce soit, & à la charge que ceux qui y seront cy-aprés receus, n'y pourront prétendre aucun rang que par l'ordre de leur reception.

Arrest du Parlement de Paris, qui démet les Maistres Violons, de l'opposition par eux formée à l'enregistrement des Lettres d'établissement de l'Academie de Danse.

EXTRAICT DES REGISTRES DE PARLEMENT

Entre Guillaume Dumanoir, Violon ordinaire du Roy, & consorts, demandeurs aux fins de deux Requestes presentées à la Cour, les premier & quatre Avril dernier; la premiere tendante à ce qu'ils fussent receus opposans à l'enregistrement des Lettres de Maistrise à Danser & établissement d'Academie pour la Danse, obtenuës par les défendeurs, cy-aprés nommez; ensemble de l'Arrest de Verification d'icelles, si aucun y a, que sur l'opposition les parties auroient audience au premier jour: Cependant défenses ausdits défendeurs & tous autres, de contrevenir audites Statuts, ny de s'immiscer en l'Art & Maistrise de la Danse, ny tenir aucune Academie, ny joüer d'instrumens, sinon aux conditions des Statuts desdits demandeurs, sur les peines portées de rupture de leurs instrumens & de prison: & la seconde à ce que la premiere fust enterinée, qu'ils fussent receus opposans à l'execution de l'Arrest du 30. Mars dernier. Faisant droit sur ladite opposition, que défenses diffinitives fussent faites ausdits défendeurs, de s'immiscer en ladite Academie à Danser; ordonner que les Statuts & Arrests d'enregistrement des joüeurs d'instrumens, seroient executez selon leur forme & teneur, défenses d'y contrevenir, d'une part: François Galland Sieur du Desert, Jean Renauld, Jean & Guillaume Reynal, Jean & François Piquet & consorts, Maistres és exercices de la Danse, Défendeurs d'autre, sans que les qualitez puissent prejudicier. Aprés que Isalis, pour lesdits Galand & consorts, a demandé la reception de l'appointement, en presence de Ravier Avocat des Demandeurs: Ouï Bignon pour le Procureur General du Roy, LA COUR ordonne que l'appointement sera receu: ce faisant sur les requestes & opposition desdits Dumanoir & consorts, a mis & met les parties hors de Cour & de procés, fait en Parlement le 30. jour d'Aoust 1662. DU TILLET.

Collationné aux Originaux, par moy Conseilleur Secretaire du Roy, Maison & Couronne de France & de ses Finances.

ESTABLISSEMENT DE L'ACADEMIE ROYALE DE DANSE EN LA VILLE DE PARIS AVEC UN DISCOURS Academique, pour prouver que la Danse dans sa plus noble partie n'a pas besoin des instumens de Musique, & qu'elle est en tout absolument indépendente du Violon.

Il estoit difficile de s'imaginer que la Danse & les instrumens qui avoient vécu en bonne intelligence depuis plusieurs siecles, se pûssent broüiller dans le nôtre, où l'une & les autres sont en leur perfection; On avoit crû que leur societé avoit esté formée sur celle de l'harmonie & du mouvement des cieux, et qu'elle devoit durer autant que le monde; Aussi la Danse proteste qu'elle n'a rien contribué à leur discord, qu'elle a esté toûjours promte à suivre leurs mouvemens, tandis qu'ils ont bien voulu s'accommoder aux siens, & conserver cette égalité qui fait & qui maintient les societez: Mais lors que le Violon enflé d'orgeuil de se voir introduit dans le cabinet du plus grand des Rois, & de se voir favorablement écouté dans tous ses divertissemens, a voulu se donner une superiorité inoüie, & que le Luth, ny pas un des autres instrumens, n'avoit jamais prétendu sur la Danse; Elle a crû devoir s'opposer à cette nouveauté, & faire connoistre son independance de la Musique: A quoy elle a si bien reüssi, que le Roy a qui la Providence a donné, avec mille autres qualitez Royales, un discernement admirable, a trouvé juste de faire une Academie de Danse, où il n'entre aucune chose de la Musique ny des instrumens, afin de faire voir qu'encore que la Danse & le Violon se soient joints en mille rencontres pour son divertissement, ils n'ont pas fondu l'un dans l'autre, & qu'il n'y a nulle raison de les confondre.

Et quoy que le jugement du plus éclairé & du plus absolu de tous les Rois, deust suffire à la Danse pour luy faire croire que toutes les personnes raisonnables la considereront à l'avenir comme indépendante des instrumens de Musique, & comme un corps qui peut facilement subsister sans estre animé par leur harmonie; Elle a bien voulu justifier cette verité par ce petit discours pour la satisfaction de sa Majesté-mesme, qui prend toûjours plaisir de voir ses sentiments autorisez par la raison, & pour la conviction entiere de ceux qui pourroient douter qu'on peut separer deux corps qui ont eu une si longue & si étroite liaison.

La Danse ne dira rien qui ne soit avantageux à la Musique, pour qui elle conservera toûjours beaucoup d'estime: elle tâchera seulement de monstrer son indépendance & ses avantages contre le Violon qui la vouloit assujettir; & quoy que les contestations qui naissent sur le sujet des rangs & des préseances soient toûjours aigres, l'on ne verra rien dans ce discours qui porte ce caractere.

La Musique & tous les instrumens dont elle se sert pour composer l'harmonie qui luy a donné tant d'estime & de reputation dans toutes les Nations policées, ont tiré leur origine des sons naturels, qui dans l'enfance du monde & par un consentement universel ont esté jugez agreables, soit qu'en effet ces sons eussent quelque proportion avec l'harmonie de nostre ame, ou qu'ils eussent seulement la faculté de flater agreablement nos oreilles, comme les belles couleurs flatent nos yeux; ainsi l'on ne peut pas contester que tous les instrumens de Musique ne soient inventez pour le plaisir de l'ouïe seulement. Et en effet, si nous consultons le goust & l'attouchement, ils nous diront qu'ils n'y trouvent rien de savoureux ny de doux; & la veuë qui se mesle de controller tout ce qui touche les autres sens, dira qu'elle n'y void rien qui ne la choque, & l'on sçait bien que de quelques ornemens qu'on pare les Violons dans les assemblées, on les trouve toûjours plus beaux quand on ne les void pas.

La Danse au contraire n'a rien que l'oreille puisse entendre, son premier employ dans la plus obscure antiquité fut de faire voir par des signes & par des mouvemens du corps les secrets sentimens de l'ame, afin de perfectionner cette expression generale que la nature avoit enseignée à tous les hommes pour se faire entendre par signes aux lieux où leur langage n'estoit pas connu. A quoy plusieurs reüssirent si bien en recherchant & en imitant par leurs gestes & par leurs visages, les caracteres de tous les desirs & de toutes les passions, qu'un auteur celebre a dit qu'on entendoit mieux leurs signes que leurs paroles. Sortant de cet employ general qui fut rendu inutile par la connoissance des langues, elle se fixa à l'expression de la joye & de la tristesse seulement, & devint une partie de la religion des Grecs, qui luy associerent alors la Musique, & qui en l'exprimant par un nom equivoqué avec l'assemblage de ses parties donnerent sujet à la confusion qu'on y a depuis voulu mettre. Elle ne s'arresta pas long-temps à cette destination particuliere, elle fut deslors employée aux exercices de la guerre, & des Nations entieres la receurent pour la marche ordinaire de leur milice. Un grand Capitaine Athenien qui n'estoit pas trop galand, luy a rendu ce témoignage qu'elle estoit tres-propre pour former les hommes aux exercices militaires. Et les Romains qui parmy leur galanteries mêloient toûjours quelque combat de gladiateurs, n'ont pas fait de difficulté de la recevoir parmy les divertissemens utiles à la Republique.

La France la reconnoist depuis long-temps pour le commencement necessaire de tous les beaux exercices; c'est elle qui corrige les défauts naturels du corps & qui en change les mauvaises habitudes; c'est elle qui luy donne cet air aisé & cette grace qui répandent tant d'agréement dans toutes ses actions; c'est elle qui enseigne à ceux qui la cultivent, l'art d'entrer agreablement dans les compagnies, & d'y gagner cette premiere & promte approbation qui fait quelquefois leur fortune, & toûjours leur joye avec celle des spectateurs; c'est elle qui leur apprend à se démêler avec bienseance & sans desordre, des lieux les plus embarrassez; c'est elle qui leur facilite l'exercice de monter à cheval & celuy de faire des armes; c'est elle qui les rend plus propres à servir leur Prince dans les batailles, & à luy plaire dans les divertissemens.

Le Violon n'entre pour rien en toutes ces choses, & s'il est quelquefois meslé avec la danse, il faut qu'il avoüe que ce n'est que dans la partie qui regarde le plaisir seulement; & encore ne peut-il pas nier que cet avantage ne luy soit commun avec tous les autres instrumens de Musique. Il ne peut pas aussi desavoüer qu'il ne soit absolument inutile à ceux qui apprennent à Danser, qui ne sçauroient suivre la cadence du Violon sans avoir auparavant appris à faire les pas, à porter leur corps & à former les figures necessaires: De sorte qu'on peut dire avec verité que le Violon n'est à la Danse, que ce que les Tambours & les Trompettes sont à la guerre: car comme ces derniers animent les combattans par des sons accommodez à la rapidité & à la ferocité de l'action, & qu'ils ne leur monstrent point en quelle figure ny de quelle maniere ils doivent combattre, pour ce que cet ordre regarde de plus nobles Officiers; le Violon ne fait autre chose qu'animer les Danseurs, qui demeureroient immobiles à tous ses mouvemens s'ils n'avoient auparavant appris de leur Maistres, ce qu'ils doivent faire tandis que les Violons joüent. Et comme il paroistroit sans doute ridicule que les Tambours & les Trompettes se voulussent attribuer quelque superiorité sur les Aydes de camp & sur les Sergens de bataille, pour avoir sonné l'attaque ou la retraite, lors que ces illustres Oficiers faisoient battre ou retirer les troupes; il faut avoüer qu'il y a eu quelque chose d'etrange en la pensée que les Violons ont eu de s'eriger en Rois & en Maistres de la Danse, pour avoir sonné tandis que par des mouvements étudiez, par des pas concertez, par des figures reglées, & par mille & mille démarches éloquentes, la Danse tâchoit de faire parler des muets aux yeux des spectateurs, & de representer des histoires, où sans prologue, sans recit, & sans aucun secours de la voix elle fait connoistre la nature, la condition, l'estat & la passion des personnes qu'elles represente.

Que s'il falloit encore comparer l'utilité du Violon avec celle de la Danse, il ne seroit pas difficile de faire voir que tout l'avantage est du costé de la derniere, puis que le Violon ne produit qu'un son agreable à la verité, mais qui se perd en l'air aprés avoir un peu flaté l'oreille, sans laisser aucune impression utile de son harmonie, au corps, ny à l'esprit, au lieu que la Danse outre les agréements qu'elle employe au divertissement des yeux, forme encore en ceux qui la pratiquent, & laisse dans l'esprit de ceux qui la voyent, des impressions de bien-seance & de démeslement qui peuvent estre de quelque avantage à la Nation, soit pour la politesse ou pour la facilité des exercices militaires.

Que s'il falloit parler des qualitez necessaires aux personnes qui Dansent & à celles qui joüent du Violon, il ne seroit pas dificule de faire voir que les Danseurs ont tout l'avantage, car ils doivent estre bien faits du corps, & l'on sçait qu'une formation heureuse & agreable est quasi toûjours une marque de la bonté de l'ame, ils doivent estre naturellement adroits & débarrasez, ils doivent avoir le corps & l'esprit souples, & ils ne sçauroient s'introduire chez les personnes de condition, sans avoir ou sans contracter des teintures d'onnesteté & de courtoisie, qui supposent presque toûjours une honneste naissance, ou du moins une bonne éducation.

Les joüeurs de Violon n'ont pas besoin de tout cela, ils peuvent estre boiteux, aveugles & bossus, sans que personne s'en scandalise, il ne leur faut que l'oreille & les bras pour bien joüer; & quoy que la plupart de ceux qui sont aujourd'huy dans les charges soient fort bien faits, & honnestes gens, ils avoüeront sans doute qu'ils pourroient avoir moins de mine & moins d'honnesteté, & ne laisser pas d'estre de fort bons Violons.

Mais pour finir par le plus grand avantage que la Danse ait jamais remporté sur le Violon, elle dira que le Roy qui n'a negligé aucune des belles connoissances qui peuvent compatir avec la Majesté Royale, n'a pas dédaigné d'employer cette merveilleuse adresse qu'il a receuë du Ciel pour tous les beaux exercices, à celuy de la Danse qu'il sçait en perfection, & qu'il a bien voulu estre Protecteur de son Academie, & luy donner pour Vice-Protecteur, Monsieur le Comte de Saint-Aignan, qu'on sçait estre un des plus spirituels & des plus galans hommes de sa Cour.

Letters Patent of the King for the Establishment of a Royal Academy of Dance in the City of Paris. Verified in Parliament on March 30, 1662

LOUIS BY THE GRACE OF GOD KING OF FRANCE AND OF NAVARRE, Welcomes all those present and to come. Although the Art of the Dance has always been recognized as one of the most honorable and necessary for forming the body, and giving it the first and most natural dispositions for all sorts of exercises, and among others for the exercise of arms, and consequently has been considered one of the most advantageous and useful for our Nobility, and for others who have the honor of approaching us, not only in wartime in our armies, but even in peacetime in our Ballets: Nevertheless, during the disorders and confusion of the last wars[1] there have been introduced into the said Art, as into all the others, such a great number of abuses as has almost brought them to their irreparable ruin, that several people, as ignorant and unskilled as they were in this Art of the Dance, have managed to show it publicly; so that it is astonishing that the small number of those capable of teaching it have through their application so long resisted the essential faults with which the infinite number of ignorant people, in the person of most of Upper Society, have tried to disfigure and corrupt dance: Which brings about that we see few people among our Court and entourage who are able and capable of entering directly into our Ballets, and other similar Dance diversions, despite the fact that we would have called upon them. Since this does call for action, and since we do desire to reestablish the said Art in its first perfection, and embellish it as much as possible: We have judged apropos to establish in our good city of Paris a Royal Academy of Dance, on the model of those of Painting and Sculpture, composed of thirteen Adepts (*Anciens*) and those most experienced in the practice of the said Art, so that they may in any place of their choosing in the said city, pursue the exercise of all sorts of Dance following the Statutes and rules that we have listed as twelve principle articles. FOR THESE REASONS, and for other good considerations that have moved us, we have by these presents signed with our hand, and with our full power and Royal authority said, decreed, and ordered, let us say, we say, decree, and order, want and it pleases us that, a Royal Academy of Dance be without cease established in our said city of Paris, that we have thirteen of the most experienced in the said Art, and whose skill and capacity is known to us through our experience of them in our Ballets, where we have done them the honor of calling them these several years, to wit François Galland of the Desert, the Ordinary Dancing Master of the Queen our very dear Wife, Jean Renauld Ordinary Master of our very dear and only brother the Duke of Orleans, Thomas le Vacher, Hilaire d'Olivet, Jean and Guillaume Reynal, brothers, Guillaume Queru, Nicolas de l'Orge, Jean François Piquet, Jean

Grigny, Florent Galland Desert, and Guillaume Renauld; who will assemble once a month, in such house as will be chosen by them and taken at common cost to confer amongst themselves about Dancing, to plan and deliberate upon the means of perfecting it and correcting the abuses and faults that can have or may yet still pervade it; they will maintain and run the said Academy following and conforming to the said Statutes and Rules attached here under the seal of our Chancellery: which we want to be kept and observed following their form and tenor: Expressly forbidding all persons of whatever high quality they may be to countervene the efforts herein contained, and further efforts that may come to pass. We want the above named and others who will compose the said Academy to enjoy the right of *Committimus*[2] in the same manner as does the Academy of Painting and Sculpture, in all personal, possessive, hypothecary, or mixed causes, as much in pleading as in defending before the Maistres des Requetes ordinaires of our Hotel, or the Requestes of the Paris Palace, they may choose, just as do the Commensal Officers of our House, and be discharged of all Taxes and Guardianship as well as of any Patrol or Watch. We want the said Art of the Dance to remain for ever exempt of any Letters of Mastery, and if by chance or in any other possible manner, there had been or were to be any such Letters of Mastery, we presently revoke them and declare them null and void and expressly forbid those who will have obtained them from using them under threat of fifteen hundred livres fine and damages and interest, payable to the said Academy. AND WE HEREBY MANDATE our loyal Parliament of Paris that they have these letters read, published, and registered and instate the said Desert, Renauld, and others of the said Royal Academy through this content in their functions, ceasing and making to cease all troubles and contrary hindrances: FOR THAT IS OUR PLEASURE. And so that this might be firm and stable for all time, we have affixed our seal to these present documents, which is our right. DELIVERED in Paris in the month of March this 1661 and the 19th year of our reign. Signed LOUYS, and on the reverse by the King, DE GUENEGAUD, to serve as Letters for the establishment of a Royal Academy of Dancing.

Visa, SEGUIER

Registered, heard, and the King's Public Prosecutor consenting to this, the intent and content of these letters is put into effect by Certificate of Verification on this day in Paris, in Parliament, March 30, 1662. DU TILLET.

STATUTES THAT HIS MAJESTY WANTS & INTENDS TO BE OBSERVED
IN THE ROYAL ACADEMY OF DANCE THAT HE WISHES TO SEE
ESTABLISHED IN THE CITY & ENVIRONS OF PARIS, IN IMITATION OF
THE ACADEMIES OF PAINTING & SCULPTURE

FIRSTLY, the said Academy will be composed of the oldest and most experienced of Dancing Masters, the most expert in Dance, in the number of thirteen, to wit François Galland Sieur du Desert, Master Ordinary of Dancing to the Queen, Jean Renauld Dancing Master of Monsieur the King's Brother, Thomas le Vacher, Hilaire d'Olivet, Guillaume Queru, Jean and Guillaume Reynal, Nicolas de l'Orge, Jean François Piquet, Jean Grigny, Florent Galland Desert, and Guillaume Renauld.

II

The said thirteen Ancients will meet once a month at a place or house that will be chosen by them and taken at common cost, to confer amongst themselves on the state of Dance, to take council and deliberate on the means for perfecting it, and to correct the abuses that can have been introduced or that could be introduced.

III

Two of the said Ancients will be chosen in turn to meet on every Saturday with other Dancing Masters, or with others who may want to teach Dance, in order to instruct them on the manner to Dance, and to show them the old and the new Dances, that will have been or will be invented by the thirteen Ancients; so that those who desire instruction can learn how to demonstrate and to avoid the abuses and the bad habits that they may have contracted.

IV

All sorts of persons of whatever quality or high condition they may be, Masters, sons of Masters, and others, will come to said place and will be received there to receive instruction in these things, and learn them from the mouth of the Ancients and by their instruction given to the other Masters of the said Art.

V

The other Ancients of the named thirteen can also be present in said place or hall, with the said Deputies, on the said day, to give their opinion on what will be presented there, and the instruction and teaching touching the said Dances, even if they are not called upon to be there that week.

VI

The other Masters teaching Dance in the said village and environs of Paris can aspire to be among the number of Ancients and Academicians and to be received in the said Academy, if they are judged by the Ancients in a majority vote to be worthy and capable. The candidates will have to demonstrate the exercise of all sorts of Dances, old and new, as well as steps from Ballets, on a day set aside for such auditions. They will pay the sum of 150 livres if they are sons of Masters, and 300 livres if they are other, which sums will be applied to the ornaments, and common expenditures of the said Academy.

VII

All those who want to call themselves Dancers in the said city and environs will have to register their names and addresses on a register that will be held by the Academicians. If they do not, they will forgo any privilege in the said Academy, never to join the ranks of the said Ancients and Academicians.

VIII

Those of the said Ancients, and others who Dance, who will have or want to invent and compose a new Dance will not be able to show it unless it has been previously viewed and examined by the said Ancients and approved by them in a majority vote when they are assembled on days set aside for such deliberation.

IX

The deliberations undertaken concerning the affairs of Dance by the said Ancients convened as specified above, will be carried out according to the form and tenor indicated by the said Ancients and by others who make Dance their profession and aspire to join the Academy, with the disciplinary actions mentioned and 50 livres of fine for any breach of these rules.

X

The said Ancient Academicians and their children will be able to show and teach all kinds of Dances in the city and its environs and elsewhere throughout the realm, without being constrained or obliged under any pretext to acquire Letters of Mastery nor any other authority beyond what is conferred upon them by the said Academy, in the manner and the forms indicated here.

XI

Since the King needs persons capable of participating and Dancing in his Ballets and similar divertissements, when his Majesty honors the said Academy with notice, the Ancients will be expected to furnish incessantly from amongst themselves or others the number of dancers needed by his Majesty.

XII

The common affairs of the said Academy will be pursued, maintained, and defended by the said Academicians, at their common expense whose fund will be earned between themselves, and they will decide on all necessary measures in a majority vote when they are assembled to that purpose as described.

Registered

Registered, heard, and the King's Public Prosecutor consenting to this, it will be executed according to form and tenor, following the Certificate of Verification on this day, at Paris in Parliament, March 30, 1662. DU TILLET.

DELIBERATION OF THE ROYAL ACADEMY OF DANCE, CONTAINING
THE RECEPTION OF SIEUR BERNARD DE MANTHE IN THE PLACE OF
THE LATE SIEUR LE VACHER, AND THE ARRANGEMENTS OF RANKS
AND MEETINGS OF THE ACADEMICIANS, OF APRIL 16, 1662

Assembled in the Academy Sirs François Galand sieur du Desert, Dancing Master to the Queen, Jean Renauld Dancing Master of the King, in reversion of Monsieur Prevost, and Dancing Master of Monsieur, the King's brother, Guillaume Queru, Hilaire d'Olivet, Bernard de Manthe, Jean Reynal, Nicolas de l'Orge, Guillaume Renauld, Jean Piquet, Florent Galand du Desert, Jean de Grigny, and Guillaume Reynal, Dancing Master of Monseigneur the Dauphin.

It has been represented by the Sieur du Desert that the Sieur le Vacher named above by the King to fill one of the Academy's places, being dead, and there being a need to choose someone capable to replace him, as will please the King; he believes that the Company could not make a better choice than that of Sieur Bernard de Manthe who has the service and qualities required for that, and asked the company to deliberate on it.

UPON WHICH, the said Sieur de Manthe having left the room, it was resolved in a common voice that he would be received, and returning thereafter, he took the oath required in this case, to observe the statutes and orders of the Academy, and he took his place.

And since it had also been proposed to arrange the rank of the Academicians, so that no contestation might ever arise among them, and so that they might maintain the unity and understanding they need for their Academy to grow and flourish. It was resolved that in all of the Acts and Assemblies of general and particular nature, in Contracts and Deliberations, the said Academicians would be seated in the order that their names are written in the present Deliberation, without ever allowing that order to be changed for whatever cause or occasion might arise, and those that follow will claim no priority other than the order of their reception.

Decree of the Parliament of Paris, that dismisses the opposition of the Master Violinists to the registration of the Letters for the establishment of the Academy of Dance.[3]

EXCERPT OF THE REGISTERS OF PARLIAMENT

Enter Guillaume Dumanoir, Ordinary Violinist of the King, and consorts, petitioning on two Requests presented to the Court the first and fourth of last April; the first request relative to their being received as opposing the registration of Letters of Mastery of Dancing and establishment of the Academy of Dance obtained by its defenders named hereafter; the second, that if the Letters received a Decree of Verification that the opposition would be granted audience on the first day. Nevertheless, the opponents are prohibited from disobeying the said Statutes and from participating in the Art and Mastery of Dance: they are prohibited from forming any Academy, from playing instruments except by conditions imposed by the Statutes on pain of separation from their instruments and imprisonment. As for the second request it was decided that they be received as opposing the execution of the Decree of last 30th March. Furthermore, definitive prohibition was established against the opponents to interfere with the said Academy. It was ordered that the Statutes and Decrees about registering musicians be executed according to its form and tenor. The defenders may not alter them, as in François Galland Sieur du Desert, Jean Renauld, Jean and Guillaume Reynal, Jean and François Piquet and consorts, Dancing Masters, defenders irrespective of their rank. After Isalis on the part of Galand and his consorts, requested the reception of appointment in presence of Ravier, the Lawyer of the Petitioners: Bignon for the King's attorney general, THE COURT orders that the appointment will be received: this was done over the requests and opposition of the said Dumanoir and his consorts, who were put out of the court and out of trial, in Parliament August 30, 1662. DU TILLET.

Collated from the originals, by myself the King's general secretary, House of the Crown of France and of its Finances.

ESTABLISHMENT OF THE ROYAL ACADEMY OF DANCE IN THE CITY OF PARIS
WITH AN ACADEMIC DISCOURSE to prove that the Dance in its noblest part
does not need Musical instruments and that it is entirely independent of the
Violin.

It was difficult to imagine that Dance and instruments, having lived for
centuries in good understanding, should come to a parting of the ways in our
time when both are in their perfection. It had been believed that their society
was modeled on that of harmony and the movement of the firmament, and
that it would last as long as the world. Dance protests that it had nothing to
do with their discord, that it was always ready to follow their movements as
long as they were able to accommodate the movements of dance to conserve
that equality that constitutes and maintains societies. But when the Violin,
swelling with pride at having been admitted into the private domain of the
greatest of Kings and at having seen itself favorably received in all of his
divertissements, gave itself an unwonted superiority that not even the Luth or
any other instrument had ever wielded over Dance, Dance thought it should
oppose that innovation and let its independence from music be known.
Dance succeeded so well in this that the King, to whom Providence has given
– with a thousand other royal qualities – an admirable discernment, found it
just to establish an Academy of Dance where music and instruments have no
place. In such a way, it will be seen that, although for his amusement Dance
and the Violin came together frequently, they are no longer mutually indistinguishable, and that there is no reason to confuse them with one another.

And although the judgement of the most enlightened and absolute of all
Kings should suffice to assure Dance that all reasonable people will henceforth consider it as independent of Musical instruments and as a body that
can easily subsist without their harmonious animation, Dance wants to justify this truth by a little discourse for the satisfaction of his Majesty himself,
who is always pleased to see his feelings seconded by reason, and for the
entire conviction of those who could doubt the separation of these two bodies
that have had such a long and close union.

Dance will say nothing disadvantageous about Music for whom it will
always have much esteem. Dance will just try to show its independence and
its advantages over the Violin that wanted to subjugate it. And although
contestations that are animated by rank and precedence are always bitter,
nothing in this discourse will be of that character.

Music and all of the instruments that it uses to compose the harmony that
has accrued such esteem and reputation in all civilized Nations, were born of
natural sounds which, in the world's childhood and by a universal consent,
were judged pleasant, either because these sounds had some proportion with

the harmony of our soul or because they had the ability to flatter our ears as beautiful colors flatter our eyes. So one cannot contest that all musical instruments were invented for the pleasure of the ear alone. And, indeed, if we consult taste or touch, they will tell us that Music has nothing odorific or soft. And vision, which concerns itself with all the other senses, says it sees nothing shocking in this because we know that although Violins be adorned with ornaments in assemblies, one finds them more beautiful when they are unseen.

Dance, on the contrary, has nothing that the ear can hear. Its first use in the most ancient antiquity was to make visible the secret feelings of the soul by signs and bodily movements, in order to perfect that general expression that nature had taught to all men so that they might be understood by signs wherever their language was not understood. Some people did this so well by finding gestures and facial expressions imitating the characters of all desires and of all passions, that a famous Author said that their signs were better understood than their words. After that general use, having become less important as the knowledge of languages grew, Dance became associated with the expression of joy and of sadness alone, and it became part of the religion of the Greeks who then set it to Music. The Greeks called it by an equivocal name [*chorea*] that confused it with its other parts and created confusion that some still entertain. Dance was subsequently used in war exercises and entire Nations used dance as a military march. A great Athenian captain who was not too gallant stated that Dance was very proper for creating military exercise. And the Romans, who always included gladiatorial combat among there amusements, didn't fail to receive dance among the useful diversions of the Republic.

France has long recognized Dance as the necessary origin of all beautiful exercises. It is Dance that corrects the natural defects of the body and changes its bad habits; it is Dance that gives that comfortable air and that grace that fills actions with loveliness. Dance teaches those who frequent company to enter and cultivate it pleasantly and acquires for them that prompt approbation that sometimes earns them their fortune, and always their joy with the joy of the spectators. Dance teaches them to handle matters with seemliness and without disorder and to extract themselves from the most embarrassing places. Dance helps one to ride horseback and carry arms. It renders one more skilled at serving one's Prince in battle, and pleasing him in divertissements.

The Violin has nothing to do with all of these things and if it is occasionally mixed in with the Dance, it still must admit that this occurs only in what concerns pleasure, and that this advantage is enjoyed by all other Musical instruments. The Violin cannot deny that it is useless to all those who learn to

Dance: they could not follow the Violin's cadences before having learned how to do the steps, to carry their bodies, and to form the necessary figures. So that one can say that the Violin is to the Dance what Drums and Trumpets are to war. For as the latter animate the combatants with sounds appropriate to the rapidity and ferocity of action but do not show what figure to assume or how to fight – because that function belongs to more noble Officers – so the Violin only animates Dancers who would remain immobile in response to its movements if they hadn't learned from their masters what to do while the Violins played. And just as it would appear ridiculous for Drums and Trumpets to attribute some superiority to themselves over and above the Aides-de-camp and the Sergeants of battle for having sounded the attack or the retreat when these illustrious Officers caused the troops to advance or withdraw, so one must admit that there would be something strange in the thought that Violins have had to set themselves up as Kings and Masters of the Dance. They have only played while the Dance has tried to make mute people speak to the spectators through studied movements, concerted steps, regulated figures, and thousands and thousands of eloquent ways of moving. And Dance has told stories where, without a prologue, without a *récit*, and without any help from the voice it makes known the condition, the state, and the passions of those it represents.

If we had further to compare the usefulness of the Violin with that of Dance, it would not be difficult to show that all of the advantages are on the side of the latter, since the Violin only produces a pleasant sound in truth, but which sound is lost on the air after having briefly flattered the ears, without leaving any useful impression of its harmony for the body or the spirit, while the Dance, besides the pleasures it accrues in divertissements for the eyes, forms impressions of decorum and resourcefulness in those who practice it and in the minds of those who see it: these impressions can be of some use to the Nation, either for its politeness or for its facility in military exercises.

And if we had to speak of qualities necessary to those who Dance and to those who play the Violin, it would not be difficult to show that the Dancers have all the advantages. They must be well formed in body, and one knows that a good and agreeable physical formation is almost always a sure sign of the goodness of the soul; they must be naturally adroit and quick, they must have supple bodies and minds, and they would not be able to join persons of quality without contracting some honesty and courtesy, which almost always betrays a high birth or, at least, a good education.

Violin players don't need all that. They can be lame, blind, and hunchbacked without anyone bothering about it. They only need an ear and arms to play. And although most Violinists today look good and are honest people, they will admit that if they were less becoming and less upstanding, they would still be very good Violinists.

But to conclude with the greatest advantage Dance ever won over the Violin, Dance will say that the King, who has not neglected any of the beautiful practices that can grace his Royal Majesty, has not disdained to employ his marvelous address, received from heaven for all beautiful exercises, in dancing, which he knows to perfection, and that he himself is the Protector of his Academy. He gives as a Vice-Protector, Monsieur le Comte de Saint-Aignan, whom one knows to be one of the most witty and gallant men of his Court.

4

THE AMERINDIAN IN FRENCH HUMANIST AND BURLESQUE COURT BALLETS

The first French exploration, and aborted colonization, of the New World was contemporaneous with the era of transition from Valois humanist court ballet to the melodramatic and burlesque styles of the early baroque. In examining three distinct yet not entirely discontinuous appropriations of the savage by humanists, Protestants, and nobles, I will outline the import of New World iconography for court ballet. What qualities characterize the iconographic construction of the American primitive or Amerindian by late Renaissance ethnographers? And were related constructions operative in the domestic festival context when the Amerindian became a stock court ballet figure of burlesque ballet?[1]

The image of the Amerindian in French court ballet has negligible ethnographic significance; but so, for that matter, does European iconography of the New World.[2] Court ballet imagery and New World iconography are connected on the basis of their political purposes in and for Europe. The savage accedes to iconographical and performed presence in a way reflecting purely Eurocentric concerns that belong to internal political struggles among hegemonic individuals. French representations of the Amerindian need to be related in particular to the rivalry between France and Spain both in Europe and in the New World. These engraved and danced representations tell us about strife over religious intolerance in France, about the *politique* diplomacy of the Valois, and about the growing precariousness of the noble class in French society since 1550.

France maintained settlements in Canada between 1535 and 1543, in Florida between 1562 and 1565, and in Brazil between 1555 and 1560 and again between 1612 and 1614.[3] From the time of the first Brazilian exploits, court ballets were being developed in France as tools of international diplomacy. Before the role of the savage was danced by nobles in court ballets, however, a group of 50 Brazilians voyaged to France and appeared as themselves for the entry of Henri II and Catherine de' Medici into Rouen.[4] Prototypes of humanist court ballet under the Valois are generally thought to have begun in 1564 with the Bayonne fêtes. But the 1550 Rouen entry was seminal to the development of Americanist dance in court ballet. Those 50 Brazilians (among a supporting cast of 250 naked and painted Frenchmen and an unknown number of equally naked Frenchwomen) were apprehended by the French literary imagination as a visible alternative to the hypocrisy of courtly manners. The Amerindian quickly became a humanist allegory for the self-evidence of unadorned behavior. Montaigne employs New World imagery in the preface to his *Essais* by opposing courtly and rhetorical culture to its favorably viewed "other":

Que si j'eusse esté entre ces nations qu'on dict vivre encore sous la douce liberté des premieres loix de nature, je t'asseure que je m'y fusse très-volontiers peint tout entier, et tout nud. (E, "Au lecteur": 2)

Had I been placed among those nations which are said to live still in the sweet freedom of nature's first laws, I assure you [reader] I should very gladly have portrayed myself here entire and wholly naked.

For the French Renaissance humanist, the figure of the Amerindian embodied philosophical and social forthrightness in an unintentionally critical presence.

It is therefore not surprising that the notion of ethnicity in French courtly social dance became manifest through the demonstration of dances' stylistic plurality. The sixteenth-century French repertory contained dances of ostensibly foreign character.[5] By impersonating other nationalities, the noble playfully reproduced himself as a series of hypothetical others whose very difference spoke well for the authenticity of the noble's own predictably codified behavior.

Moreover, under the Valois, the notion of internationalism had a particularly *politique* aura. The idea of internationalist communion on the occasions of court festivities to which foreign ambassadors were invited was skillfully engineered by Catherine de' Medici to encourage religious tolerance in France. As Frances A. Yates has shown in her study of the Valois tapestries, Medici court ballets in France contained internationalist references to a *politique* alliance between France, the Netherlands, and Poland at Spain's expense. Although Valois festivities, culminating in *Le Balet des Polonais* (1573) and *Le Balet comique de la Royne* (1581), did not have many internal representations of the New World, they did reveal that internationalism per se was already the signal of an implicit subtext about religious tolerance.

During the festivities at the 1572 wedding of Marguerite de Navarre, Catherine de' Medici's daughter, with Henry of Navarre, the French Protestant leader, Catholic participants were dressed as Amazons and Protestants as Turks during the equestrian games. The Amazones or Amazonides were a mythical race of South American or African warlike females who had cut off their right breasts in order better to wield the bow. In later burlesque ballet, the Amazon is frequently costumed as an adrogyne, with part male and part female attire. Protestants, on the other hand, were dressed as Turks and thus, in the context of French festivities, inevitably suggested an anti-Catholic and antimonarchical presence. It was during these festivities that the Saint Bartholomew's massacre of Protestants took place.[6] My point in rehearsing this well-known and tragic occurrence is only that a *ballet des nations* format was instrumental in ritualizing politicoreligious tensions.

French New World ethnographers, or those whose writing appeared in French and Latin translation in France, were primarily Protestant: Jean de Léry, Girolamo Benzoni (translated and adapted by Urbain Chauveton), and the engraver Théodore de Bry. The New World vision conveyed to French readers was thus a form of Protestant polemic in response to the threats often acted on within festival contexts. The so-called ethnographers' negative commentary on Spanish Catholic colonization was meant to contribute to the Protestant cause in the wars of religion that pitted French Catholic against French Protestant during the second half of the sixteenth century. The Protestants identified with the Amerindians as victims with victims, even as their ethnography purveyed an anti-Spanish, and therefore anti-Catholic, vision of conquerors exploiting and brutalizing the indigenous populations of the Americas.[7] For our purposes here, let us note that the Amerindian in ethnographic writing was, as in the case of the humanist interpretation, a critical image directed at domestic Catholic society by expatriated Protestants. However, the context had switched from humanistic moral philosophy and Pleiade poetry to evangelism and the goals of the Reformation.

By appropriating the Amerindian as a critical figure, the French Protestant ethnographer also expressed an ambivalence about the Amerindian's reputed cannibalism. This was done by conflating a feminine Amerindian figure with traits of the Amazon. De Bry's ubiquitous savage woman with the sagging breasts has been analyzed by Bernadette Bucher as just such a paradigmatically ambivalent figure in de Bry's engravings. Sagging breasts, like those of the Amazon, were joined with secondary sexual characteristics that were clearly male: this androgynous Amazon signified pacific receptivity on the verge of threatening violence. In his analysis of Ralegh's discovery of Amazons, Louis Montrose notes: "The matriarchal, gynocratic Amazons are the radical Other figured but not fully contained by the collective imagination of European patriarchy."[8] The Amazon/androgyne's appearance in the *Grands Voyages* tempers the monstrosity of overtly cannibalistic behavior with sexual ambiguity. At its most fantastic and least ethnographic, French New World ethnographers, like burlesque court ballet choreographers, presented the androgyne as an ambivalent image of the fellow victim become dangerous foe.[9]

The androgyne replaced the morphological hybridity of the monstrous with a human, albeit sexually and socially ambiguous, figure.

It is in the figure of the androgyne that I see the most coherent connection between New World ethnography and burlesque performance. In burlesque works of the 1620s and early 1630s, the androgyne signaled critique of the monarchy as well as embodied the programmed ambiguity of burlesque satire itself and the dangers of the burlesque enterprise.

In burlesque ballet, notions of alienated courtliness and grotesque monstrosity join internationalism as modes of theatrical communication. Burlesque ballet under Louis XIII experimented with political ambivalence toward and critique of the monarchy.[10] The Amerindian was one of several roles performed by the grandee in these works to signal his dissenting position. Other recurrent roles were the Androgyne, the Moor, and the Turk.

Recalling the critical import of the Brazilian's presence in the Rouen entry for humanist critique of courtly hypocrisy, there seems to be some precedent for the use of New World imagery in the playfully satiric burlesque works of the early seventeenth century. In burlesque ballet, the object of criticism was not the moral fabric of courtliness but the growing power of monarchy. According to Rudolf zur Lippe, the social and economic instability of the noble class was directly fueled by the discovery of the New World and its resultant commercial possibilities.[11] International trade shifted the economic power base toward production in urban centers and away from feudal-agrarian society and guild-based crafts – the world of the landed warrior class. The noble's response to precapitalist markets was to invent his own internationalism: civility manuals appeared in polyglot editions developing noble virtue into a transnational, European concept and making the idea of cosmopolitanism a social reality. When the grandee dancer impersonates the Amerindian, however, he expresses the negative effects of internationalism. In burlesque works, Amerindians do not represent Christian alternatives to Spanish Catholicism or a humanist's better self, but an alarming figure of the disenfranchised noble.

One of the three most significant burlesque works, *Le Grand bal de la douairière de Billebahaut* (1626), is constructed as a "ballet des nations."[12] The entire work is thus intended as a travesty of theatrical ostentation as a tool of foreign policy. Rather than parade before the French monarch, however, the various nations parade before the grotesque Dowager of Billebahaut in honor of her rumored merits. The first *entrée* is that of the "Ameriquains," presaging the ballets of Atabalipa and the peoples of America. The Americans, dressed in feathers, are interrupted in their dance by the entry of parrots whose talk, according to the libretto, is better than their dance. American hunters pursue the parrots, mesmerizing them with music and mirrors and taking them captive. As the hunters exit with their prey, androgynes appear.

Their costumes are split down the middle, being half pants and half dress, and they carry the distaff in one hand, the sword in the other. The appearance of the androgyne on American soil, as it were, recalls the androgynous engravings of New World inhabitants. The libretto also indicates that their steps are partially on the ground and partially in the air, thus corresponding to the principal modalities of female and male movement in Renaissance social dance. Only the androgyne's *récit*, however, offers an explanation of their relevance to the New World capture of the parrots:

> Quelle gloire eut jamais de plus augustes marques?
> Le fuseau que je tiens est le fuseau des Parques,
> Par qui des Rodomans je décide les jours;
> Leur audace où je suis est en vain occupée,
> Affin de la trancher sans espoir de secours,
> J'ay de la main de Mars cette fameuse espée. (L, 3: 156)

> What glory ever had more august signs?
> The distaff I hold is the distaff of the Fates,
> By which I decide the fate of Boasters;
> Their audacity can have no effect upon me,
> In order to cut it without hope of remedy,
> I hold in my warrior's hand this famous sword.

The androgyne compresses the classical image of the three Lady Fates – Clotho, who spins the thread of life; Lachesis, who identifies the victim; and Atropos, who cuts the thread – into one ambiguously gendered figure. Furthermore, the death induced is the death of rumor, the very motor of propagandistic court ballets. It seems possible that there is a reference here to Huguenot ethnographic discourse as a form of slander and extravagant self-advertisement. The boasters are the fanfaronading parrots hunted by savages in the New World. Yet just as Protestants extended the charge of cannibalism to Catholics as believers in transsubtantiation ostensibly devouring the body of Christ, so here the victimization of the Protestants undergoes a reversal, coming out as the infliction of death on the monarchy's pretensions, a death that renders the perpetrator's identity, like his or her sex, uncertain. This sort of carnivalesque reversal is typical of burlesque works and reveals that the androgyne, while a shadow figure of the American, is actually emblematic of the burlesque enterprise as a whole. Burlesque ballet that deals in such controversial imagery, like the discourse of the Amazon in New World ethnography, opens, in the words of Montrose, "a conceptual space for reversal and negation . . . within the world picture of a patriarchal society."[13]

Burlesque ballet in metaphoric terms is an America on whose shores dissident nobles took refuge and from which they disparaged the monarch through grotesque self-portraiture, equivocal images of their own estrangement in a savage court.

NOTES

PROLOGUE

1. This theory is developed in Mark Franko, *The Dancing Body in Renaissance Choreography (c. 1416–1589)* (Birmingham: Summa Publications, 1986). The concept of mannerism itself involves the culture of manners in which life becomes an art. The culture of manners, however, can be thought of either as an aptitude for simulation (reconstruction of the rule) or as the generation of subtly differing forms (reinvention). My interpretation of *civilité* since Castiglione is dynamic and evolutive rather than static. I do not envisage it as a series of rigid precepts engendering stylish behavior as much as a technique for rendering precepts natural, lending them convincing life. In the art historical context, mannerism also refers to quotation or appropriation of earlier art in a creative process that increases art's self-referentiality. With self-referentiality comes an artistic autonomy from literary-historical sources and their narrative legibility. Through increased self-reference, non-verbal arts can construct their own internal history. In the following pages, I will show that this process in late Renaissance and early baroque fine art is also a process of court ballet performance. Art history and performance history of the mannerist interval have in common their attempt to deflect the legibility of the human body. But performance history unveils a political dimension to autonomy whose story is unique. For a discussion of the issues surrounding mannerism, see James V. Mirollo, *Mannerism and Renaissance Poetry: Concept, Mode, Inner Design* (New Haven, Conn.: Yale University Press, 1984).

2. Apart from the work of French dancer Christine Bayle for her company L'éclat des muses, the most remarkable reconstruction of baroque dance I have seen is preserved on film in Shirley Wynne's *Baroque Dance, 1675–1725*, made in collaboration with Allegra Fuller Snyder in 1979.

3. See his *Morales du grand siècle* (Paris: Gallimard, 1948), p. 28. Bénichou, e.g., writes that Corneille's tragedy is "doubly a performance, since the grandeurs represented on the stage already have spectacular value in life" (p. 29). See also Jean-Jacques Demorest, "Une notion théâtrale de l'existence," *L'Esprit Créateur* 11, no. 2 (Summer 1971): 77–91.

4. See Norbert Elias, *The Court Society* (New York: Pantheon, 1983).

5. See Erica Harth, *Ideology and Culture in Seventeenth-Century France* (Ithaca, N.Y.: Cornell University Press, 1983).

6. Historical studies by Prunières (1914), Christout (1967), and McGowan (1978) have laid the indispensable groundwork for all subsequent research.

7. For my purposes here, Aristotelian qualities can be characterized principally as linear plot progression and the imitation of action. Aristotle's *theoria*, however, is pertinent to dance (see p. 30). Court ballet lasted roughly one hundred years. Marie-Françoise Christout cites the definitive decline of court ballet – within which she includes comedy-ballet – in 1672 with *Fêtes de l'Amour et de Bacchus*. See her *Le Ballet de cour de Louis XIV, 1643–1762: Mises en scène* (Paris: A. et J. Picard, 1967), pp. 124–5. On the other hand, Françoise Dartois-Lapeyre believes *Le Triomphe de l'Amour* (1681) to be the last court ballet. See her "Révélation d'un genre: La Tragi-comédie-ballet," *La Recherche en Danse* 2 (1983): 54, note 17. Court ballet was succeeded by ballet in opera.

8. See Renate Baader, "La Polémique anti-baroque dans la doctrine classique," *Baroque*

6 (1973): 133–48, and Michael Moriarty, *Taste and Ideology in Seventeenth-Century France* (Cambridge University Press, 1988). Moriarty suggests that "the courtier's taste-discourse is a means of affirming, against all the appearances, their independence from royal control, a last aristocratic self-assertion against the pressures of political, social and economic subordination to the monarchy" (p. 152). In a similarly materialist interpretation, I am suggesting that the courtier's dance practices of the burlesque form a kind of bad taste-discourse constituting an earlier form of dissent. The aesthetics of a mannerist grotesque are explored by Giancarlo Maiorino in *The Portrait of Eccentricity: Arcimboldo and the Mannerist Grotesque* (University Park: Pennsylvania State University Press, 1991).

9. Thomas Postlewait asks, "How are we as historians and readers of history veiled from the event, even when we have these undisputed facts before us?" For an examination of the problems raised by the interpretation of theatrical events as history, see his "Historiography and Theatrical Event," *Theatre Journal* 43, no. 21 (May 1991): 157–98.

10. I will refer to Margaret M. McGowan's *Le Balet comique by Balthazar de Beaujoyeulx, 1581* (Binghamton: Medieval and Renaissance Texts and Studies, 1982). This facsimile edition of the libretto will hereafter be cited as *Le Balet comique*. All English translations are cited or adapted from the Carol MacClintock and Lander MacClintock version in *Musicological Studies and Documents*, no. 25 (1971), published by the American Institute of Musicology. It will be referred to in notes as MacClintock and MacClintock.

11. See Paul Lacroix, *Ballets et mascarades de cour sous Henri IV et Louis XIII (de 1581 à 1652)* (Geneva: chez J. Gay et fils, 1868–70; rpt. Geneva: Slatkine, 1968). This work will be referred to hereafter in notes as Lacroix. Lacroix was followed in his efforts by Victor Fournel, *Les Contemporains de Molière, recueil de comédies rares ou peu connues, jouées de 1650 à 1680, avec l'histoire de chaque théâtre* (Paris, Firmin Didot Frères, 1866). Volume 2 of this collection is devoted to court ballet librettos and has been reprinted in facsimile (Geneva: Slatkine, 1967). Both Lacroix and Fournel published learned introductions to their collections of librettos. See Lacroix, "Notice sur les ballets de cour," in Lacroix, vol. 1, pp. v–xxvi, and Fournel, "Histoire du ballet de cour," in *Les Contemporains de Molière*, vol. 2, pp. 173–221. I will return to their remarks with regard to burlesque ballet. Bibliographies of the anthologized and uncollected librettos can be found in McGowan (1978) and Christout (1967). But, in the early seventeenth century, burlesque ballets were as numerous as political pamphlets and lampoons: many survive only as titles. See *Recueil des plus excellens ballets de ce temps* (Paris: Touss. du Bray, 1612), Pierre François Godard de Beauchamps, *Recherches sur les théâtres de France depuis l'année onze cens soixante et un, jusques à présent* (Paris: Prault, 1735; rpt. Geneva: Slatkine, 1968), and Duc de la Vallière, *Ballets, opéra et autres ouvrages lyriques* (Paris: chez Cl. J. Baptiste Bouche, 1760; rpt. London: H. Baron, 1967).

12. The major exception being Françoise Christout, *Le Ballet de cour de Louis XIV*.

13. Margaret M. McGowan has afforded sustained attention to choreographic practice within the perspective of the literary trope of praise. See her recent *Ideal Forms in the Age of Ronsard* (Berkeley and Los Angeles: University of California Press, 1985), particularly the chapter "Dancing Forms," pp. 209–41. But in general, historians account for choreography in the very terms of the original theorists, without delving beneath them. See, e.g., "Théorie et théoriciens," in Christout, *Le Ballet de cour de Louis XIV*: pp. 137–53.

14. Henry Prunières's *Le Ballet de cour en France avant Benserade et Lully* (Paris: Henri Laurens, 1914) stresses the Italian sources of court ballet: the double influence of "mascarade," for its mixture of high and low style, and the "intermezzo," for the combination of song and choreographic figures in a pastoral setting. Frances A. Yates's major contributions to the history of court ballet in the late Renaissance can be found in *The French Academies of the Sixteenth Century* (London: Warburg Institute, 1947), *The Valois Tapestries* (London: Routledge & Kegan Paul, 1959), and *Astraea: The Imperial Theme in the Sixteenth Century* (London: Routledge & Kegan Paul, 1975).

15. First published in 1963, *L'Art du ballet de cour en France* was reissued by the Centre National de Recherches Scientifiques (Paris) in 1978. It will be referred to hereafter in notes as *L'Art*. Unfortunately, it has yet to be translated into English. McGowan's special contribution is her analysis of the sociohistorical contexts of court ballet in France between 1581 and 1643. Since this work, McGowan has continued to deepen the theoretical basis for her interpretation of late Valois court ballet as a practice of harmony in the Platonic sense. In Chapter 2, I will suggest an alternate contemporary theory, the Heraclitean, which renders Renaissance choreography more problematic. I will further discuss McGowan's interpretation of court ballet choreography as an idealization in Chapter 5.

16. I have reviewed McGowan's monograph introduction to her edition of *Le Balet comique de la Royne* in *Romanic Review* 75, no. 4 (November 1984): 504–6, and she evaluated my recent findings in "The Semiotics of Dance: A State of the Art in the Renaissance," in *Continuum* 1 (Rethinking Classicism) (1989): 249–257.

17. See Roy C. Strong, *Splendor at Court* (Boston: Houghton Mifflin, 1975).

18. Christout refers to the period between 1660 and 1672 as "Le Triomphe du Faste" ("the Triumph of Opulent Display") in *Le Ballet de cour de Louis XIV*, pp. 101–35. On the major librettist of noble style court ballets, see Charles I. Silin, *Benserade and His Ballets de Cour* (Baltimore: Johns Hopkins University Press, 1940). I will discuss Silin's work in Chapter 4. For an overview of the evolution of court ballet from the perspective of music history, see Robert M. Isherwood, *Music in the Service of the King: France in the Seventeenth Century* (Ithaca, N.Y.: Cornell University Press, 1973).

19. For example, with regard to the important and little understood phenomenon of burlesque ballet, I nuance and deepen McGowan's notion of satire. See *L'Art*, pp. 148–9. McGowan says that burlesque ballets "criticize institutions and open people's eyes to the society and the world they live in." Still, such satire appears as the one aspect of court ballet not sufficiently historicized by McGowan. The content of this satire brought the very foundations of court ballet into question, particularly between 1624 and 1627. My interest is to rehistoricize these works, which were dismissed as "silly."

20. John Guthrie, e.g., writes, "By 'the Baroque era' is meant that period in which a particular dance style was in fashion, and which covers approximately one century, from 1660–1760." "Quelques considérations sur le style de la danse à l'époque baroque," in *Les Goûts-Réünis* (Paris: l'Institut de musique et de danse anciennes, 1982), p. 96 (my translation).

21. The transition between the sixteenth and seventeenth century has also been referred to as mannerist. The periodization of mannerism is a problematic issue too complex to confront in these pages. See Frank Warnke, "Mannerism in European Literature: Period or Aspect?" in *Revue de Littérature Comparée* 56 (1982): 255–60, and John Steadman, *Redefining a Period Style: "Renaissance," "Mannerist" and "Baroque" in Literature* (Pittsburgh, Pa.: Duquesne University Press, 1990). I address ramifications of the idea of mannerism for court ballet throughout the text.

22. See his *La Littérature de l'âge baroque en France: Circé et le paon* (Paris: Librairie José Corti, 1954), p. 233. Rousset sets the French baroque period – from Montaigne to Puget – between 1580 and 1665, after which the forces of neoclassicism and cultural homogeneity consolidate in France. In a broader perspective, Frank J. Warnke refers to the baroque as "the style dominant in European literature from the last decades of the sixteenth century to the last decades of the seventeenth – the style that appears tentatively in Tasso and Montaigne, reaches its fulfillment in Donne, Crashaw, Marvell, Browne, Milton, Corneille, Pascal, Vondel, Gryphius, Marino, and Gongora, and occurs vestigially in Dryden and Racine." See his *Versions of Baroque: European Literature in the Seventeenth Century* (New Haven, Conn.: Yale University Press, 1972), p. 1.

23. Victor L. Tapié, *La France de Louis XIII et de Richelieu* (Paris: Flammarion, 1967), p. 94.

24. José Antonio Maravall, *Culture of the Baroque: Analysis of a Historical Structure*, trans. Terry Cochran (Minneapolis: University of Minnesota Press, 1986), p. 35.

25. For a good resume and critique of the notion of "general crisis" in the seventeenth century, see A. D. Lublinskaya, *French Absolutism: The crucial phase, 1620–1629*, trans. Brian Pearce (Cambridge University Press, 1968).
26. For a historical overview of the relationship of dance to law, see Marianne Panzer, *Tanz und Recht* (Frankfurt am Main: Moritz Diesterweg, 1938).
27. See Rudolf zur Lippe, *Geometrisierung des menschen und repräsentation des privaten im französischen absolutismus* (Frankfurt am Main: Syndikat Reprise, 1979), the second volume of *Naturbeherrschung am menschen*. Louis Marin also pursues ideological analysis of spectacle in *Le Portrait du roi* (Paris: Minuit, 1981). See, in particular, his chapter entitled "Le roi magicien ou la fête du prince," pp. 236–50. In the earlier part of his study, *Körpererfahrung als entfaltung von sinnen und beziehungen in der ära des italienischen kaufmannskapitals*, zur Lippe argues that fifteenth-century Italian dance uncovered a new relationship between physical and mental work allowing for human self-realization independent of the cycle of productive labor. This premise of a post-Marxian social psychology is alluring although suspect by virtue of a modernist infatuation with dance as self-expression. As interesting and sensitive as zur Lippe's analysis of Renaissance dance culture can be, his fundamental premise does not materialize from the primary sources themselves because he focuses on the *historical potential* of Renaissance dance, not on its ideologically determined forms in history. The historical realization of this potential should be studied in the late nineteenth century when self-expression was more explicitly at artistic issue than in the fifteenth century. In his second volume, zur Lippe argues that as dance became the tool of absolutism in the late sixteenth and early seventeenth centuries, it lost the human potential for self-realization. Court ballet then manipulated physical display, and as a part of politics, it too became self-alienating. The burlesque period may prove an exception to this rule. But that does not make it heir to the Italian courtly social dance tradition such as zur Lippe describes it (see chapter 4).

    The twentieth-century German school of dance historians before zur Lippe added little or nothing to court ballet scholarship. Oskar Bie devotes four pages of his *Der Tanz* (Berlin: Julius Bard, 1919) to French court ballet, which he calls a "neronische Schwärmerei" ("a riotousness worthy of Nero," p. 282). Curt Sachs makes no contribution to court ballet historiography in *World History of the Dance* (New York: Norton, 1973). "Within the history of dance," he writes, "the beginnings of the ballet do not much concern us" (p. 392). Similarly, John Schikowski devotes a mere six pages of anecdotes to court ballet under Louis XIII and Louis XIV in his *Geschichte des Tanzes* (Berlin: Buchmeister Verlag, n.d.), pp. 106–12. A sketchy article by Helmut Günther, "Ballet de Cour: Beginn einer selbstbewussten Ballettkunst," recognizes the period as heralding a self-conscious art form. See *Das Tanzarchiv* (Oct. 1973): 137–42. For German scholarship on Molière's comedy-ballet from a musicological perspective, see Friedrich Böttger, "Die 'Comédie-Ballet' von Molière-Lully," Ph.D. Friedrich-Wilhelms University: Berlin, 1931.
28. See Pierre Legendre, *La Passion d'être un autre: Etude pour la danse* (Paris: Seuil, 1978). Legendre's work is part of the explosion of inquiries into the body that took place in French intellectual life during the 1970s. Legendre's argument, however, is not guided by a historicized interdisciplinary approach to dance history. For Legendre, all the aesthetic, sociological, and anthropological modes of reasoning, the common entry points to dance scholarship, miss the point. Rather, dance is the symptom of a blind spot at the origin of Western institutions themselves. Dance has both an exemplary and a shadow status. Those institutions are founded on a mythologized dogma that has cathected human desire. Legendre argues that we want to be that powerful "other" seen in the dancing body as having transferred its primitively savage desire to internalized idolatry. Dance is a way to induce love of the Law. This idea is already clearly sketched out in Plato's *Laws*, but Legendre deploys the problem-idea against the backdrop of his philosophical interpretation of legality. Nevertheless, he ends up iterating some of the very clichés initially attacked: dance is all and nothing. He does outline, however, the many pitfalls and dead ends of Western dance problematics. Le-

gendre's other books, *Jouir du pouvoir* and *L'Amour du censeur*, extend his reflection on the meaning of legality. For a summary of his point of view, see the interview with Legendre, "Le droit et toute sa rigueur," *Communications* 26 (L'objet du droit) (1977): 3–14.

29. Zur Lippe, *Geometrisierung*, p. 15.

30. Clearly, there are connections to be made with claims regarding "absolute dance" in the twentieth century.

31. This "crise de classe" had an economic, a social, and a political basis. See Davis Bitton, *The French Nobility in Crisis, 1560–1640* (Stanford, Calif.: Stanford University Press, 1969).

32. See René Pintard, *Le Libertinage erudit dans la première moitié du XVIIe siècle* (Paris: Boivin, 1943).

33. Or to assert "royal power at the expense of the traditional elites," in the formulation of Roger Mettam, *Power and Faction in Louis XIV's France* (Oxford: Blackwell Publisher, 1988), p. 44. Mettam militates against the ubiquitous use of the term "absolutism" to designate the real historical milieu of the seventeenth century, which was constituted by a dynamic balance of forces, the crown being only one of them. Mettam attributes the overuse of this term to the study of literary and curial sources that exaggerate the power of the monarchy because those dependent on patronage – writers and courtiers – are the most likely subjects of royal propaganda. Yet the type of resistance exerted from within court ballet production shows that nobles were neither entirely duped nor entirely censored by their proximity to the patronage network. Their experience indicates that absolutism was sensed as a threat rather than as a historical reality. While the degree to which absolutism shaped social life is open to debate, Louis's manipulation of the arts addresses his political aspirations. Those aspirations may not themselves have transformed social life, but they surely affected it. Lublinskaya relates that one of Richelieu's financial reforms instituted during the 1620s was to cut nobles' pensions by more than half. This would explain the ubiquitous poor noble of burlesque ballets. She also relates that Richelieu was assailed by a "paper war" of satirical pamphlets during these years. She could have added that the minister's support

of melodramatic ballet led to the opposition of burlesque ballet as an antigenre. Richelieu was also confronted with a hail of satirical ballets, a point most historians neglect to mention. See Lublinskaya, *French Absolutism*, pp. 272–6 and 316.

34. I differ with McGowan when she divides burlesque ballet dancing uniquely into the comedic and the imitative sorts (see *L'Art*, p. 190). Some burlesque dance suggested the nonpresence of critique through an emphasis on cryptic physical presence and should therefore be thought of as potentially autonomous in a modernist sense. That is, in an attempt to deflect legibility, some burlesque dancing took place in a self-induced semantic vacuum. (The other two forms of dancing that complete McGowan's taxonomy are geometrical and courtly social dancing.) This notion is further developed in Chapter 4.

35. Francis Sparshott calls autonomous or "pure" dance "a practice that is defined in terms of body movements performed simply for their own sakes." See his *Off the Ground: First Steps to a Philosophical Consideration of Dance* (Princeton, N.J.: Princeton University Press, 1988), p. 386. This definition would place the requisite dance in the artistic realm of purely formalist constructions as defined most pointedly by Clement Greenberg. It is interesting to note, however, that self-referentiality in dance has historical roots in ideological struggle. The issue of autonomy is, historically speaking, not purely formalist.

36. Yates, *The Valois Tapestries*.

37. Mikhail Bakhtin, *Rabelais and His World*, trans. Helene Iswolsky (Cambridge, Mass.: MIT Press, 1968), pp. 33–4. Joan DeJean identifies these survivals in the novel as the "libertine text" in *Libertine Strategies: Freedom and the Novel in Seventeenth-Century France* (Columbus: Ohio State University Press, 1981).

38. Clearly, Bakhtin is unsure where to place seventeenth-century burlesque performance. While burlesque court ballets employ carnivalesque procedures – sexual reversals, obscenity – they are not the expressions of popular culture they were in the Renaissance. Bakhtin is divided in his interpretation, maintaining that "the tradition of the grotesque is not entirely extinct; [that] it continues to live and to struggle for its existence in the lower

canonical genres" (p. 101), but also admitting that burlesque court ballet was "obviously linked to the mood of the rebellious aristocracy of that time" (p. 102). Because it reflects unsavory aristocratic politics, Bakhtin reluctantly concludes that the burlesque lacks regenerative force: "the ambivalent improprieties related to the material bodily lower stratum were turned into erotic frivolity. The popular utopian spirit and the new historic awareness began to fade" (p. 103). His attraction to the form is due to the adaptations of Rabelais's novels in court ballets. See H.-E. Clouzot, "Ballets tirés de Rabelais au XVIIe siècle," *Revue des Etudes Rabelaisiennes* 5 (1907): 90–7.

39. Bakhtin links the process of rebirth through carnivalesque laughter to an eventual revolution of the oppressed. *Rabelais and His World*, p. 49.

40. I will pursue the link between burlesque ballet, Molière's comedy-ballets, and political opposition in Chapter 4 and in the Epilogue.

41. I do not think this question is collapsible into the thesis proposed by Robert Garapon that farce simply pervades court entertainment throughout the baroque era. Garapon gives much too broad a definition of farce while failing to identify the determining characteristics of court ballet. See his "La Permanence de la farce dans les divertissements de cour au XVIIe siècle," *Cahiers de l'Association Internationale des Etudes Françaises* 9 (June 1957): 117–27.

42. See Mikhail Bakhtin, *Problems of Dostoevsky's Poetics*, trans. Caryl Emerson (Minneapolis: University of Minnesota Press, 1984), pp. 106–37.

43. See Sachs, *World History of the Dance*, p. 393. Fournel also calls it the golden age of ballet (*Les Contemporains de Molière*, p. 184).

44. On the noble style from a technical viewpoint, see Wendy Hilton, *Dance of Court and Theater: The French Noble Style, 1690–1725* (Princeton, N.J.: Princeton University Press, 1981). For other stylistic viewpoints, see Francine Lancelot, "Les Ornements dans la danse baroque," in *Les Goûts-Réünis*, 72–8, and Christine Bayle, "De la composition chorégraphique . . . à la composition chorégraphique," 79–89, in ibid.

45. Susan Manning discusses this twentieth-century choreographic issue in *Feminism and Nationalism in the Dances of Mary Wigman* (Berkeley and Los Angeles: University of California Press, in press).

46. This account in no way presupposes that geometrical dances can be "reconstructed." Rather, the research aimed ultimately at a theoretical profile pertinent to all geometrical dances of the period. That theory could be redeployed in the performance of what I call a historical construction. I devote fuller discussion to connections between hermeneutics and performance in the Epilogue.

47. Other important events predate this piece and prefigure court ballet. See Frances Yates on the Fontainebleau fêtes (1564), the Bayonne fêtes (1565), and the "Paradis d'amour" (1572) in *French Academies*, pp. 251–7, and *The Valois Tapestries*, pp. 85–6. But the most important of all fêtes predating *Le Balet comique* is *Le Balet des Polonais* (1573), for which a libretto does survive. See Prunières, *Le Ballet de cour en France*, pp. 55–7; Yates, *The Valois Tapestries*, pp. 67–72; and McGowan, *L'Art*, pp. 41–2. Curiously, the copious references to dance in the segment of the *Polonais* libretto entitled "Chorea nympharum" have never been analyzed by these writers. I will discuss "Chorea nympharum" in Chapter 1.

48. Norbert Elias develops the notion of *homo clausus* in the introduction to the 1968 edition of *The Civilizing Process: The History of Manners*, trans. Edmund Jephcott (New York: Urizen Books, 1986), pp. 221–63. Joan DeJean discusses this introduction in the final chapter of her *Libertine Strategies*, "The Other in the Grand Siècle," pp. 157–63.

49. See Octave Nadal, "L'Ethique de la gloire au dix-septième siècle," *Mercure de France* 308 (Jan.–Apr. 1950): 22–34.

50. "Homo ludens" is a term I adopt from Johan Huizinga rather than Bakhtin. See *Homo Ludens: A Study of the Play Element in Culture* (Boston: Beacon, 1950). Given the lack of conceptual distance between those "doing" carnival and the idea that carnival expresses in Bakhtin's mind, the notion of play is appropriate and helpful here in contrasting Bakhtin with Elias. I do not intend, however, to imply any confusion between the

51. The term *"homo strategicus"* was suggested to me by Jean-Pierre Etienvre, "Du jeu comme métaphore politique," *Poétique* 56 (Nov. 1983): 410.

52. See the respective introductions to their collections of librettos by Lacroix and Fournel. In a review article about Fournel, Louis Liévin encapsulated this view as follows: "They were not demented, they were depraved. The court was profoundly corrupted." He also speaks of "these gross and immoral spectacles." See Louis Liévin, "Le Ballet de cour et les moeurs sous Louis XIV," *Revue Contemporaine* (1870); 117 and 127. This judgement is to be expected in one who believes dance is only a natural manifestation, never a cultural and rhetorical construction employing the body as a figure.

53. For a general introduction to Molière's comedy-ballet, see Robert McBride, "Ballet" A Neglected Key to Molière's Theatre," *Dance Research* 2, no. 1 (Spring 1984): 3–18.

54. As a librettist, Benserade is generally prized for the literary value of his verse in the literary wasteland that is court ballet. Benserade is also praised for the way his verse points the way to the more lyric qualities associated with the development of a French operatic style in singing. In other words, Benserade's contribution is particularly valued because it allows court ballet to develop into something other than itself: opera. See Mme L. Maurice-Amour, "Benserade, Michel Lambert et Lulli," *Cahiers de l'Association Internationale des Etudes Françaises* 9 (June 1957): 53–76. For an account of the way Benserade's verse fostered a freer combination of syllable lengths and rhythmic units than in either measured music or *air de cour* employed by burlesque ballet, thereby favoring a less rhetorical, more passionate, delivery, see Patricia Ranum, "Audible Rhetoric and Mute Rhetoric: The 17th Century French Sarabande," *Early Music* 14, no. 1 (Feb. 1986); 26–7.

55. See Urbain-Victor Chatelain, *Le Surintendant Nicolas Foucquet, protecteur des lettres des arts et des sciences* (Geneva: Slatkine Reprints, 1971), pp. 461–88.

56. Fouquet was neither a noble nor disloyal to the king, but his sumptuary ostentation was perceived as provocative by the young Louis XIV. According to Daniel Dessert, the *affaire Fouquet* was trumped up by Colbert to protect himself from similar charges following the death of Mazarin. In Dessert's analysis, both Louis and Fouquet were victims of their own naiveté, manipulated by a post-Fronde ruling elite covering its tracks. See Daniel Dessert, *Argent, pouvoir et société au Grand Siècle* (Paris: Fayard, 1984).

57. Molière contributed *La Princesse d'Elide* and *George Dandin* respectively to these festivities. See Jean-Marie Apostolidès, *Le Roi-Machine: Spectacle et politique au temps de Louis XIV* (Paris: Minuit, 1981), esp. pp. 59–65. Apostolidès hypothesizes that court ballet survived until the monarchical discourse "filled it to bursting," at which point it "exploded" (p. 62). In a sense this statement is worked out in greater detail by the present study. Yet I cannot agree with the way Apostolidès theorizes the evolution of court ballet prior to comedy-ballet. He maintains that the visual dominated the written in *Le Balet comique* and that the subsequent history of librettos from Bordier to Molière through Benserade shows a gradual encroachment of the text on visual material. In contrast, my interpretation proposes that the text dominated early composite spectacle, lost its power in the subsequent burlesque period, and regained strength with Benserade and, however ambivalently, with Molière. See ibid., pp. 60–2.

58. See Walter Benjamin, *Illuminations*, ed. Hannah Arendt (New York: Schocken, 1976), p. 223. I am not proposing a postauratic reconstruction: dance is too reliant on presence to become a simulacrum of itself. Instead, I propose that the contents of the "aura" in reconstruction be shifted and relocated by theory rather than presupposed by a slavish obeisance to images.

59. The phrase "Dance as Text" as the title of this book is borrowed from a special session of the Modern Language Association in 1984, organized by Susan Foster, in which I participated.

60. The idea of a bodily writing came into vogue again toward the end of the nineteenth century through Mallarmé's reflections on dance. See Mary Lewis Shaw, "Ephemeral Signs: Ap-

28. Ibid.
29. On the relationship of the labyrinth to textuality, see Doob, *The Idea of the Labyrinth*. In his unpublished paper, "On the Bed of Polyclitus: Ancient Sculpture and Renaissance Aesthetics" (read at the conference, Mannerism at the Crossroad: Eccentricity and Interdisciplinarity, Indiana University, Bloomington, March 28, 1990), Leonard Barkan suggested that the human figure subsumed by geometrical patterning in Renaissance art signifies a move toward "decorative independence." He also proposed that geometry was later replaced by a turned or twisted body. Both of these ideas confirm my findings in contemporaneous court ballet. Although both geometry and writing – of which one can already see a hint in the chaotic meandering of the transitions in geometrical dance – come about in fine art through quotations of classical sources, they also intentionally ambiguate the narrative content of those sources, thus shaping an autonomous, self-reflected history within the art work. We shall see in what follows that the turned and twisted body is essential to the choreographic aesthetic of burlesque ballet. It already exists in embryo in geometrical dance.
30. Bocangel on movement in sculpted human figures, quoted by Maravall, *Culture of the Baroque*, p. 176.
31. See Brantôme, *Oeuvres complètes,* vol. 5, p. 59.
32. Librettos indicate that such disjointed transitions are a feature of much court ballet choreography and are not limited to geometrical dances alone.
33. *Vandosme,* p. 24.
34. *Chaînes* ("chains") are mentioned in *Le Balet comique, Le Ballet de Monseigneur le duc de Vandosme, Le Balet de la reyne* (1609), *Le Ballet du veritable amour* (1618), and *Le Ballet de la Royne representant la Beauté de ses nymphes* (1619).
35. Brantôme, *Oeuvres complètes,* vol. 5, p. 59.
36. See Julia Kristeva's theory of the semiotic *chora* in *Revolution in Poetic Language,* trans. Margaret Waller (New York: Columbia University Press, 1984). Kristeva adapts the term *chora* from Plato's *Timaeus* (50e–51b), a text that is also at the origin of what James Miller calls the *"choreia topos"* (40c–d).

37. Jean-Antoine de Baïf, "Au roy," in *Euvres en rime* (Paris: Alphonse Lemerre, 1883), p. 230.
38. D. P. Walker, "The Influence of Musique Mesurée à l'Antique Particularly on the Airs de Cour of the Early Seventeenth Century," *Musica disciplina* (1948): 142.
39. Ibid., pp. 8–9. See also, Walker, "La musique des intermèdes Florentins de 1589 et l'humanisme," in *Les Fêtes de la Renaissance,* ed. Jean Jacquot (Paris: C.N.R.S., 1973), vol. 1, pp. 132–44.
40. See Michel Foucault, *The Order of Things: An Archaeology of the Human Sciences* (New York: Vintage, 1973), esp. p. 42.
41. Ibid.
42. For a fuller discussion of the phenomenon of *fantasmata,* see *The Dancing Body,* pp. 58–66. In that study, I show that an Italian dance aesthetic originating in the fifteenth century had a decisive influence on the syntax of the sixteenth-century French *basse danse.* This influence of the Italian aesthetic on the French led me to posit a common theory of kinetic theatricality perceptible despite national differences in style and dress. In what follows, I see the same Italian aesthetic as equally influential on French geometrical dance. See also Mark Franko, "The Notion of *Fantasmata* in Fifteenth-Century Italian Dance Treatises," *Dance Research Annual* 17 (1987): 68–86; "Deux métamorphoses de Perrault," in *Corps Ecrit* 26 (1988): 123–9; and "La Théâtralité du corps dansant," in *Le Corps à la Renaissance,* ed. Jean Céard, Marie Madeleine Fontaine, and Jean-Claude Margolin (Paris: Aux Amateurs de Livres, 1990), pp. 133–42; and Rudolf zur Lippe, *Naturbeherrschung am Menschen* 1, p. 163–81.
43. Domenico da Piacenza, *De arte saltandi e choreas ducendi* (Paris: Bibliothèque nationale), Ms. it. 972, fol. 2 (my translation). Again, it should be stressed that *fantasmata* is an unacknowledged manifestation of Renaissance Neoplatonism since it finds its earliest expression in the writing of Plotinus, the founder of Neoplatonic philosophy. See Miller, "Holding the Pose," in *Measures of Wisdom,* pp. 140–232.
44. Zur Lippe critiques Ingrid Brainard's contention that the pose was above all an expressive tool. See *Naturbeherrschung am Menschen* 1, pp. 170–1. He argues that poses were pri-

marily expressive of theoretical consciousness of dance. If we must say that the pose expresses at all, then it expresses self-reflection and is mimetic of the act of dancing coming to consciousness. This is quite different from Brainard's assertion of a pantomimic pose. While I find zur Lippe's analysis of the Medusa image brilliant, his interpretation of the falcon suffers from misplaced emphasis. He pictures the falcon as gliding on the air in search of prey. But Domenico describes the falcon as taking off from the earth: the bird's movement is symbolic of movement's rebirth from stillness, and the meaning of the term "falcon" in Domenico's writing should be qualified by its surrounding context. In zur Lippe's reading, both the Medusa and the falcon images correspond to allegorical moments of repose. In fact, the falcon serves to represent the resumption of motion for Domenico. The broader problem is that zur Lippe equates *fantasmata* with the pose, overlooking that *fantasmata* designates the whole dialectical rapport between pose and movement. See ibid., p. 167. By the same token, zur Lippe does not recognize the ideological context of moderation in all of its ramifications. He sees moderation in choreographed dances as a way to overcome the church's misgivings about physical movement. By introducing moderation, the Renaissance would achieve access to bodily movement as an end in itself. "Obstinacy and Possession," he writes, "are the outer poles of a lively art" (pp. 198-9). But these outer poles – utter control and utter abandonment of control – structure the very notion of moderation that, like virtue itself, is defined as an avoidance of extremes. Thus, moderation is not simply an alibi whose performance qualities allow something else to happen, it is the very structure through which the self is allowed to appear or in which the self is constructed as an appearance. By acknowledging yet sidestepping this ideological net, zur Lippe injects a different paradigm into the historically determined ideology of Renaissance dance. In other terms, he counterbalances Renaissance ideology with what he considers to be dance's virtual historical potential. Thus, there is a considerable to and fro in zur Lippe's text between the virtual and the historical. The historical potential of self-expression is, in my view, activated much more pertinently – both theoretically and visually – in American modern dance of the late nineteenth and early twentieth century by dancers such as Isadora Duncan. Nevertheless, the notion of the *posa* in its theoretical formulation by Domenico is certainly relevant to early modern dance since the latter developed in part from statue posing. See Nancy Lee Chalfa Ruyter, *Reformers and Visionaries: The Americanization of the Art of Dance* (New York: Dance Horizons, 1979), pp. 17-30, and Katherine M. Adelman, "Statue-Posing in the Late Nineteenth Century Physical Culture Movement," in *Proceedings: 5th Canadian Symposium on the History of Sport and Physical Education* (Toronto: University of Toronto, 1982), pp. 308-17.

45. C. Mazzi, "Il 'Libro dell'arte del danzare' di Antonio Cornazano," *La Bibliofilia* 17 (1915): 11. Zur Lippe discusses the reticence of later Italian dance masters – from Cornazano and Ebreo da Pesaro to Negri and Caroso a century later – with regard to the pose. See *Naturbeherrschung am Menschen* 1, pp. 173-4. Nevertheless, he maintains that the pose was foundational to Western theatrical dance. I would amend this by the following: (1) it is not the pose as such that is foundational but the fantasmatic process in which the pose plays an essential part; (2) the fantasmatic process is manifestly present in French baroque dance, as the following description of a dancer attests: "Quelquefois il laissoit passer une cadence entière sans se mouvoir, non plus qu'une statuë, & puis partant comme un trait, on le voyoit à l'autre bout de la sale, avant que l'on eust le loisir de s'appercevoir qu'il estoit parti" ("Now and then he would let a whole rhythmic unit go by, moving no more than a statue and then, setting off like an arrow, he would be at the other end of the room before anyone had time to realize that he had departed"). Father François Pomey, "Description d'une Sarabande dansée," in *Le Dictionnaire royal augmenté* (Lyons: 1671), cited in Ranum, "Audible Rhetoric and Mute Rhetoric," pp. 34-5.

46. Maravall, *Culture of the Baroque*, p. 252.

47. See Ingrid Brainard, *The Art of Courtly Dancing in the Early Renaissance* (West New-

ton, Mass.: Brainard, 1981), p. 53. This book is an abbreviated reworking of Brainard's "Die Choreographie der Hoftänze in Burgund, Frankreich und Italien im 15. Jahrhundert" (Ph.D. diss., Georg August University, 1956). The dissertation contains more detailed study of Domenico's concept of fullness and void in dance technical terms.

48. Werner Jaeger, *Paideia: The Ideals of Greek Culture*, trans. Gilbert Highet (Oxford: Oxford University Press, 1962), vol. 1, pp. 125–6. "Rhythm then," writes Jaeger, "is that which imposes bonds on movement and confines the flux of things . . . the original conception which lies beneath the Greek discovery of rhythm in music and dancing is not *flow* but *pause*, the steady limitation of movement" (p. 126).

49. See Emile Benveniste, "La notion de 'rythme' dans son expression linguistique," in *Problèmes de linguistique générale* (Paris: Gallimard, 1966), vol. 1, p. 329. The key text of reference for the etymology of the term *rhythm* is Aristotle, *Metaphysics* 1:4:985b. Domenico da Piacenza alludes to the same Aristotelian passage in describing what he means by fullness and void in movement. Domenico links fullness and void to natural and accidental movement, on the beat versus between the beat, and speech and silence respectively (see da Piacenza, *De Arte saltardi*, Ms. It., p. 2r). Aristotle links fullness to the solidity of bodies and the void to "what is not," presumably space. He concludes, however, that "Void is as real as Body." Aristotle shows that everything is caused by the interaction of these two principles that yield shape, arrangement, and position. The examples he gives of these three qualities are written characters. While neither Aristotle nor Domenico da Piancenza is concerned with geometrical dance, one can see that the creators of geometrical dance were concerned with absorbing earlier theory in a potent choreographic structure.

50. Benveniste, "La notion de 'rythme'," p. 333. Benveniste specifies what rhythm meant: "Form in the instant that it is assumed by what moves, is mobile and fluid, form which has no organic consistency: it belongs to the *pattern* of a fluid element, to an arbitrarily fashioned character . . . 'configurations' with neither fixity nor natural necessity and result-

ing from an arrangement constantly subject to change" (ibid.).

51. The term *fantasmata* itself may reflect Plato's *phantasmein* meaning "to simulate." This would be true because both movement and pose are designated by the term *fantasmata* in their mutual tendency to deny one another and thus simulate each other. Furthermore, in Platonic art theory, a written character would indeed be a simulacrum: the copy of a referent (a thing in nature) that is a likeness of the essential idea. The written character for Plato is the copy of a copy: a simulacrum. Thus, if the body imitates a written character, it is third-generation copy.

52. See Wlad Godzich's interesting treatment of Ruskin's distinction between *aesthesis* and *theoria* in "The Tiger on the Paper Mat," foreword to Paul de Man, *The Resistance to Theory* (Minneapolis: University of Minnesota Press, 1986), pp. ix–xviii.

53. *Aristotle's Poetics* (New York: Hill & Wang, 1961), p. 10.

54. In the last of the Valois court ballets (1584–5), dancers spelled out the names of the king and queen, Henry and Louise, with their bodily postures. See Roy C. Strong, "Festivals for the Garter Embassy at the Court of Henri III," *Journal of the Warburg and Courtauld Institutes* 22 (1959): 68–9.

55. Michel Foucault, "Body/Power," in *Power/Knowledge: Selected Interviews and Other Writings, 1972–1977*, ed. by Colin Gordon (New York: Pantheon, 1972), p. 55.

2. UT VOX CORPUS, 1581

1. Sparshott, *Off the Ground*, p. 50.

2. This is clearly one of the dangers of a phenomenological approach to dance.

3. Yates, *The Valois Tapestries*, p. 54.

4. There is doubtless a profound historical link between the organization of bodies in theatrical space (choreography) and the notion of a national topography (chorography). The secondary and rhetorical meaning of the term *chorographia* is the description of a nation. See Richard A. Lanham, *A Handlist of Rhetorical Terms* (Berkeley and Los Angeles: University of California Press, 1969), p. 23.

5. It was commissioned and danced by Queen Louise de Lorraine and the members of the court of Henri III. Yates stresses that Cath-

erine de' Medici, the Queen Mother, was the mastermind of Valois productions. The performance may have taken place either in the Louvre's Grande Salle or in the Salle de Bourbon of the Petit Palais. The attribution of a place for the performance of *Le Balet comique* is not simply a matter carelessly glossed over by generations of negligent commentators, as Germaine Prudhommeau suggests in her article "A propos du *Balet comique de la Reine*," *La Recherche en Danse* 3 (1984): 15–24. Contradictions are inherent in the primary material. The libretto only states "la grande salle de Bourbon," which can be read as a cross between the "grande salle du Louvre" and the "salle de Bourbon" in the Palais du Petit Bourbon, where many ballets were performed. "On voyoit tout cela reluire," notes Brantôme, "dans une salle du bal, au Pallais ou au Louvre" ("One saw the radiance [of the ballets] in a ballroom in the Palais or the Louvre"). See his *Oeuvres complètes*, Vol. 5, p. 77. The manuscript program for the *Magnificences* in the Bibliothèque nationale (Fonds français 15, 831, fol. 92) states "Le ballet de la Royne au Louvre" ("the Queen's ballet at the Louvre"). It is reproduced in Frances A. Yates, "The *Joyeuse Magnificences* (1581)," in *Astraea*, pp. 169–72. Furthermore, the *Mémoires* of l'Estoile state, "Le dimanche 15e, la Royne first son festin au Louvre, lequel elle finist par un ballet de Circé et de ses nymphes" ("On Sunday the fifteenth, the Queen had her festivity at the Louvre, which she completed by a ballet about Circe and her nymphs"). See *Mémoires*, vol. 2, p. 33. While the two above-mentioned sources do not agree on the date of performance, they do concur on the place. Despite these sources giving the Louvre as the place of the ballet's performance, Prudhommeau gives no hard evidence to back her opinion in favor of the Palais du Petit Bourbon, but because the space of the Palais was appreciably larger than that of the Louvre, it is easier and perhaps more pleasing to imagine the ballet in it. See Dianne L. Woodruff, "The Ballet Comique in the Petit Bourbon: A Practical View," in *Proceedings of the Society of Dance History Scholars* (1986): 91–129. It should be added that the hypothesis of the Palais is not new. It was proposed twenty-five years ago by Wilma S. Deierkauf-Holsboer in *L'Histoire de la*

mise en scène dans le théâtre français à Paris de 1600 à 1673 (Paris: Nizet, 1960), p. 28.

6. Yates views this development in music and dance of the late Renaissance as fundamentally academic. The compromise "is characteristic of the whole academic attitude in which classicism does not involve a violent break with the past." For a remarkably penetrating analysis of the aesthetics of this approach in music, see her *The French Academies*, pp. 56–8.

7. Antoine de Baïf, "Letters Patent and Statutes of Baïf's Academy" cited in Yates, *The French Academies*, p. 320.

8. That these three goals are eminently rhetorical can easily be demonstrated by comparing them to the three genres of rhetorical discourse: the deliberative, the juridical, and the epideictic. See Franko, "The Rhetorical Code," in *The Dancing Body*, pp. 14–17.

9. Walker, "The Influence of musique mesurée à l'antique," pp. 145–6. In this article Walker explains that *Le Balet comique*'s composers "were consciously imitating *musique mesurée*" and that the homophonic songs only lacked "a regular poetic meter," being otherwise "indistinguishable from *musique mesurée*." See also Frances A. Yates, "The Measured Poetry and Music," in *The French Academies*, pp. 36–76, and Edouard Frémy, *Origine de l'Académie française des derniers Valois, de poésie et musique (1570–76), du palais (1576–85)* (Geneva: Slatkine, 1969).

10. See Plato's *Symposium* in *The Collected Dialogues*, ed. Edith Hamilton and Huntington Cairns (Princeton, N.J.: Princeton University Press, 1973), p. 540 (187).

11. See Stephen Orgel, *The Jonsonian Masque* (New York: Columbia University Press, 1981).

12. See Harry Levin, *The Myth of the Golden Age in the Renaissance* (Oxford: Oxford University Press, 1969).

13. A similar though more elementary form of wish fulfillment is at work in Mellin de Saint Gelais's "mascarade de six dames habillees en sibylles" (Saint Germain en Laye, 1554) in which all good things are prophesied for the royal family. See *Oeuvres* (Lyon: A. de Harsy, 1574), pp. 13–14.

14. The king is also an effective though nonactive performer in the 1610 *Ballet de Monseigneur le duc de Vandosme*.

15. Frances A. Yates develops the notion of the

Renaissance exercising a "refined and learned type of magic" in court ballets. See her *Astraea*, pp. 159–62.

16. Ibid.

17. On the theological and political ramifications of grace, see Eduardo Saccone, "Grazia, Sprezzatura, Affetazione in *The Courtier*," in *Castiglione: The Ideal and the Real in Renaissance Culture*, edited by Robert W. Hanning and David Rosand (New Haven, Conn.: Yale University Press, 1983), pp. 45–67, and Franko, *The Dancing Body*, pp. 67–78.

18. Rudolf zur Lippe, Geometrisierung, p. 16.

19. See Miller, *Measures of Wisdom*, p. 169.

20. D'Aubignac defines the "act" as that which occurs between two songs. See his *La Pratique du theatre* (Geneva: Slatkine, 1971), 3, 5, p. 195. Intervals between the acts were marked by the sound of violins, he tells us in 1635, and were occasionally accompanied by dances and ballets. There is only one other example of an exclusively musical segment identified as an interlude in court ballet. In *Le Ballet du roy ou la vieille cour* (Paris, 1635), we read that "un concert de luths . . . ayant fait l'intermède, la Déesse de la Seine . . . fit un récit" ("a lute concert . . . having done the intermezzo, the Goddess of the Seine . . . performed a récit"). See Lacroix, vol. 5, p. 64. The term *intermezzo* is used more often in an arbitrary way. For example, in *Les Resveries d'un extravagant* (Dijon, c. 1633), sixteen *entrées* of an arbitrary nature are followed by "Intermède: Les Fourberies," consisting of fourteen other *entrées* that complete the ballet (Lacroix, vol. 5, pp. 9–19). Nor is there any reason why an episode entitled "Intermede des quatre Chevaliers des adventures" in the *Adventure de Tancrede* (Paris, 1619) should be so called (Lacroix, vol. 2, p. 179). Furthermore, two scene changes are called intermezzi in the *Explication allegorique du ballet de Madame* (Lacroix, vol. 2, pp. 64–5).

21. It is presumably from similar transitional dissolutions of pattern into choreographic flux that eleven new patterns successively emerge.

22. A similar color coding may have worked to the same effect in *Au balet de Madame* (Tours, 1593). In that ballet, ten nymphs are divided in two groups. Five are "habillees de blanc ayant les corps incarnatz" ("dressed in white with red bodies") and the other five are "habillees d'incarnat ayant les corps blancs"

("dressed in red with white bodies"). See Marcel Paquot, "Comédies-Ballets représentées en l'honneur de Madame, Soeur du Roi Henri IV," in *Revue Belge de Philologie et d'Histoire* 10 (1931): 969.

23. Pontus de Tyard, *Solitaire Second* (Geneva: Droz, 1980), p. 83.

24. Furthermore, Beaujoyeulx lacks consistency in his terminology because "ballet" signifies alternately dance and song together or dance alone, whereas "poetry" denotes either sung verse or, on occasion, dramatic poetry. Beaujoyeulx will write to the king: "Ce sera votre histoire poetique, ou bien si lon veut, comique" ("This will be your poetic, or, if you prefer, your theatrical history"). *Le Balet comique*, a.iij.; MacClintock and MacClintock, p. 28.

25. For example, it is difficult to interpret the successive notations of the terms *récit* and *ballet* in the margins of a descriptive libretto of *Ballet du soleil pour la reine* (Paris: 1621) as indications of simultaneous use. At the most, one can say that the terms *récit* and *ballet* indicate close sequence rather than overlapping of word and dance. According to André Verchaly, the *récit* was a sung monody with instrumental accompaniment. See his "Poésie et air de cour en France jusqu'à 1620," in *Musique et poésie au XVIe siècle* (Paris: C.N.R.S., 1954), p. 222.

26. Menestrier, *Des Ballets anciens*, p. 207.

27. In keeping with this conclusion, the preface to *Ballet de la prosperité des armes de la France* (Paris: 1641) calls dancing segments "acts" that are separated by *récits* as if by interludes: "Les recits separent les actes, et les entrees de danseurs sont autant de scenes" ("The *récits* separate the acts, and the *entrées* by dancers constitute the scenes"). Lacroix, vol. 5, p. 230.

28. Beaujoyeulx stresses that "l'invention est principalement composee de ces deux parties" ("the invention is composed principally of these two parts"), i.e., the act and the intermezzo. He seems conscious of attributing meaning to the intermezzo in the title: "Le titre et inscription de ce livre est sans exemple" ("The title and inscription of this book is unusual"). *Le Balet comique*, "Au lecteur"; *MacClintock and MacClintock*, p. 33. Thus, he refers to the title *Le Balet comique*, in which the term *ballet* is the noun and whose adjective refers to drama. The most accurate

translation of this title would be *Theatrical Ballet*.

29. Charles Delmas, "*Le Ballet comique de la reine* (1581): structure et signification," *Revue d'Histoire du Théâtre* 2 (1970): 148.
30. Ibid., p. 145.
31. Ibid.
32. *Le Balet comique*, pp. 22v–23r; MacClintock and MacClintock, p. 55.
33. Unfortunately, no visual or descriptive data relate the frozen posture of the "captives" to the postures assumed within the holding patterns of the geometrical dance in the *entrée* immediately preceding it.
34. *Le Balet comique*, p. 39v; MacClintock and MacClintock, p. 60.
35. *Le Balet comique*, p. 48r; MacClintock and MacClintock, p. 79.
36. Pontus de Tyard, *Solitaire second*, p. 84.
37. Ibid., p. 83.
38. Giovanni Maria Artusi, *Seconda parte dell'Artusi overo della imperfettioni della moderna musica* (Venice: Vincenti, 1603), p. 5.
39. Pontus de Tyard, *Solitaire second*, p. 103.
40. Gioseffo Zarlino, *Le Istitutioni harmoniche del reverendo M. Gioseffo Zarlino da Chioggia* (Venice: Francesco Senese, 1562), p. 17.
41. Giovanni Maria Artusi, *L'Arte del contrapunto* (Venice: Vincenti, 1598–9), p. 10.
42. And by the same token, Foucault probably went too far in casting Renaissance culture under the aegis of a resemblance theory of metaphor. The ground of proportion establishes only a very provisory likeness in *Le Balet comique*. The body as metaphor operates equally well through semantic polarity despite the great chain of being and Foucault's world folded in on itself.
43. Lacroix, vol. 4, p. 212. For further information of Colletet's ballets, see McGowan, *L'Art*, pp. 155–67.
44. Colletet cited in Lacroix, vol. 4, p. 212. In musical theory, the production of sound is envisaged by conceptualizing the movement of bodies in air: "Corpo sonoro e quello che percosso . . . manda fuori alcun suono" ("A sonorous body is one that beats . . . sends forth a sound"). See Artusi, *L'Arte*, p. 10. Zarlino will say that sounds take their principle from movement ("havendo li suoni il loro principio dal movimento"). *Le Institutioni harmoniche*, p. 13.
45. Foucault, *The Order of Things*, p. 29.
46. "L'Apparente est celle que la voix, et les instruments forment" ("The Apparent is the kind formed by voices and instruments"). "Latent" or "secret" harmony, as Garel explains, has nothing to do with the audition of sound and is "*proportionale.*" See Elie Garel, *Les Oracles françois ou explication allegorique du Balet de madame, soeur aisnee du roy* (Paris, P. Chevalier, 1615), p. 211.
47. *Le Balet comique de la Royne* has never, to my knowledge, been reconstructed.
48. Sparshott, *Off the Ground*, p. 52.
49. Ibid. Sparshott writes well on why dance did not formerly attain the status of a fine art and did not become the object of a theoretical reflection. Yet at times, he pictures the failure of dance to compel thinkers – primarily Hegel – to espouse its importance as shortcomings one can trace back to the historical reality of performance. Occasionally, the theory that he critiques for having excluded dance blurs his apprehension of dance history per se. Sparshott presents dance history before the twentieth century as if it unfolded in a continuous present with regard to its possible effects. He considers the cultural meaning of dance in and for a given historical period as "uncritical." Although it is true that many dance historians have not raised the proper questions, history is still important as that institutional context he makes such good use of in examining twentieth-century dance (p. 78). Without the proper context – a historicized horizon of expectation – we must assume that dance only begins to become interesting in the twentieth century and that, even in our own time, the interplay of ideas and sensory experience should be kept to a minimum.
50. Historicizing is something that aestheticians are in general loath to do. But that is no reason to obligingly confine dance history to a fact-finding rather than a fact-interpreting mode. Or rather, that *is* a reason to distinguish critical dance theory from conventional history and aesthetics alike. Dance theory should be a historicized aesthetics asking fundamental questions about the construction of meaning in dance without assuming that a historically uninformed, uniquely phenomenological perception theory will furnish answers.

51. The phrase is Artusi's in *L'Arte*, p. 1.
52. As an opposition of fast and slow, high and low, it reiterates the noble ethos inherent in the earlier *basse danse*. For more information on the *basse danse* in this connection, see Franko, "Renaissance Conduct Literature and the Basse Danse: The Kinesis of *Bonne Grâce*," in *Persons in Groups: Social Behavior as Identity Formation in Medieval and Renaissance Europe*, ed. Richard Trexler (Binghamton: Medieval and Renaissance Texts and Studies, 1985), pp. 55–66.
53. See also Francis Sparshott, "On the Question: Why Do Philosophers Neglect the Aesthetics of the Dance?" *Dance Research Journal* 15, no. 1 (Fall 1982): 11.

3. INTERLUDE

1. It will be noticed that Renaissance reconstruction as I analyze it here is closely linked to the concept of a reinventive mannerism mentioned earlier (see the Prologue, note 1). On practical applications of these ideas, see the Epilogue.
2. Michel de Montaigne, *Les Essais* (Paris: Garnier, 1962), bk. 2, chap. 6, p. 416; *The Complete Essays of Montaigne*, trans. Donald Frame (Stanford, Calif.: Stanford University Press, 1965), p. 274. All English translations of the *Essais* are drawn from Donald Frame's translation and will be referred to hereafter in notes as Frame. Pagination of the English translation will be cited in the text after a slash.
3. See Chapter 2.
4. See Chapter 4.
5. It should be remembered that prior to retreating from public life to write his *Essais*, Montaigne was mayor of Bordeaux and an occasional diplomat.
6. *Essais*, 2, 37, pp. 171–2; Frame, p. 576. "It is true, and striking," writes Hugo Friedrich, "that Montaigne cannot disguise an impulse toward polemical irritation whenever he encounters a formal and rhetorical idea of culture." *Montaigne*, trans. R. Rovini (Paris: Gallimard, 1968), p. 94.
7. "Il advient à la plus part de roidir leur contenance et leurs parolles pour en acquerir reputations" ("It happens to most men to stiffen their countenance and their words in order

thereby to acquire a reputation"). *Essais*, 2, 13, p. 3; Frame, p. 459.
8. In "Des livres," the inflation of "fantastiques elevations" ("fantastic flights") is an effect of poorly accomplished imitation and even plagiarism: "Ce qui les faict ainsi se charger de matiere, c'est le deffiance qu'ils ont de se pouvoir soustenir de leurs propres graces; il faut qu'ils trouvent un corps où s'appuyer" ("What makes them so load themselves with material is the distrust they have of being able to sustain themselves by their own graces; they have to find a body to lean on"). *Essais*, 2, 10, p. 452; Frame, p. 299. "Il leur faut plus de corps. Ils montent à cheval parce qu'ils ne sont assez forts sur leurs jambes" ("The less wit they have, the more body they need. They mount on horseback because they are not strong enough on their legs") (ibid., p. 453; Frame, p. 299).
9. Jean Starobinski analyzes the relationship of custom to nature in the context of Montaigne's attitudes toward medicine in "The Body's Moment," *Yale French Studies* 64 (1983): 273–305.
10. The reverence is an example in point: "Il est des peuples où on tourne le doz à celuy qu'on salue, et ne regarde l'on jamais celuy qu'on veut honorer. . . . "Où, pour signe de subjection, il faut hausser les espaules et baisser la teste . . . Où l'on saluë mettant le doigt à terre, et puis le haussant vers le ciel" ("There are countries where they turn their back to the person they greet, and never look at the one they wish to honor. . . . Where, for a sign of subjection you must shrug your shoulders and lower your head. . . . Where people greet one another by putting their finger to the ground and then raising it to heaven"). *Essais*, 1, 23, pp. 116–19; Frame, pp. 79–82.
11. *Essais*, 3, 13, p. 534; Frame, p. 827. See also 1, 23, p. 116; Frame, p. 79: "J'estime qu'il ne tombe en l'imagination humaine aucune fantaisie si forcenee qui ne rencontre l'exemple de quelque usage public, et par consequent que nostre discours n'estaie et ne fonde" ("I think that there falls into man's imagination no fantasy so wild that it does not match the example of some public practice, and for which, consequently, our reason does not find a stay and a foundation"). See also 3, 13, p. 538; Frame, p. 830: "La coustume a desjà,

sans y penser, imprimé si bien en moy son caractere en certaines choses, que j'appelle excez de m'en despartir" ("Habit, imperceptibly, has already so imprinted its character upon me in certain things that I call it excess to depart from it").

12. Although there is a tension in the *Essais* between nominalism and realism, *coustume* may act as an expedient though surrogate universal, Antoine Compagnon has called custom "la définition de l'universel empirique comme seul critère du naturel, à l'exclusion pleinement nominaliste d'une eventuelle essence" ("the definition of the empirical universal as sole criterion of the natural, to the nominalist exclusion of a possible essence"). Antoine Compagnon, *Nous, Michel de Montaigne* (Paris: Seuil, 1980), p. 176.

13. Montaigne establishes the conceptual framework of court ballet performance by envisaging permeable boundaries between the traditional and subversive ones to come. His thinking evidences that, without improvisation, there can be no historical context.

14. See Arlette Jouanna, *Ordre social: Mythes et hiérarchies dans la France du XVIe siècle* (Paris: Hachette, 1977).

15. See John Stuart Mill, *Philosophy of Scientific Method* (New York: Hafner, 1950), pp. 13–64.

16. Similarly, a nominalist position in "Des noms" and "Des pouces" stresses the parallelism between gestures and proper names in Montaigne's thought.

17. With the possible exception of Montaigne's own proper name. See Compagnon, *Nous, Michel de Montaigne.*

18. While I prefer the term "rehearsal" in this context, anthropologist Victor Turner's notion of "cultural performance" might also be applicable here. For Turner, cultural performance deals reflexively with anthropological, social, and metaphysical categories. Whatever symbolic form such performance might take, it is "liminal" for Turner: cultural performance lies between the subjunctive and the indicative, between what is and what might be. Performance attempts to reconcile and transform while pointing out "the fundamental indeterminacy that lurks in the cracks and crevices of all our sociocultural 'constructions of reality.'" See his *The Anthropology of Performance* (New York: PAJ Publications, 1986), p. 60.

19. *Essais*, 1, 26, p. 163; Frame, p. 112. This passage leads directly into the already quoted one on learning capers.

20. François Rigolot, *Les Métamorphoses de Montaigne* (Paris: P.U.F., 1988), p. 203.

21. This misapprehension stems from another, more evident in an earlier study for this chapter, "Les Jeux de Montaigne," in *Les Jeux à la Renaissance*, ed. Philippe Ariès and Jean-Claude Margolin (Paris: Vrin, 1982). There, Rigolot writes, "If hunting is the quintessential noble leisure activity, dance is more of a popular and rustic pastime" (p. 329). Rigolot does not take into account that dancing in the Renaissance was a courtly as well as a popular pastime.

22. Only an inquiry into cultural performance transcending the immediate boundaries of the critical literary endeavor can reveal that Montaigne's concept of movement *does* have a cultural and rhetorical precedent. One might, then, well ask whether the sharp distinctions drawn by Rigolot between historical and poetic knowledge and inquiry are truly in the deeper interests of literary exegesis. Should we not rather rehearse the questions of literature within the broader confines of cultural performance?

4. POLITICAL EROTICS OF BURLESQUE BALLET, 1624–1627

1. But it should be noted that even initial unity is presented as risqué and spirited rather than sober and serious. The color green frequently has off-color connotations in French, making it part of the semantic field of *gaillard* (galant and spirited).

2. Bakhtin, *Rabelais and His World*, p. 255.

3. Rosemund Tuve, *Elizabethan and Metaphysical Imagery* (Chicago: University of Chicago Press, 1947), p. 136.

4. "Ballet dansé par le roy (la délivrance de Persée)," (1617) in Lacroix, vol. 2, p. 111.

5. See Francis Bar, *Le Genre burlesque en France au XVII siècle: Etude de style* (Paris: Editions D'Artrey, 1960), p. XIII. Bar admits that burlesque ballet preceded burlesque poetry in France. He sees ballet as part of an older current of burlesque prose literature (p. 409). He

is careful, however, not to identify the verse in burlesque ballet librettos with burlesque poetry, except for two or three ballets, among them *Les Fées*. Perhaps in order to distance burlesque poetry from its use in burlesque performance, Bar mistakenly asserts that the *récits* were not spoken in the ballets but only read by the audience in their libretti (ibid., note 28). He certainly demonstrates detachment from the traditions of French court ballet when he asserts that any mention of dance in burlesque verse automatically deprives the character depicted as dancing of all "heroic dignity" (p. 182). Although one would expect this often to be the case in burlesque verse, the context of dance extends beyond the burlesque precisely to include heroic dignity. Furthermore, many of the dance types Bar quotes in the section of his chapter on technicisms entitled "Danses" seem in no way ironic.

6. See Stephen Orgel, "Nobody's Perfect: Or Why did the English Stage Take Boys for Women?" in *Displacing Homophobia: Gay Male Perspectives in Literature and Culture*, ed. Ronald R. Butters, John M. Clum, and Michael Moon (Durham, N.C.: Duke University Press, 1989), pp. 7–29.

7. Linda L. Carroll has analyzed similar phenomena in fifteenth-century Italian comedy. See her "Who's on Top? Gender as Societal Power Configuration in Italian Renaissance Drama," *Sixteenth Century Journal* 20, no. 4 (Winter 1989): 531–58.

8. *Le grand bal de la douairière de Billebahaut* (Paris, 1626) in Lacroix, vol. 3, p. 155. Another scene with an androgyne appears in *Le Ballet des deux magiciens* (Paris, 1636) in which "trois Sardanapales sortent avec des habits d'hommes et de femmes, une masse d'armes d'un costé, et une quenouille de l'autre, faisant connoistre qu'ils ne se soucient pas de se rendre blâmables pour avoir leur plaisir" ("Three Sardanapalus characters dressed as men and women, a heap of weapons on one side and a distaff on the other, made clear that they were unconcerned with drawing blame for their pleasures") (Lacroix, vol. 5, p. 137).

9. *Le Ballet politique* (1627), Bibliothèque nationale, imprimés G.30574, p. 1.

10. See *L'Art*, pp. 134–6. This seems too local an explanation for the dramatic lowering of taste standards in burlesque works. Court ballet was not a commercial enterprise dependent on mass consumption and therefore did not need to cater to the ostensible tastes of lower classes. It may, however, have shared some theoretical attributes with twentieth-century media culture. See, in this connection, Andrew Ross's thesis that contemporary popular culture may transcend mass manipulation in *No Respect: Intellectuals and Popular Culture* (New York: Routledge, 1989).

11. See Bar, *Le Genre burlesque*, p. XII.

12. These three motifs are featured in the opening *récit* of a debauched Bacchus in *Le Ballet du roy representant les Bacchanales* (1623):

> Vive la paix et ses délices;
> Je ne cherche point les combats
> Qu'avec les flacons et saucisses,
> Où mon coeur prend tous ses esbats
> Ma gloire
> C'est de boire.
>
> Lorsque je dors le mieux,
> Le bon vin me reveille,
> Et n'ay point d'yeux
> Que pour voir la bouteille.
>
> Je n'espargne point force escus
> Pour faire baiser a des coupes
> Ces damoiselles de Bacchus
> Que l'on coiffe avec des estouppes.
>
> Long life peace and delights;
> I seek out no combat
> If it is not with bottles and sausages,
> Where my heart finds its pleasure.
> My glory
> Is in drink.
>
> When I sleep the best,
> Good wine wakes me,
> I only have eyes
> For the bottle.
>
> I don't spare money
> To make them kiss at cups
> Those young Bacchic ladies
> Who can be corked with hemp.

Lacroix, vol. 22, p. 313.

13. Ferdinand Brunetière, "La Maladie du burlesque," *Revue des Deux Mondes* 5 période, vol. 34 (July–August 1906): 680.

14. DeJean, *Libertine Strategies*, p. 142. She places the sublime beyond categories of elevated or base style, in hyperbolic imagination: "The libertine makes no such distinc-

tions between beautiful and nonbeautiful, and even scorns harmony in favor of the fiery disorder of thought exploding simultaneously in multiple directions." Ibid., p. 143.

15. Sun King imagery was originated with Louis XIII and only passed on to Louis XIV. See McGowan, *L'Art*, pp. 182–4.

16. Lacroix, vol. 3, pp. 19–32. Bakhtin also remarks that "ambivalent praise of a malady, especially syphilis and gout, was common" in carnival. *Rabelais and His World*, p. 161.

17. See "Vers pour *Le Ballet du roy representant les bacchanales*," in Lacroix, vol. 2, p. 315. Joan DeJean notes that two erudite libertines, Charles Sorel and Théophile de Viau, collaborated on this ballet. See *Libertine Strategies*, p. 30, note 3.

18. See Fournel, *Les Contemporains*, vol. 2, pp. 295–324. For a list of all of Louis XIV's roles in court ballet, see Philippe Hourcade, "Louis XIV travesti," in *Cahiers de Littérature du XVIIe siècle* 6 (1984): 257–71.

19. Bakhtin has shown that travestied prophecies are a carnivalesque motif. *Rabelais and His World*, p. 235.

20. Lacroix, vol. 3, p. 124. Courtiers also ridiculed themselves and others as arbiters of fashion. In *Le Balet du Sérieux et du Grotesque* the following *récit* for the Count Harcourt as a grotesque courtier implies that his ruff and hat were "d'une figure enorme" ("for an enormous face"):

> Je suis un Courtisan qui viens donner
> la loy
> Et reformer l'abus qui regne en ces
> contrées,
> Et soustiens que tous ceux qui feront
> leurs entrées,
> Sont des extravagans s'ils ne sont
> comme moy.
>
> I am a Courtier coming to publish the
> law
> And reform the abuses reigning in
> these parts,
> I hold that all who do their *entrées*,
> Are extravagant if they do not study
> me.

The same character also asserts that those who maintain normal proportions are only suited to dance in ballets. Lacroix, vol. 3, p. 321.

21. One *récit*, for example:

> Toute sorte de fard naist de nostre
> sçavoir
> La laideur est par luy si belle qu'on
> l'adore;
> La vieille en devient jeune, et d'un
> divin pouvoir,
> Ce qui voit son couchant retourne à
> son aurore.
>
> All kinds of disguise are born of our
> knowledge
> Through it, ugliness is adorably
> beautiful;
> The old become young and of divine
> power,
> That which is at its twilight returns to
> its dawn.

Lacroix, vol. 3, p. 20.

22. Ibid., p. 22. Bourgeois are pictured as having more money than visible pomp:

> Maintes fois ces galants [courtisans]
> monstrent tout leur thresor,
> Dont la vanité mesme est la visible
> source;
> Si comme eux aux cordons nous ne
> portons point d'or,
> Nous en avons souvent beaucoup plus
> dans la bourse.
>
> Often these galants [courtiers] show all
> their treasure,
> Whose vanity is its visible source;
> If like them, we wear no cord laced
> with gold,
> We often have much more in our purse.

Ibid.

23. See Elie Garel, *Les Oracles françois ou explication allegorique du Ballet de madame, soeur aisnée du roy* (Paris: P. Chevalier, 1615), Bibliothèque de l'arsenal: Ra3 61, in 12, pp. 56–7.

24. See Etienne Thuau, *Raison d'etat et pensée politique à l'epoque de Richelieu* (Paris: Colin, 1966), p. 27.

25. Cross dressing is probably the most omnipresent motif of burlesque ballet. In *Ballet de monseigneur* le prince (1622) Monsieur Guillemin plays a "femme amoureuse de trois amans nyais" ("woman in love with three silly men") and Sieur de Boisrobert plays "la Demoiselle de Lavande" (Lacroix, vol. 2, pp.

64. Apostolidès, *Le Roi-Machine*, p. 99.
65. See Carroll, "Who's on Top?" It should be added that the notion of play could be understood as that of dance improvisation. In this connection, there are parallels to be drawn between the two dance genres under discussion. On improvisation in Italian courtly social dance, see Barbara Sparti, "Style and Performance in the Social Dances of the Italian Renaissance: Ornamentation, Improvisation, Variation and Virtuosity," in *Proceedings of the Society of Dance History Scholars* (Riverside, Calif.: Society of Dance History Scholars, 1986), pp. 31–52.
66. In addition to *Les Fées*, the most prominent examples of burlesque style were to be found in *Le Ballet de la Douairière de Billebahaut* (1626) and *Le Ballet du chateau de Bissestre* (1632).
67. *Les Fées* was written by René Bordier, set to music by Antoine Boesset, designed by Daniel Rabel, and probably choreographed by Henri, duc de Nemours. Much information on it can be found in John H. Baron's study, *Les Fées des forests de St. Germain, ballet de cour, 1625*, in *Dance Perspectives* 62, vol. 16, (New York: Dekker, 1975). See also, Margaret McGowan, *The Court Ballets of Louis XIII* (London: Victoria and Albert Museum, 1986). My interpretation of the piece differs with Baron's in that I extend its symbolic significance beyond "the five attributes most desirable in a gentleman at court" (p. 18) to the attributes of dancing and ballets per se. In studying *Les Fées*, I have supplemented Lacroix with the original libretto, *Les Fées des forests de St. Germain: Ballet* (Paris: René Giffart, 1625), Mazarine 4761.Yf.1000, from which I cite to avoid the errors of Lacroix's transcription. All page references are, however, to Lacroix. A prose synopsis of the work, without *récits*, gives a clearer idea of the fourth *entrée* and its battle scenes. See *Les Fées des forests de St. Germain – Ballet: Dansé par le roy en la salle du Louvre le 9. jour de fevrier 1625* (Paris: Jean Sara, 1625). This synopsis and an English translation of it are provided in Appendix 2.
68. Games, particularly one called "la Blanque," are important in other burlesque ballets such as *Le Balet des fols aux dames* (1627) in Lacroix, vol. 4; see also "La Blanque," in *Recueil des ballets qui ont esté joues devant la Majeste du Roy* (c. 1615), in Lacroix, vol. 2, pp. 37–53, and *Mascarades des eschecs et du maistre de l'Academie d'Hyrlande* (1607), a work presumably organized, as was *Les Fées*, by le Duc de Nemours.
69. See *Fables choisies* 12, 3 (Paris: Garnier, 1962), pp. 321–2. The apes in the illustrations for this piece appear to have lions' manes.
70. See Sonnet 68 in Saint-Amant, *Oeuvres* (1629; rpt. Paris: Didier, 1971), p. 289. Bakhtin also lists virility ("reproductive force") as a carnivalesque motif. See *Rabelais and His World*, p. 175.
71. Furetière explains the game as follows: "Un jeu qui consiste en une aiguille de fer mobile dans un cercle, aux bords duquel il y a plusieurs chiffres ou divisions, et où l'on perd ou on gagne suivant les nombres sur lesquels l'aiguille s'arreste" ("A game which consists of an iron needle moving in a circle, at whose edges are several numbered compartments, and in which one wins or loses depending on the numbers the needle settles on"). See his *Dictionnaire universel*.
72. Maravall has linked gaming with the wager as a play of tactics in the baroque mentality. In this vision, substantial essences are replaced with temporary appearances thanks to which the interplay of the individual with society becomes largely strategic. The individual needs to analyze circumstances and passing appearances, not essences. "With things and human beings," writes Maravall, "which appear in our life endowed with the indeterminable and scarcely apprehensible reality of the occasion, the mode of operating can be nothing other than gaming." See Maravall, *Culture of the Baroque*, pp. 190–7.
73. "Pour un jeu de balle forcee," in *Oeuvres poétiques de Amadis Jamyn* (Paris: 1878), p. 51.
74. For example, the librettist of the *Mascarades des eschecs et du maistre de l'Academie d'Hyrlande* (1609) recommends his piece "tant pour l'invention que parce qu'elle fut fait en deux jours, et parfaitement representé" ("as much for its inventiveness as because it was realized in two days and perfectly performed"). Librettists pride themselves on turning insurmountable time constraints to their advantage when creating choreography and scenography. Of the *Ballet de la reyne* we read: "bien qu'on n'eust eu que cinq jours

pour le preparer, et voire meme qu'on n'eust pas loisir de la repeter une seule fois, si re- üssit-il tres-heureusement" ("although we only had five days to prepare it and, indeed, it was not even rehearsed once, it was performed quite successfully"). Lacroix, vol. 2, p. 207. See also *Le Ballet des improvistes* (Paris, 1636) in which "[le roi] a resolu d'en danser un [ballet] à l'improviste, dont la diversité des vers, des pas, des gestes et des habits, fera confesser que la variété mérite absolument la qualité d'une des plus agreables choses de la nature, et que l'on en peut faire de fort belles avec peu de peine et sans longue estude" ("[the king] wanted to dance an impromptu [ballet] in which diversity of verse, steps, gestures and costume would show that variety can produce the same quality as the most beautiful things in nature and that beautiful work can be done without much trouble and long preparation"). Lacroix, vol. 5, p. 150. There are also hints at novel postures in the verse for *Le Ballet des postures* in Lacroix, vol. 4, p. 318.

75. See Abby E. Zanger, "Paralyzing Performance: Sacrificing Theater on the Altar of Publication," *Stanford French Review* 12, nos. 2–3 (1988): 179.

76. See Charles Sanders Peirce, *Philosophical Writings of Peirce*, ed. Justus Buchler (New York: Dover, n.d.), pp. 98–119.

77. Many of the parallel leg positions in the illustration suggest the *grue* of the *gaillarde*. See Thoinot Arbeau, *Orchesographie*, p. 39v. All English citations from this work are drawn from the Mary Stewart Evans translation reedited by Julia Sutton (New York: Dover, 1967), pp. 76–77, referred to hereafter in notes as Evans.

78. Saint Hubert, *La Maniere de composer et faire reussir les ballets*, pp. 12–13.

79. Le. P. Claude-François Menestrier, "Remarques pour la conduite des ballets," in *L'Autel de Lyon* (1658), reprinted in Christout, *Le Ballet de cour de Louis XIV*, p. 221.

80. Lacroix, vol. 2, pp. 157–8. In the same ballet, a courtier plays the part of a madwoman to testify to his love of a lady:

> Pour Monsieur le Baron de Palluau
> representant une folle:
>
> Il est vray, je confesse, Amour,
> Que pour jouer quelque bon tour,

> Il faut aller à ton escolle.
> La beauté dont je suis espris
> Est enfin cause que j'ay pris
> Le geste et l'habit d'une Folle

For Monsieur the Baron de Palluau playing a madwoman:

> It is true, I confess, Love,
> That to play a good trick,
> One must attend your school
> The beauty I am in love with
> Is herself the reason that I have adopted
> The gesture and the outfit of a madwoman.

Ibid., p. 159.

81. See, e.g., Ronsard's sonnet 180 from *Amours de Cassandre*, which begins, "Amour et Mars sont presque d'une sorte" ("Amour and Mars are almost of one kind"), in *Oeuvres complètes*, vol. 1, p. 78.

82. Bakhtin, *Rabelais and His World*, p. 176.

83. The term *bilboquet* actually has three meanings in seventeenth-century French. It is variously a cup and ball toy, a little figure that is always upright, and a light and frivolous person.

84. DeJean, *Libertine Strategies*, p. 166.

85. Lincoln Kirstein, *Movement and Metaphor: Four Centuries of Ballet* (New York: Praeger, 1970), p. 74.

86. See *L'Art*, p. 141. Despite the mimetic criteria intermittently applicable to all the arts of the Renaissance, McGowan does allow that court ballet rendered "essences" of things and people as well as "intellectual concepts" visible in performance.

87. See, e.g., Craig Owens, "The Allegorical Impulse: Toward a Theory of Postmodernism," in *Art after Modernism: Rethinking Representation*, ed. Brian Wallis and Marcia Tucker (New York: The New Museum of Contemporary Art, 1984), pp. 203–35.

88. Benjamin, *The Origin of German Tragic Drama*, p. 175.

89. See McGowan, *L'Art*, p. 138.

5. MOLIÈRE AND TEXTUAL CLOSURE

1. See *Le Bourgeois Gentilhomme* in Molière, *Théâtre complet*, vol. 2, p. 717. Christout characterizes the period between 1653 and 1660 as one of preciosity and fantasy in *Le*

Ballet de cour de Louis XIV. The ninth discourse of Michel de Marolle's *Mémoires* (Paris: Sommaville, 1656–7) deals extensively with court ballet. It is significant that, by mid-century, Marolles distances himself from burlesque ballet. He excludes from the category of court ballet "ces danses impudiques qui se font quelquefois en des Maisons particulières, où l'on mêle des actions impures, et de mauvaises équivoques, qui réjouissent les ames basses" ("these prurient dances that are sometimes done in private mansions where impure acts are combined with bad jokes to regale low souls") (in part 3, p. 110).

2. Louis himself had already danced to great approbation in *Le Ballet de la nuit* (1653), *Les Noces de Pélée et de Thétis* (1654), *Le Ballet du temps* (1654), *Le Ballet des plaisirs* (1655), *Le Ballet des bienvenus* (1655), and *Le Ballet de Psyché* (1656), to name but the most prominent. He also participated in innumerable shorter works and *mascarades*. Christout provides useful synopses of these and other works in *Le Ballet de cour de Louis XIV*, pp. 67–99. Louis XIV would continue to perform theatrically until 1670 and socially until 1679. See Rebecca Harris-Warrick, "Ballroom Dancing at the Court of Louis XIV," *Early Music* 14, no. 1 (Feb. 1986): 41–50.

3. In 1651, the nine-year-old Louis XIV made his first appearance as a dancer in Benserade's *Ballet de Cassandre.* He was seated in a "grotesque" chariot led by Cassandre, who sang the "branle de Cassandre." See Benserade, *Ballet de Cassandre, dansé au Palais Cardinal; le premier ou le roy a dansé dans le mois de Fevrier 1651* (Bibliothèque nationale, Yf Réserve 1209). This work is also in Lacroix, vol. 6, p. 273.

4. Louis XIV, King of France and Navarre, *Mémoires for the Instruction of the Dauphin*, trans. Paul Sonnino (New York: Free Press, 1970), p. 102.

5. The *Lettres patentes du roy pour l'establissement de l'Académie royale de danse en la ville de Paris* are reproduced in Appendix 3 from the original text (Paris: Pierre le Petit, 1663) with an English translation (hereafter referred to as *Letters Patent*).

6. *Letters Patent*, p. 4.

7. Louis XIV, *Mémoires*, p. 102.

8. See Chapters 1, 2, and 4, and the "Discours academique" in Appendix 3.

9. *Letters Patent*, p. 15. The *Letters Patent* also stipulate that the Academy will supply or recommend dancers needed for Louis's court ballets.

10. Ibid., pp. 33–4.

11. And, of course, the *Letters Patent* also paved the way for asserting the converse: the monarch would henceforth monopolize spectacle. In the early 1660s, plans were already under way for Versailles, the privileged locus of power and its entrancing spectacle. By 1664, Louis XIV mounted his first major production, *Les Plaisirs de L'île enchantée*, followed in 1668 by *Le Grand divertissement royal de Versailles.* In both of these works, Louis XIV mobilized all the spectacular technology at his disposal. But much of this technology is salvaged from earlier court ballet. For example, the festival structure spreading these performances out over several day's time and including all manner of diversions had not been seen since *Le Balet comique.* Also from *Le Balet comique* came the overarching conceit of the return of a golden age in *Les Plaisirs*, while its plot had already been adapted from Ariosto for *Le Ballet de Monseigneur le duc de Vandosme.* On these two theatrical events in the context of Louis XIV's manipulation of all the arts through his academies, see Apostolidès, *Le Roi-Machine*, pp. 93–113.

12. The division of labor was an issue, as indicated by resistance to the *Letters Patent* expressed in Guillaume du Manoir, *Le Mariage de la musique avec la danse, et la danse* (Paris: chez. G. de Luyne, 1664).

13. Fournel, *Les Contemporains de Molière* 2, p. 186. Prunières makes a similar comment, *Le Ballet de cour*, p. 142.

14. *Letters Patent*, p. 36.

15. See Franko, *The Dancing Body*, pp. 26–43, 68–78.

16. Molière engaged a dancer, Daniel Mallet, for the troupe in 1644, probably to work in such ballets. See Fournel, *Les Contemporains de Molière*, p. 185.

17. His collaborators included Lully, Torelli, Pellison, Beauchamps, Le Brun, and Vigarani.

18. I am fully aware that this hypothesis goes strongly against the grain of traditional Molière criticism, which has tended to view *Les Fâcheux* as an accident. See, e.g., Maurice Pellisson, *Les Comédies-Ballets de Molière* (1914; rpt. Paris: Editions d'Aujourd'hui,

1976), p. 59. Jean-Denis Marzi is one of the few to argue the deliberate construction of the play in " 'Les Fâcheux': A Study in Thematic Composition," *USF Language Quarterly*, 22, nos. 1–2 (Fall–Winter 1983): 27–9. Hallam Walker also comes close to an important insight in stating that the play's "unifying action" is "to divert." See " 'Les Fâcheux' and Molière's Use of Games," *L'Esprit Créateur* 11, no. 2 (Summer 1971): 27. For another analysis that takes *Les Fâcheux* seriously, see Ronald W. Tobin, "Le Chasseur enchâssé: La Mise en abyme dans *Les Fâcheux*," *Cahiers de Littérature du XVIIe Siècle* 6 (1984): 407–17.

19. Ibid. A similar note is struck in *L'Amour médecin*, when the allegories of Comedy, Music, and Dance proclaim, "Unissons-nous tous trois d'une ardeur sans seconde" ("Let us unite all three with unmatched ardor"). Ibid., vol. 2, p. 96.

20. See d'Aubignac, *La Pratique du theatre*, p. 260. For a fuller discussion of d'Aubignac's theory relative to gesture and speech in Corneille, see Mark Franko, "Act and Voice in Neo-Classical Theatrical Theory: D'Aubignac's *Pratique* and Corneille's *Illusion*," *Romanic Review* 128, no. 3 (May 1987): pp. 311–26.

21. See Louis Eugene Auld, "The Unity of Molière's Comedy-Ballets: A Study of Their Structure, Meanings, and Values" (Ph.D. diss., Bryn Mawr College, 1968); and Claude Abraham, *On the Structure of Molière's Comédies-Ballets* (Paris: Papers on French Seventeenth Century Literature, 1984).

22. See W. D. Howarth, *Molière: A Playwright and His Audience* (Cambridge University Press, 1982), p. 215.

23. There are presently signs of an increasing awareness of this problem. See Charles Mazouer, "Il faut jouer les intermèdes des comédies-ballets de Molière," *XVIIe Siècle* 165, no. 4 (Oct.–Dec. 1989): 375–81.

24. Pellisson *Les Comédies-Ballets de Molière*, p. 44. Pellisson even denies that court ballets contained any degree of fantasy (p. 122).

25. As such, they would be absorbed into the general corpus of court ballets as an "ingenious and gallant entertainment which," in the words of Fournel," preceded and prepared the way for opera." See "Histoire du ballet de cour," in *Les Contemporains de Molière*, p. 173. The same view is taken by Jacques Bernard Durey de Noinville, *Histoire du théâtre*

de l'Académie royale de musique en France (Paris: Duchesne, 1757).

26. Defaux is actually caught in the contradictory posture of devalorizing court ballet while valorizing Molière's use of it. Symptomatic of this conflict is his statement that *Le Bourgeois gentilhomme* is the apogee of Molière's second, "reflexive" style coupled with the subsequent assertion that the same play is a "pure spectacle without any reflexive dimension" (Gérard Defaux, *Molière ou les Métamorphoses du Comique: De la comédie morale au triomphe de la folie* [Lexington, Ky.: French Forum, 1980], pp. 30, 164). Defaux sees all court spectacle as an expression of superficiality, while literature is characterized, by contrast, as the sole conveyor of moral values. The "reflexive dimension" he perceives in Molière's theater is one through which Molière would point out the shortcomings of dance even as he uses dance to brilliant effect in fully one-third of his output. For a critique of Defaux's theory, see John Cairncross, "Facteurs 'réflexifs' et faits répertoriables chez Molière," *Papers on French Seventeenth-Century Literature* 13, no. 24 (1986): 149–187, and no. 25: 77–91.

27. In Defaux's words, Molière took this "eminently artificial, conventional and flat genre" and "breathed a soul into it," "provided it with a depth and significance which it did not have until then." Defaux thinks court ballet was "a pure spectacle, a gratuitous divertissement which engaged people in no way, a sort of allegorical and mythological tapestry reduced to the harmony of its own colors." See *Les Métamorphoses du comique*, p. 218.

28. See, e.g., Samuel S. Taylor, "Le Geste chez les 'maîtres' Italiens de Molière," *XVIIe Siècle*, 132 (July–Sep. 1981): 285–301.

29. "Art dance tended to follow a continuum running from mime to purely formalized movement, while the gestures of comedy, at the other end of the same continuum, proceeded from mime to completely realistic stage business in which sense of rhythm all but disappeared." See Auld, "The Unity of Molière's Comedy-Ballets," p. 45.

30. While this idea seems quite well taken for the first act, it is less compelling for the remainder of the play.

31. See Robert McBride, "Molière, le Languedoc et le ballet des incompatibles," in *La Vie thé-*

âtrale dans les provinces du Midi, ed. by Y. Giraud (Paris: Edition Place, 1980).

32. With regard to Molière's innovative use of song in the comedy-ballets, see Helen Purkis, "Le Chant pastoral chez Molière," Cahiers de l'Association Internationale des Etudes Françaises 28 (May 1976): 133–44.

33. Other uses of dance to satiric purposes – particularly as regards doctors – derive directly from the burlesque ballet tradition and are not particularly original.

34. This idea was experimented with in an earlier play of the same year, Les Amants magnifiques. In it the protagonists observe each interlude as spectators would a performance.

35. See Chapter 2.

36. This instance appears innovative. Other instances do allude to prior traditions. At the end of act 2, four assistants to the tailor dress Jourdain to music in his new robe. "Mettez cet habit à Monsieur," orders the master tailor, "de la manière que vous faites aux personnes de qualité" ("Dress him in the way you would a nobleman") (TC, 2:733). This ceremony is not an original use of dance, but a representation of its ceremonial use. At the end of the act, the tailors rejoice over Jourdain's gratuities by dancing for joy. Here again, dance expressing emotion is simply absorbed into the narrative as a plausible action. Dancing extends the expression of emotion in a naturalistic way rather than distinguishing itself by and for its nonverbal, self-reflexive qualities. The third interlude at the end of act 3 is that of the cooks who dance before they serve dinner to Jourdain and his noble guests. Along with the two drinking songs of the following act, these are performance elements recalling the tradition of the entremets (an entertainment between the courses of a meal), and thus justify their presence in the narrative fabric as a recognizable tradition.

37. See Abby E. Zanger, "The Spectacular Gift: Rewriting the Royal Scenario in Molière's Les Amants magnifiques," Romanic Review 81, no. 2 (Mar. 1990): 173–88.

38. See Vallot, d'Aquin, and Fagon, "Remarques sur l'année 1653," in Journal de la Santé du Roi Louis XIV (Paris: Auguste Durand, 1862), p. 13.

39. See Apostolidès, Le Roi-Machine, pp. 114–31.

40. See my discussion of Noverre and Diderot in the Epilogue.

41. In Le Balet des fols aux dames (1627) lowlife are said to be less entertaining than are down-and-out courtiers:

> Un Crocheteur, un Biberon
> Un Gagne-Petit, un Laron
> Resjouïront nostre assistance,
> Et sur tous il fera beau voir
> Un Gentilhomme au desespoir
> Pour avoir perdu sa finance.
>
> A Picklock, a Drunkard
> A Knife-Grinder, a Thief
> Will entertain our audience,
> And above all it will be amusing
> To see a Noble in despair
> For having lost his finances.

Lacroix, vol. 4, p. 11.

42. The connection between these two scenes is particularly clear in the 1958 film of Le Bourgeois Gentilhomme directed by Jean Meyer for the Comédie Française. In Meyer's performance, Jourdain's repetition of the vowels negated their rudimentary structural coherence as building blocks of language.

43. If the dancing lesson was first experimented with in Les Fâcheux, the Turkish ceremony had a precursor in Monsieur de Pourceaugnac. However, in that work, the dancing and singing of the doctors and lawyers was used to confuse the protagonist.

44. Yates, The Valois Tapestries, p. 88.

45. Ibid.

46. Jacques de Lafons, Le Dauphin (1609), p. 144, cited in Thuau, Raison d'etat, p. 18.

47. In the court ballet tradition, reference to Turks is traditionally reference to Protestants or to anti-Catholic forces in general.

48. See Larry W. Riggs, Molière and Plurality: Decomposition of the Classical self (New York: Lang, 1989), p. 8.

49. Riggs, Molière and Plurality, p. 13.

50. Especially in her Ideal Forms.

51. See Djelal Kadir, Questing Fictions: Latin America's Family Romance (Minneapolis: University of Minnesota Press, 1986), pp. 86–104.

52. I adapt these terms from Michel De Certeau's "Des outils pour ecrire le corps," Traverses 14–15 (Panoplies du corps) (April 1979): 3.

53. Kadir, Questing Fictions, p. 70.

54. DeJean raises similar questions and concludes that "the Libertine awareness, with only rare exceptions, is unable to go beyond the sense of invasion by other voices in order to reassert power over the aggressor" (*Libertine Strategies*, p. 188). But DeJean does not overlook the dissident potential of this failure (pp. 197–8). The libertine, for DeJean, is always a victim and complicitous with his or her persecutor (p. 125).

55. Kadir, *Questing Fictions*, p. 87: "America as baroque discourse, one might say, is tautologically synonymous to itself."

EPILOGUE

1. Dore Hoyer (1911–1967) was the only exponent of German *Ausdruckstanz* who was able to continue performing it brilliantly after the second world war. Her career was cut short by suicide in 1967. She wrote *Affectos humanos* in 1962. Susanne Linke's reconstruction of this work had its theatrical premiere June 15, 1988, at the Forum Niederberg in Velbert, West Germany.

2. Among these one could cite as examples the dance-dramas of Régine Astier, the work of Catherine Turocy in the United States, or of Christine Bayle in France.

3. Let us note as examples Oskar Schlemmer's Bauhaus dances by Debra McCall, Nikolai Foregger's *Machine Dances* reconstructed by Mel Gordon, the compositions of Isadora Duncan by Lori Belilove and, in a different style, by Annabelle Gamson, and the latter's work on Mary Wigman. Most recently one could cite Millicent Hodson's reconstruction of Nijinsky's *The Rite of Spring* for the Joffrey Ballet and the reconstructions by the Martha Graham Dance Company of its own early works such as *Heretic* (1929) and *Celebration* (1934) among others. Sally Banes has spoken of "the current mania for reconstruction" in the context of Schlemmer's probable influence on Alwin Nikolais. See her review of Nikolais in *Dance Magazine* 57, no. 2 (Feb. 1983): 27.

4. Hal Foster, *Recodings: Art, Spectacle, Cultural Politics* (Port Townsend, Wash.: Bay Press, 1985), p. 41. Or, as Jean Baudrillard might say, as a monument to and compensation for the loss of historical sensibility per se. See "L'Histoire: Un Scénario rétro," in *Simulacres*

et simulation (Paris: Éditions Galilée, 1981), pp. 69–76.

5. See his *L'Impureté* (Paris: Grasset, 1985).

6. Foster, *Recodings*, p. 20.

7. There are indications that similarly oriented work has recently been conducted in France spearheaded by François Raffinot. Not having seen his work, I must reserve comment. It is clear, however, from several interviews that his work must be understood in the context of the French fascination with the baroque. Pierre Charpentrat points out that this "fashion" began in the 1950s. See his *Le mirage baroque* (Paris: Minuit, 1967). A constructive approach is also beginning to emerge in the work of Klaus Abromeit in Berlin.

8. Umberto Eco, *Postscript to "The Name of the Rose"* (New York: Harcourt Brace Jovanovich, 1984), p. 66. Mary Ann Caws makes reference to the rapport between modernism and mannerism in "Representing Bodies from Mannerism to Modernism: Cloaking, Remembering, and the Elliptical Effect," in *The Art of Interference: Stressed Readings in Verbal and Visual Texts* (Princeton, N.J.: Princeton University Press, 1989), pp. 25–50.

9. This theory of mannerist art is outlined by Claude-Gilbert Dubois in *Le Maniérisme* (Paris: P.U.F., 1979).

10. Manfredo Tafuri, *The Sphere and the Labyrinth: Avant-Gardes and Architecture from Piranesi to the 1970s*, trans. Pelligrino d'Acierno and Robert Connolly (Cambridge, Mass.: MIT Press, 1990), p. 29.

11. Novack continues: ". . . Two distinctive audience responses . . . indicate dramatic change – change which cannot be explained simply by observing alteration or development of movement techniques; they provide ample evidence of a shift in larger patterns of cultural values." *Sharing the Dance: Contact Improvisation and American Culture* (Madison: University of Wisconsin Press, 1990), p. 223.

12. Two theater publications have recently given attention to the dance field in the context of reconstruction. See Rob Baker, "Sixty Years Old, but Still Looks New: Reconstructing Cubo-futurist, Constructivist and Bauhaus Theatre Pieces," *Theatre Crafts* 18, no. 4 (Apr. 1984), 46–9, 84–7, and the issue of *Drama Review* devoted to reconstruction (vol. 23, no. 3, Fall 1984). Neither has gone

tinuum, 1982), p. 241. "One might ask," writes Schlemmer, "if the dancers should not be real puppets moved by strings, or better still self-propelled by means of a precision mechanism, almost free of human intervention, at most directed by remote control? Yes! . . . The effect such an experiment would produce can be found described in Heinrich Kleist's essay on the Marionette." Schlemmer, "Man and Art Figure," in *The Theater of the Bauhaus*, ed. Walter Gropius (Middletown, Conn.: Wesleyan University Press, 1979), p. 29.

31. Yet this conflict arises from the mistaken idea that modernism had the intention to eliminate all subjectivity. We have seen that, historically, the move away from dance as a moral emblem of harmony toward burlesque self-expression was accompanied by an episodic dehumanization of the body's outer form. Since the eighteenth century, the possibility of an expressivity given over to "mechanical" reproduction of gesture engendered the theoretical figure of the marionette to replace the human performer. It is therefore not surprising that modernism would inherit the marionette figure along with a confusion over subjectivism and subjectivity. For a discussion of this problem in the context of twentieth-century American poetry, see Andrew Ross, *The Failure of Modernism: Symptoms of American Poetry* (New York: Columbia University Press, 1986).

32. For an interesting discussion of this problem within the context of English acting techniques of the eighteenth century, see George Taylor, "'The Just Delineation of the Passions': Theories of Acting in the Age of Garrick," in *The Eighteenth-Century English Stage*, ed. Kenneth Richards and Peter Thomson (London: Methuen, 1972), pp. 51–72.

33. I refer throughout to Walter Herries Pollock's translation (New York: Hill & Wang, 1957), p. 12.

34. Diderot, *Paradox*, p. 14.

35. Ibid., p. 19. "Extreme sensibility makes middling actors; middling sensibility makes the ruck of bad actors; in complete absence of sensibility is the possibility of the sublime actor" (p. 20).

36. Ibid., p. 16. Thus she can observe herself. "In such a vision," he adds, "she has a double personality" ("dans ce moment elle est dou-

ble"). The mask or marionette image is used several times by Diderot in the *Paradox*. For example, he speaks of the actor using the metaphor of a child enveloped within a large light mannekin, a kind of moving scarecrow (pp. 67–8). At another point the actor is referred to as "a great courtier, accustomed since he first drew breath to play the part of a most ingenious puppet" (*un pantin merveilleux*) (p. 46).

37. All quotations from Noverre are my own translations of *Lettres sur la danse et les arts imitateurs* (Paris: Editions Lieutier, 1952). All page references will be to the French edition.

38. Ibid., p. 39.

39. It existed also, of course, as a separate art form. For an excellent discussion of the pivotal position of pantomime among the performing arts of the eighteenth century, see Angelica Gooden, *Actio and Persuasion: Dramatic Performance in Eighteenth-Century France* (Oxford: Oxford University Press, 1986).

40. Noverre, *Lettres*, p. 93.

41. There seem to be two stages to Diderot's thought on acting. Approximately twenty years prior to the *Paradox*, Diderot's point of view was not so very different from that of Noverre. See in particular *Entretiens sur le fils naturel* (1757) and *Discours de la poésie dramatique* (1758). For a nonparadoxical perspective on Diderot's shift, see Yvon Belaval, *L'Esthétique sans paradoxe de Diderot* (Paris: Gallimard, 1950); see also Michael Fried, *Absorption and Theatricality: Painting and the Beholder in the Age of Diderot* (Berkeley and Los Angeles: University of California Press, 1980); and Joseph R. Roach, *The Player's Passion: Studies in the Science of Acting* (Newark: University of Delaware Press, 1985). Philippe Lacoue-Labarthe draws all of the ramifications of the paradoxical position in "Diderot, le paradoxe et la mimésis," *Poétique* 43 (Sep. 1980): 265–81.

42. Indeed, the end result Diderot is after is naturalness, always a relative concept in theater history. But the important point is that he claims it can be best achieved through a technique of artifice.

43. Kleist, "On the Marionette Theater," p. 239.

44. Ibid.

45. The concept of physical expressivity is understood historically as an external, corporal

trace of a secret event hidden from view: the scene of emotions' impact on the soul. I am adapting the language of Johann Jacob Engel in *Idées sur le geste et l'action théâtrale* (1795; reprint, Paris: Ressources, 1979), pp. 96–7. For a discussion of expression theory, see my "Expressivism and Chance Procedure: The Future of an Emotion," *Res* 21 (Spring 1992): 142–60.

46. See Appendix 1.

47. Kleist, "On the Marionette Theater," p. 241.

48. The moral connotations of Diderot's theatrical theory can be deduced from his novel *Le Neveu de Rameau*. The paradox that Rameau incarnates for the philosopher is that, despite its emotional vacuity, flattery seems to be the very source of passions. Implicit here is the notion that the passion must be as empty of real feeling as the imitation of the passion. Although this is certainly not articulated in the *Paradox*, it is clearly implied in *Le Neveu de Rameau*. He who knows how to flatter already imitates, and he who imitates flattery on the stage is merely repeating the socially recognizable forms in which people express feelings, according to this cynical view. In other terms, flattery in all its guises is close to constituting an artifical code of the passions. The concept of expressivity is partially deconstructed here by the very eighteenth-century discourse that espoused it as the sole mode of theatrical communication.

49. Schlemmer, *The Letters and Diaries*, pp. 126–7.

50. All citations come from Craig's original publication of this essay in the review significantly entitled *The Mask* (1908): 3.

51. Ibid., p. 7.

52. Ibid., p. 8.

53. Ibid., p. 11.

54. It is also reminiscent of Diderot inasmuch as it theatricalizes theory.

55. Zur Lippe, *Naturbeherrschung am Menschen* 1, pp. 28–34.

56. Ibid., p. 31.

57. Roy Wagner's elucidation of the "in-between" character of the anthropologist could equally well be applied to the situation of the reconstructor, "participating simultaneously in two distinct worlds of meaning and action." See *The Invention of Culture* (Chicago: University of Chicago Press, 1981), p. 9.

58. Foster discusses the work of Grand Union and Meredith Monk as reflexive choreography: dances that write rather than offering themselves to be read. See her *Reading Dancing*, pp. 227, 237 note 3.

59. Ibid., pp. 187, 221, 227.

APPENDIX 2

1. According to Furetière, the "forest" is both a royal preserve and a dangerous lawless domain: a "jungle." St. Germain was a residence of the royal court outside of Paris, in Laye. The constant references in the synopsis to the country coming to the city involve both a reminder that ballet is a "holiday" fantasy and that some unpleasant aspects of nature menace the enclosure of culture.

2. Of Music as a Female Colossus, Marolles notes: "La première entrée représente la musique sous la figure d'une grande femme, ayant plusieurs luths pendus autour d'un vertugadin d'où ils furent décrochés par certains musiciens fantasques qui sortirent de dessous ses jupes; et, comme ils en faisoient un concert, la grande femme dont la teste s'elevoit jusqu'aux chandeliers qui descendoient du plafond de la salle, battoit la mesure" ("The first *entrée* represents music in the figure of a big lady with several luths hung from her farthingale, later taken by fantastic musicians who issued from under her skirts; and, as they played a concert, the big lady whose head reached up to the chandeliers hanging from the ceiling, beat the measure"). *Archives curieuses de l'histoire de France depuis Louis XI jusqu'à Louis XVIII, ou collection de pièces rares et intéressantes . . . publiées d'après les textes conservés à la Bibliothèque royale* (Paris: Beauvais, 1834–40), vol. 6, p. 66. Neither the libretto nor the synopsis, however, mentions dancers entering from beneath the skirts of Music.

3. A sign of their nobility.

4. Music's *récit* appears to have a "cor de chasse" ("a hunting horn") attached to her nose. The libretto indicates that this first song and dance are cacophonous and grotesque, respectively.

5. The implicit reference is to the aesthetic of novelty governing burlesque invention.

APPENDIX 3

1. France entered the Thirty Years' War overtly in 1635. After the Peace of Westphalia in 1648,

hostilities with Spain continued until 1659. At the time of Louis's personal accession to power, France had experienced twenty-four years of armed conflict externally, and the return of the disorders of the Frondes were a real possibility.

2. The privilege of *committimus*, according to Furetière, makes those protected by the king free agents before the law and allows them to represent their own interest personally before the king's Masters of Requests.

3. The case against the Academy is documented in Guillaume du Manoir, *Le Mariage de la musique avec la danse*. The violin was the instrument most closely associated with dancing in the seventeenth century. Furetière calls it "le Roy des instruments" ("the King of instruments") because it has "plus d'effet sur l'esprit que tous les autres instruments" ("more *effect* on the mind than all other instruments"). Therefore, the violin is "le plus propre à faire danser" ("the most apt for making people dance"). Similarly, de Pure writes that the violin is the only instrument "qui soit capable du mouvement François" ("that is capable of French movement"). See *Idées des spectacles anciens et nouveaux*, p. 195.

APPENDIX 4

1. Théodore de Bry's *Grands Voyages*, published in thirteen volumes between 1590 and 1634, corresponds most strikingly to the era of burlesque court ballet.

2. See Bernadette Bucher, *La Sauvage aux seins pendants* (Paris: Hermann, 1977).

3. See Frank Lestringant, *Le Huguenot et le sauvage: L'Amérique et la controverse coloniale en France, au temps des guerres de religion (1555–1589)*. Paris: Aux amateurs de Livres, 1990.

4. See Margaret M. McGowan, "Forms and Themes in Henri II's Entry into Rouen," *Renaissance Drama* 1 (1968): 199–252; Jean-Marie Massa, "Le Monde Luso-Brésilien dans le joyeuse entrée de Rouen," in *Les Fêtes de la Renaissance*, vol. 3, ed. Jean Jacquot

(Paris: C.N.R.S., 1975), pp. 105–16; Steven Mullaney, "Strange Things, Gross Terms, Curious Customs: The Rehearsal of Cultures in the Late Renaissance," *Representations* 3 (Summer 1983): 46–8.

5. Arbeau's *Orchesography* (1588) has a branle d'Ecosse and de Malte, the Allemande, the Pavane d'Espagne, the Canaries, and the Morisque.

6. As Yates has noted, this was the occasion of an important, though poorly documented court ballet of the Valois period, *Le Paradis d'amour*: "The setting represented Hell and Paradise, and the heavens with the revolving spheres of the stars. In the 'Paradise' were twelve nymphs. It was defended by the King and his brothers, and the attacking rebels whom they sent to Hell were Navarre and his Huguenot companions." See Yates, *The Valois Tapestries*, p. 61.

7. This point is developed by Bucher in *La Sauvage aux seins pendants*. It was only after the Saint Bartholomew massacre of 1572 that Protestants began to take the project of resettlement as a historical necessity rather than as a rampart from which to proselytize at a distance.

8. Louis Montrose, "The Work of Gender in the Discourse of Discovery," *Representations* 33 (Winter 1991): 25.

9. The androgyne was inspired, in Bucher's words, by "a syncretism of ethnic, cultural, zoological, mythological, and biblical forms." Bucher, *La Sauvage*, p. 24.

10. See Chapter 4.

11. See Rudolf zur Lippe, *Naturbeherrschung am Menschen* 1, pp. 151–6.

12. Another burlesque work employing this motif is Guillaume Colletet's *Le Ballet des nations* (1622). See Marcel Paquot, "Les 'Vers du ballet des nations' de Guillaume Colletet," *Revue Belge de Philologie et d'Histoire* 10 (1931): 53–68. Paquot argues convincingly for the date 1622 rather than 1650 as claimed by Lacroix. The entire libretto is reproduced in this article.

13. Montrose, "The Work of Gender," p. 26.

BIBLIOGRAPHY

Abraham, Claude. *On the Structure of Molière's Comédies-Ballets*. Paris: Papers on French Seventeenth Century Literature, 1984.

Adelman, Katherine M. "Statue-Posing in the Late Nineteenth Century Physical Culture Movement." *Proceedings: 5th Canadian Symposium on the History of Sport and Physical Education*, pp. 308–17. Toronto: University of Toronto Press, 1982.

Adorno, Theodor. *Aesthetic Theory*. Translated by C. Lenhardt. London: Routledge & Kegan Paul, 1984.

Aignan, Duc de Saint. "Ballet Impromptu." In *Extrait de Mercure de mai, 1618*.

Albertini, Rudolf von. *Das Politische Denken in Frankreich zur Zeit Richelieus*. Marburg: Simons Verlag, 1951.

Allut, Paul. *Recherches sur la vie et sur les oeuvres du P. Claude-François Menestrier*. Lyon: R. Scheuring, 1856.

Apostolidès, Jean-Marie. *Le Roi-Machine: Spectacle et politique au temps de Louis XIV*. Paris: Minuit, 1981.

Arbeau, Thoinot [Tabourot, Jean]. *Orchesographie. Et Traicte en forme de dialogue, par lequel toutes personnes peuvent facilement apprendre et practiquer l'honneste exercice des dances*. Lengres: Jehan des preyz, 1588. Reprint. Bologna: Forni Editore, 1969. This book was translated by Mary Stewart Evans and reedited by Julia Sutton as *Orchesography*. New York: Dover, 1967.

Archives curieuses de l'histoire de France depuis Louis XI jusqu'à Louis XVIII. Paris: Beauvais, 1834–40.

Aristotle. *Metaphysics*. Introduction and commentary by W. D. Ross. Oxford: Oxford University Press, 1958.

Aristotle's Poetics, edited by Frances Fergusson. New York: Hill & Wang, 1961.

Arnaud, Charles. *Etude sur la vie et les oeuvres de l'Abbé d'Aubignac et sur les théories dramatiques du XVIIe siècle*. Paris: A. Picard, 1887.

Artusi, Giovanni Maria. *L'Arte del contrapunto*. Venice: Vincenti, 1598–9.

L'Artusi overo delle imperfettioni della moderna musica. Venice: Vincenti, 1600.

Seconda parte dell'Artusi overo della imperfettioni della moderna musica. Venice: Vincenti: 1603.

Auerbach, Erich. *Scenes from the Drama of European Literature*. Minneapolis: University of Minnesota Press, 1984.

Auld, Louis Eugene. "The Unity of Molière's Comedy-Ballets: A Study of Their Structure, Meanings, and Values." Ph.D. diss., Bryn Mawr College, 1968.

Baader, Renate. "La Polémique anti-baroque dans la doctrine classique." *Baroque* 6 (1973): 133–48.

Baïf, Jean-Antoine de. *Les Mimes, enseignements et proverbes*. Paris: 1576.

Euvres en rime. Paris: Alphonse Lemerre, 1881–90.

Baker, Rob. "Sixty Years Old, but Still Looks New: Reconstructing Cubo-futurist, Constructivist, and Bauhaus Theatre Pieces." *Theatre Crafts* 18, no. 4 (April 1984): 46–9, 84–7.

Bakhtin, Mikhail. *Rabelais and His World*. Translated by Helene Iswolsky. Cambridge, Mass.: MIT Press, 1968.

Problems of Dostoevsky's Poetics. Translated by Caryl Emerson. Minneapolis: University of Minnesota Press, 1984.

Balet de la revanche du Méspris d'Amour. London: 1617.

Ballet à Troyes. 1629.

Ballet dansé à Dijon devant mgr. le prince le 11 février. 1627.

Furetière, Antoine. *Dictionnaire universel.* Rotterdam: 1690.

Garel, Elie. *Les Oracles François ou explication allegorique du Balet de madame, soeur aisnee du roy.* Paris: P. Chevalier, 1615.

Garapon, Robert. "La Permanence de la Farce dans les Divertissements de Cour au XVIIe siècle." *Cashiers de l'Association Internationale des Etudes Françaises* 9 (June 1957): 117–27.

Gooden, Angelica. *Actio and Persuasion: Dramatic Performance in Eighteenth-Century France.* Oxford: Oxford University Press, 1986.

Goodman, Paul. *Speaking and Language: Defense of Poetry.* New York: Random House, 1971.

Gropius, Walter, ed. *The Theater of the Bauhaus.* Middletown, Conn.: Wesleyan University Press, 1979.

Gross, Nathan. *From Gesture to Idea: Esthetics and Ethics in Molière's Comedy.* New York: Columbia University Press, 1982.

Guicharnaud, Jacques. "Les Trois niveaux critiques des *Amants magnifiques.*" In *Molière, Stage and Study: Essays in Honor of W. D. Moore,* edited by W. D. Howarth and Merlin Thomas, pp. 21–42. Oxford: Oxford University Press, 1973.

Günther, Helmut. "Ballet de cour: Beginn einer selbstbewussten Ballettkunst." *Das Tanzarchiv* 5 (Oct. 1973): 137–42.

Guthrie, John. "Quelques considérations sur le style de la danse à l'époque baroque." In *Les Goûts-réünis,* pp. 96–9. Paris: l'Institut de musique et de danse anciennes, 1982.

Harpham, Geoffrey Galt. *On the Grotesque: Strategies of Contradiction in Art and Literature.* Princeton, N.J.: Princeton University Press, 1982.

Harris-Warrick, Rebecca. "Ballroom Dancing at the Court of Louis XIV." *Early Music* 14, no. 1 (Feb. 1986): 41–50.

Harth, Erica. *Ideology and Culture in Seventeenth-Century France.* Ithaca, N.Y.: Cornell University Press, 1983.

Herzel, Roger. "Le Jeu 'naturel' de Molière et de sa troupe." *XVIIe Siècle* 132 (1981): 279–84.

Hilton, Wendy. *Dance of Court and Theater: The French Noble Style, 1690–1725.* Princeton, N.J.: Princeton University Press, 1981.

Hourcade, Philippe. "Louis XIV travesti." *Cahiers de Littérature du XVIIe siècle* 6 (1984): 257–71.

Howarth, W. D. *Molière: A Playwright and His Audience.* Cambridge University Press, 1982.

Huizingua, Johan. *Homo Ludens: A Study of the Play Element in Culture.* Boston: Beacon, 1950.

Isherwood, Robert M. *Music in the Service of the King: France in the Seventeenth Century.* Ithaca, N.Y.: Cornell University Press, 1973.

Jacquot, Jean, ed. *Les Fêtes de la Renaissance.* Paris: C.N.R.S., 1956.

Le Lieu théâtral à la Renaissance. Paris: C.N.R.S., 1963.

Jaeger, Werner. *Paideia: The Ideals of Greek Culture.* Translated by Gilbert Highet. Oxford: Oxford University Press, 1962. Three volumes.

Jamyn, Amadis. *Oeuvres poétiques de Amadis Jamyn.* Paris: 1878.

Johnston, Jill. "The New American Modern Dance." *Salmagundi* 33–4 (Spring–Summer 1976): 149–74.

Jouanna, Arlette. *Ordre social: Mythes et hiérarchies dans la France du XVIe siècle.* Paris: Hachette, 1977.

Joukovsky, Françoise. "De qui est le livret du *Ballet Comique de la Reine?*" *Bibliothèque d'Humanisme et Renaissance* 38 (1976): 343–4.

Kadir, Djelal. *Questing Fictions: Latin America's Family Romance.* Minneapolis: University of Minnesota Press, 1986.

Kirby, E. T. "The Mask: Abstract Theatre, Primitive and Modern." *Drama Review* 16, no. 3 (Sep. 1972): 5–21.

Kirstein, Lincoln. *Movement and Metaphor: Four Centuries of Ballet.* New York: Praeger, 1970.

Dance: A Short History of Classical Theatrical Dancing. New York: Dance Horizons, 1969.

Kleist, Heinrich. "On the Marionette Theater." In *German Romantic Criticism,* edited by A. Leslie Willson, pp. 238–44. New York: Continuum, 1982.

Kristeva, Julia. *Revolution in Poetic Language.* Translated by Margaret Waller. New York: Columbia University Press, 1984.

Lacoue-Labarthe, Philippe. "Diderot, le paradoxe et la mimésis." *Poétique* 43 (Sep. 1980): 265–81.

Lacroix, Paul. *Ballets et mascarades de cour sous Henri IV et Louis XIII (de 1581 à 1652).* 6 vols. Geneva: chez J. Gay et fils, 1868–1870. Reprint. Geneva: Slatkine, 1968.

Lancaster, H. Carrington. "Relation between French Plays and Ballets from 1581–1650." *PMLA* (1916): 379–94.

Lancelot, Francine. "Les Ornaments dans la danse baroque." In *Les Goûts-Réünis*, pp. 72–8. Paris: l'Institut de Musique et de Danse Anciennes, 1982.

Lanham, Richard A. *A Handlist of Rhetorical Terms*. Berkeley & Los Angeles: University of California Press, 1969.

Larmessin, Nicolas de. *Les Costumes grotesques et les métiers*. Paris: Henri Veyrier, 1974.

Lauzun, Philippe. *Un Ballet agenais au commencement du XVIIe siècle*. Agen: Fernand Lamy, 1879.

Lawrence, Francis. "Artist, Audience and Structure in *L'Impromptu de Versailles*." *Oeuvres et Critiques* 6, no. 1 (Summer 1981): 125–32.

Le Ballet nouvellement dansé à Fontainebleau par les dames d'amour. 1625.

Le Ballet politique. 1627. Bibliothèque nationale, imprimés G. 30574.

Le Magnifique et royal ballet danse à Lyon en présence de deux roynes, sous le nom de l'Aurore et Céphale. Paris: 1622. Bibliothèque de l'institut: 35262 27e.

Leclerc, Hélène. "Circé ou *Le Ballet Comique de la Royne* (1581): Métaphysique du son et de la lumière." *Theatre Research-Recherches Théâtrales* 3, no. 2 (1961): 101–20.

Legendre, Pierre. *L'Amour du Censeur: Essais sur l'ordre dogmatique*. Paris: Seuil, 1974.

Jouir du pouvoir: Traité de la bureaucratie patriote. Paris: Minuit, 1976.

"Le Droit et toute sa rigueur: Entretien avec Pierre Legendre." *Communications* 26 (1977): 3–14.

La Passion d'être un autre: Etude pour la danse. Paris: Seuil, 1978.

Lejay, Gabriel-Franc. "Liber de choreis dramaticis." In *Bibliotheca rhetorum praecepta et exempla complectens quae ad poeticam facultatem pertinent, discipulis pariter ac magistris perutilis*. Paris: Gregorium Dupuis, 1725.

Le Jeune, Claude. "Le Printemps." In *Les Maîtres musiciens de la Renaissance française VI*, edited by Henri Expert. 1603. Reprint. Paris: Alphonse Leduc, 1901.

Les Ballet de Turlupin représenté à gentilly. 1643.

Les Fées des forests de Saint Germain: Ballet dansé par sa majeste. Paris: Rene Giffart, 1625.

Les Fées des forests de St. Germain: Ballet dansé par le roy en la salle du Louvre le 9. jour de février 1625. Paris: Jean Sara, 1625.

L'Estoile, Pierre de. *Mémoires-Journaux de Pierre de l'Estoile*. Paris: Alphonse Lemerre, 1888.

Lestringant, Frank. *Le Huguenot et le sauvage: L'Amérique et la controverse coloniale en France, au temps des guerres de religion (1555–1589)*. Paris: Aux amateurs de Livres, 1990.

Lettres patentes du roy pour l'establissement de l'Academie royale de danse en la ville de Paris. Paris: Pierre le Petit, 1663.

Levin, Harry. *The Myth of the Golden Age in the Renaissance*. Oxford: Oxford University Press, 1969.

Levin, Michael. "Postmodernism in Dance: Dance, Discourse, Democracy." In *Postmodernism – Philosophy and the Arts*, edited by Hugh J. Silverman. New York: Routledge, 1990.

Liévin, Louis. "Le Ballet de cour et les Moeurs sous Louis XIV." *Revue Contemporaine* (1870): 108–34.

Louis XIV. *Mémoires for the Instruction of the Dauphin*. Translated by Paul Sonnino. New York: Free Press, 1970.

Lublinskaya, A. D. *French Absolutism: The crucial phase, 1620–1629*. Translated by Brian Pearce. Cambridge University Press, 1968.

McBride, Robert. "Moliere, Le Languedoc et le ballet des incompatibles." In *La Vie Théâtrale dans les provinces du Midi*, edited by Y. Giraud, pp. 131–7. Paris: Edition Place, 1980.

"The Triumph of Ballet in *Le Bourgeois Gentilhomme*." In *Form and Meaning: Aesthetic Coherence in Seventeenth-Century French Drama: Studies Presented to Harry Barnwell*, edited by William D. Howarth, Ian McFarlane, and Margaret M. McGowan, pp. 127–41. Amersham: Avebury, 1982.

"Ballet: A Neglected Key to Molière's Theatre." *Dance Research* 2, no. 1 (Spring 1984): 3–18.

McCall, Debra. "Reconstructing Schlemmer's Bauhaus dances: A Personal Narrative." In *Oskar Schlemmer: The Baltimore Museum of Art*, pp. 149–59. (1986).

MacClintock, Carol, and MacClintock, Lander, trans. and eds. *Le Balet comique de la Royne*. Musicological Studies and Documents, no. 25. New York: American Institute of Musicology, 1971.

McGowan, Margaret M. "Forms and Themes in Henri II's Entry into Rouen." *Renaissance Drama* 1 (1968): 199–252.

L'Art du ballet de cour en France, 1581–1643. Paris: C.N.R.S., 1978.

Ideal Forms in the Age of Ronsard. Berkeley & Los Angeles: University of California Press, 1985.

"Le Balet Comique" by Balthazar de Beaujoyeulx, 1581 (Binghamton: Medieval and Renaissance Texts and Studies, 1982).

The Court Ballet of Louis XIII. London: Victoria and Albert Museum, 1986.

"The Semiotics of the Dance: A State of the Art in the Renaissance." Review of *The Dancing Body in Renaissance Choreography* by Mark Franko. *Continuum* 1 (Rethinking Classicism) (1989): 249–57.

Magendie, Maurice. *La Politesse mondaine et les théories de l'honnêteté, en France au XVIIe siècle, de 1600 à 1660.* Paris: Slatkine, 1970.

Magne, Emile. *Les Plaisirs et les fêtes en France au XVIIe siècle.* Geneva: Editions de la Frégate, 1944.

Maiorino, Giancarlo. *The Portrait of Eccentricity: Arcimboldo and the Mannerist Grotesque.* University Park: Pennsylvania University Press, 1991.

Manning, Susan. *Feminism and Nationalism in the Dances of Mary Wigman.* Berkeley & Los Angeles: University of California Press, 1993.

Manning, Susan, and Benson, Melissa. "Interrupted Continuities: Modern Dance in Germany." *Drama Review* 30, no. 2 (Summer 1986): 30–45.

Manoir, Guillaume du. *Le Mariage de la musique avec la danse, et la danse.* Paris: G. de Luyne, 1664.

Maravall, Jose Antonio. *Culture of the Baroque: Analysis of a Historical Structure.* Translated by Terry Cochran. Minneapolis: University of Minnesota Press, 1986.

Marin, Louis. "Interview." *Diacritics* (June 1977): 44–53.

Le Portrait du roi. Paris: Minuit, 1981. Translated by Martha M. Houle under the title *Portrait of the King.* Minneapolis: University of Minnesota Press, 1988.

Marolles, Michel de. *Mémoires.* Paris: Sommaville, 1656–7.

Martin, Henriette. "La Camerata du comte bardi et la musique florentine du XVIe siècle." *Revue de Musicologie* (1932–33): 63–74.

Martin, John. *Introduction to the Dance.* New York: Dance Horizons, 1965.

Martin, Randy. *Performance as Political Act: The Embodied Self.* Westport: Greenwood, 1990.

Marzi, Jean-Denis. "*Les Fâcheux:* A Study in Thematic Composition." *USF Language Quarterly* 22, nos. 1–2 (Fall–Winter 1983): 27–9.

Massa, Jean-Marie. "Le Monde Luso-Brésilien dans le joyeuse entrée de Rouen." In *Les Fêtes de la Renaissance,* edited by Jean Jacquot. Paris: C.N.R.S., 1975, vol. 3.

Maurice-Amour, Mme. L. "Benserade, Michel Lambert et Lulli." *Cahiers de l'Association Internationale des Etudes Françaises* 9 (June 1957): 53–76.

Mazouer, Charles. "Il Faut jouer les intermèdes des comédies-ballets de Molière." *XVIIe Siècle* 165, no. 4 (Oct.–Dec. 1989): 375–91.

Mazzi, C. "Il 'libro dell'arte del danzare' di Antonio Cornazano." *La Bibliofilia* 17 (1915): 1–30.

Mémoires de la Reine Marguerite. Paris: 1628.

Menestrier, Le P. Claude-François. "Remarques sur la conduite des ballets." In *L'Autel de Lyon.* Lyon: 1658.

Des representations en musique anciennes et modernes. Paris: 1681.

Des ballets anciens et modernes selon les regles du theatre. Paris: René Guignaud, 1682.

Mersenne, Marin. *Harmonie universelle contenant la théorie et la pratique de la musique.* 1636. Reprint. Paris: C.N.R.S., 1964.

Méthivier, Hubert. *La Fronde.* Paris: P.U.F., 1984.

Mettam, Roger. *Power and Faction in Louis XIV's France.* London: Blackwell Publisher, 1988.

Michaud and Poujoulut, eds. *Nouvelle Collection des mémoires pour servir à l'histoire de France depuis le XIIIe siècle jusqu'à la fin du XVIIIe.* Paris: Guyot, 1851.

Mill, John Stuart. *Philosophy of Scientific Method.* New York: Hafner, 1950.

Miller, James. *Measures of Wisdom: The Cosmic Dance in Classical and Christian Antiquity.* Toronto: University of Toronto Press, 1981.

Mirollo, James V. *Mannerism and Renaissance Poetry: Concept, Mode, Inner Design.* New Haven, Conn.: Yale University Press, 1984.

Mishriky, Salwa. *Le Costume de déguisement et la théâtralite de l'apparence dans le "Bourgeois Gentilhomme."* Paris: Pensée universelle, 1983.

Molière, Jean-Baptiste. *Théâtre complet.* Paris: Gallimard, 1956.

Montaigne, Michel de. *Essais.* Paris: Garnier, 1962. This work was translated into English by Donald Frame as *The Complete Essays of Montaigne.* Stanford, Calif.: Stanford University Press, 1965.

Montgrédien, Georges. "Molière et Lulli." *XVIIe Siècle* 73 (1973): 3–15.

Montrose, Louis. "The Work of Gender in the Discourse of Discovery." *Representations* 33 (Winter 1991): 1–41.

Moreau, Pierre. "Ronsard et la danse des astres." In *Mélanges d'histoire littéraire (XVIe–XVIIe siècle) offerts à Raymond Lebègue,* pp. 75–82. Paris: Nizet, 1969.

Moriarty, Michael. *Taste and Ideology in Seventeenth-Century France.* Cambridge University Press, 1988.

Mullaney, Steven. "Strange Things, Gross Terms, Curious Customs: The Rehearsal of Cultures in the Late Renaissance." *Representations* 3 (Summer 1983): 40–67.

Nadal, Octave. "L'Ethique de la gloire au Dix-Septièmè Siècle." *Mercure de France* 308 (Jan.–Apr. 1950): 22–34.

Negri, Cesare. *Le Gratie d'amore.* 1602. Reprint. Milan: Forni Editore, 1969.

Noinville, Durey de, Jacques Bernard. *Histoire du théâtre de l'Académie royale de musique en France.* Paris: Duchesne, 1757.

Novack, Cynthia J. *Sharing the Dance: Contact Improvisation and American Culture* Madison: University of Wisconsin Press, 1990.

Noverre, Jean-Georges. *Lettres sur la danse et les arts imitateurs.* Paris: Editions Lieutier, 1952.

Orgel, Stephen. *The Illusion of Power: Political Theater in the English Renaissance.* Berkeley & Los Angeles: University of California Press, 1975.

The Jonsonian Masque. New York: Columbia University Press, 1981.

"Nobody's Perfect: Or Why Did the English Stage Take Boys for Women." In *Displacing Homophobia: Gay Male Perspectives in Literature and Culture,* edited by Ronald R. Butters, John M. Clum, and Michael Moon, pp. 7–29. Durham, N.C.: Duke University Press, 1989.

Owens, Craig. "The Allegorical Impulse: Toward a Theory of Postmodernism." In *Art After Modernism: Rethinking Representation,* edited by Brian Wallis and Marcia Tucker. pp. 203–35. New York: The New Museum of Contemporary Art, 1984.

Panzer, Marianne. *Tanz und Recht.* Frankfurt am Main: Moritz Diesterweg, 1938.

Paquot, Marcel. "Madame de Rohan, auteur de comédies-ballets?" *Revue Belge de Philologie de d'Histoire* 8, no. 8 (1929): 801–29.

"Comédies-ballets représentées en l'honneur de Madame, Soeur du Roi Henri IV." *Revue Belge de Philologie et d'Histoire* 10 (1931): 965–95.

"Les 'Vers du *Balet des Nations*' de Guillaume Colletet." *Revue Belge de Philologie et d'Histoire* 10 (1931): 53–68.

"La Manière de composer les ballets de cour d'après les premières théoriciens français." *Cahiers de l'Association Internationale des Etudes Françaises* 9 (June 1957): 183–97.

Les Etrangers dans les divertissements de la cour de Beaujoyeulx à Molière (1581–1673). N.p., La Renaissance du Livre, n.d.

Parthenay, [Catherine de], douane de Rohan. *Ballets allégoriques en vers, 1592–1593,* edited by Raymond Ritter. Paris: E. Champion, 1927.

Pascal, Blaise. *Pensées et opuscules.* Paris: Hachette, 1971.

Peirce, Charles Sanders. *Philosophical Writings of Peirce,* edited by Justus Bucher. New York: Dover, n.d.

Pellisson, Maurice. *Les Comédies-Ballets de Molière.* 1914. Reprint. Paris: Editions d'Aujourd'hui, 1976.

Piacenza, Domenico da. *De arte saltandi e choreas ducendi.* Paris: Bibliothèque nationale, Ms. it. 972.

Pintard, René. *Le Libertinage erudit dans la première moitié du XVIIe siècle.* Paris: Boivin, 1943.

Pirrotta, Nino. "Temperaments and Tendencies in the Florentine Camerata." *Musical Quarterly* 40, no. 2 (1954): 169–89.

Plato. "Symposium." In *The Collected Dialogues,* edited by Edith Hamilton and Huntington Cairns, pp. 526–74. Princeton, N.J.: Princeton University Press, 1973.

Plotinus. *Enneads.* Translated by A. H. Armstrong. Cambridge, Mass.: Harvard University Press, 1984.

Postlewait, Thomas. "Historiography and Theatrical Event." *Theatre Journal* 43, no. 21 (May 1991): 157–98.

Prudhommeau, Germaine. "A propos du *Balet*

Comique de la Reine." *La Recherche en Danse* 3 (1984): 15–24.

Prunières, Henry. *Le Ballet de cour en France avant Benserade et Lully.* Paris: Henri Laurens, 1914.

Purkis, Helen M. C. "Les Intermèdes à la cour de France au XVIe siècle." *Bibliothèque d'Humanisme et Renaissance* 20 (1958): 296–309.

"Le Chant pastoral chez Molière." *Cahiers de l'Association Internationale des Etudes Françaises* 28 (May 1976): 133–44.

Quintilian. *The Institutio Oratoria of Quintilian.* Cambridge, Mass.: Harvard University Press, 1976.

Rabelais, François. *Le Cinquiesme livre.* 1564. Reprint. In *Oeuvres complètes.* Paris: Gallimard, 1955.

Ranum, Patricia. "Audible Rhetoric and Mute Rhetoric: The 17th Century French Sarabande." *Early Music* 14, no. 1 (Feb. 1986): 22–39.

Recueil des plus excellens ballets de ce temps. Paris: Touss. du Bray, 1612.

Recueil des vers du Balet de la Royne. Paris: 1609.

Relation de ce qui s'est passe à Toulouse le 3.10 et 1. Février pour le mariage de Madame Soeur du Roy, avec le Prince de Savoye. Toulouse: 1619.

Renard, Joseph. *Catalogue des oeuvres imprimées de Claude-François Menestrier.* Lyon: de Pitrat ainé, 1883.

Riggs, Larry W. *Molière and Plurality: Decomposition of the Classicist Self.* New York: Lang, 1989.

Rigolot, François. "Les Jeux de Montaigne." In *Les Jeux à la Renaissance,* edited by Philippe Ariès and Jean-Claude Margolin, pp. 325–41. Paris: Vrin, 1982.

Les Métamorphoses de Montaigne. Paris: P.U.F., 1988.

Ripa, Cesare. *Iconologie ou nouvelle explication de plusieurs images.* Paris: 1677.

Roach, Joseph R. *The Player's Passion: Studies in the Science of Acting.* Newark: University of Delaware Press, 1985.

Ronsard, Pierre de. *Elegies, mascarades et bergeries.* Paris: 1565.

Oeuvres complètes, edited by Gustave Cohen. Paris: Gallimard, 1950.

Rosow, Lois. "French Baroque Recitative as an Expression of Tragic Declamation." *Early Music* 11 (Oct. 1983): 468–79.

Ross, Andrew. *The Failure of Modernism: Symptoms of American Poetry.* New York: Columbia University Press, 1986.

No Respect: Intellectuals and Popular Culture. New York: Routledge, 1989.

Rougemont, Martine de. "L'Acteur et l'orateur: Étapes d'un débat." *XVIIe Siècle* 132 (1981): 329–34.

Rousset, Jean. *La Littérature de l'âge baroque en France: Circé et le paon.* Paris: Librairie José Corti, 1954.

Ruyter, Nancy Lee Chalfa. *Reformers and Visionaries: The Americanization of the Art of Dance.* New York: Dance Horizons, 1979.

Saccone, Eduardo. "Grazia, sprezzatura and affetazione in Balthazar Castiglione's Book of the Courtier." In *Castiglione: The Ideal and the Real in Renaissance Culture,* edited by Robert W. Hanning and David Rosand, New Haven, Conn.: Yale University Press, 1983).

Sachs, Curt. *World History of Dance.* New York: Norton, 1973.

Saint-Amant. *Oeuvres.* 1629. Reprint. Paris: Didier, 1971.

Saint Gelais, Mellin de. *Oeuvres.* Lyon: A. de Harsy, 1574.

Saint Hubert. *La Manière de composer et faire reussir les ballets.* Paris: chez François Targa, 1641.

Scarpetta, Guy. *L'Impureté.* Paris: Grasset, 1985.

Schechner, Richard. *Between Theater and Anthropology.* Philadelphia: University of Pennsylvania Press, 1985.

Scherer, Jacques. *La Dramaturgie classique en France.* Paris: Nizet, 1977.

Schikowski, John. *Geschichte des Tanzes.* Berlin: Buchmeister Verlag, n.d.

Schimberg, André. *L'Education morale dans les collèges de la compagnie de Jésus en France sous l'ancien régime (XVI, XVII et XVIII siècles).* Paris: Honoré Champion, 1913.

Schlemmer, Oskar. *The Letters and Diaries of Oskar Schlemmer.* Middletown, Conn.: Wesleyan University Press, 1972.

Théâtre et abstraction. Translated by Eric Michaud. Lausanne: L'Age d'homme, 1978.

Shaw, Mary Lewis. "Ephemeral Signs: Apprehending the Idea Through Poetry and Dance." *Dance Research Journal* 20, no. 1 (Summer 1988): 3–9.

Schwartz, Judith L., and Schlundt, Christena L. *French Court Dance and Dance Music: A*

Guide to Primary Source Writings, 1643–1789. New York: Pendragon, 1987.

Silin, Charles I. *Benserade and His Ballets de Cour.* Baltimore: Johns Hopkins University Press, 1940.

Snyders, George. *Dramaturgie et société: Rapports entre l'oeuvre théâtrale, son interprétation et son public aux 16e et 17e siècles.* Paris: C.N.R.S., 1967.

Solerti, Angelo. *Le Origine del melodramma.* Turin: 1903.

Gli albori del melodrama. Milan: 1905.

Musica, ballo e drammatica alla Corte Medicea da 1600 al 1637. Florence: 1905. Reprint. Bologna: Forni, 1969.

Sparshott, Francis. "On the Question: Why Do Philosophers Neglect the Aesthetics of Dance?" *Dance Research Journal* 15, no. 1 (Fall 1982): 5–30.

Off the Ground: First Steps to a Philosophical Consideration of Dance. Princeton, N.J.: Princeton University Press, 1988.

Sparti, Barbara. "Style and Performance in the Social Dances of the Italian Renaissance: Ornamentation, Improvisation, Variation and Virtuosity." *Proceedings of the Society of Dance History Scholars* (Riverside: Society of Dance History Scholars, 1986): 31–51.

Spink, J. S., *French Free-Thought from Gassendi to Voltaire.* London: Athlone Press, 1960.

Starobinski, Jean. "The Body's Moment." *Yale French Studies* 64 (1983): 273–305.

Steadman, John M. *Redefining a Period Style: "Renaissance," "Mannerist" and "Baroque" in Literature.* Pittsburgh, Pa.: Duquesne University Press, 1990.

Stella, Mary Newton. *Renaissance Theatre Costume and the Sense of the Historic Past.* London: Rapp & Whiting, 1975.

Strong, Roy C. "Festivals for the Garter Embassy at the Court of Henri III." *Journal of the Warburg and Courtauld Institutes* 22 (1959): 60–70.

Splendor at Court. Boston: Houghton Mifflin, 1975.

Art and Power: Renaissance Festivals, 1450–1650. Woodbridge: Boydell, 1984.

Tafuri, Manfredo. *The Sphere and the Labyrinth: Avant-Gardes and Architecture from Piranesi to the 1970s.* Translated by Pelligrino d'Acierno and Robert Connolly. Cambridge, Mass.: MIT Press, 1990.

Talamon, René. "La Marquise du *Bourgeois Gentilhomme.*" *Modern Language Notes* 50, no. 6 (June 1935): 347–75.

Tapié, Victor L. *La France de Louis XIII et de Richelieu.* Paris: Flammarion, 1967.

Baroque et classicisme. Paris: Pluriel, 1980.

Taylor, George. " 'The Just Delineation of the Passions': Theories of Acting in the Age of Garrick." In *The Eighteenth-Century English Stage,* edited by Kenneth Richards and Peter Thomson, pp. 51–72. London: Methuen, 1972.

Taylor, Samuel S. "Le Geste chez les 'maîtres' italiens de Molière." *XVIIe Siècle* 132 (July–Sep. 1981): 285–301.

Thuau, Etienne. *Raison d'état et pensée politique à l'époque de Richelieu.* Paris: Colin, 1966.

Tobin, Ronald W. "Le Chasseur enchâssé: La Mise en abyme dans *Les Fâcheux.*" *Cahiers de Littérature du XVIIe Siècle* 6 (1984): 407–17.

"Fifth Service: Rehearsal and Reversal in *Le Bourgeois Gentilhomme.*" In *Tarte à la crème: Comedy and Gastronomy in Molière's Theater,* pp. 103–22. Columbus: Ohio State University Press, 1990.

Turner, Victor. *The Anthropology of Performance.* New York: PAJ Publications, 1986.

Tuve, Rosemond. *Elizabethan and Metaphysical Imagery.* Chicago: University of Chicago Press, 1947.

Tyard, Pontus de. *Solitaire Second.* Geneva: Droz, 1980.

Vallière, Duc de la. *Ballets, opéra, et autres ouvrages lyriques.* Paris: chez Cl. J. Baptiste Bouche, 1760. Reprint. London: H. Baron, 1967.

Vallot, d'Aquin, and Fagon. "Remarques sur l'année 1653." In *Journal de la Santé du Roi Louis XIV,* pp. 13–17. Paris: Auguste Durand, 1862.

Verchaly, André. "Poésie et air de cour en France jusqu'à 1620." In *Musique et poésie au XVIe siècle.* Paris: C.N.R.S., 1954, pp. 211–24.

Vers pour "Le Ballet du roy" représentant les comédiens italiens. C. 1636.

Wadsworth, Phillip A. *Molière and the Italian Theatrical Tradition.* 2nd edition. Birmingham: Summa, 1987.

Wagner, Roy. *The Invention of Culture.* Chicago: University of Chicago Press, 1981.

Walker, Daniel Pickering. "Musical Humanism in the 16th and 17th Centuries." *Music Review*

2, no. 1 (1941–2): 1–13; no. 2: 111–12; no. 3: 220–7; no. 4: 288–308; 3, no. 1; 55–71.

"The Influence of Musique Mesurée à L'antique Particularly on the Airs de Cour of the Early Seventeenth Century." *Musica Disciplina* (1948): 141–63.

ed. *Musique des intermèdes de "La Pellegrina"*. Paris: C.N.R.S., 1962.

"La Musique des intermèdes florentins de 1589 et l'humanisme." In *Les Fêtes de la Renaissance*, edited by Jean Jacquot, vol. 1, pp. 132–44. Paris: C.N.R.S., 1973.

Studies in Musical Science in the Late Renaissance. London: Warburg Institute, 1978.

Walker, Hallam. "*Les Fâcheux* and Molière's Use of Games." *L'Esprit Créateur* 11, no. 2 (Summer 1971): 21–33.

Warburg, Aby. "I costumi teatrali per gli intermezzi del 1589." *Atti dell'Accademia del R. Istituto Musicale di Firenze anno XXXIII: Commemorazione della riforma melodrammatica*. Florence: Galletti e Cocci, 1895.

Warnke, Frank J. *Versions of Baroque: European Literature in the Seventeenth Century*. New Haven, Conn.: Yale University Press, 1972.

"Mannerism in European Literature: Period or Aspect?" *Revue de Littérature Comparée* 56 (1982): 255–60.

Weise, George. "Le Maniérisme, histoire d'un terme." *L'Information d'Histoire de l'Art* (May–June 1962): 113–125.

Woodruff, Dianne L. "*The Ballet Comique* in the Petit Bourbon: A Practical View." *Proceedings of the Society of Dance History Scholars*. Riverside: Society of Dance History Scholars, 1986, pp. 91–129.

Yates, Frances A. *The French Academies of the Sixteenth Century*. London: Warburg Institute, 1947.

The Valois Tapestries. London: Routledge & Kegan Paul, 1959.

Astraea: The Imperial Theme in the Sixteenth Century. London: Routledge & Kegan Paul, 1975.

Zanger, Abby E. "Acting as Counteracting in Molière's *The Impromptu of Versailles*" *Theatre Journal* 38, no. 2 (May 1986): 180–95.

"Paralyzing Performance: Sacrificing Theater on the Altar of Publication." *Stanford French Review* 12, nos. 2–3 (1988): 169–86.

"The Spectacular Gift: Rewriting the Royal Scenario in Molière's *Les Amants magnifiques*." *Romanic Review* 81, no. 2 (Mar. 1990): 173–88.

Zarlino, Gioseffo. *Le Istitutioni harmoniche del reverendo M. Gioseffo Zarlino da Chioggia*. Venice: Franceso Senese, 1562.

Zonta, Giuseppe. *Trattati d'amore del cinquecento*. Bari: Scrittori d'Italia, 1912.

zur Lippe, Rudolf. *Naturbeherrschung am menschen*. 2 vols. Frankfurt am Main: Syndikat Reprise, 1979.

INDEX

Index